Eros and Alienat

"Sears takes social reproduction feminism and queer Marxism in exciting new directions as he historicizes penetration and orgasms. He expands the concept of alienated labor to all life-making and founds a queer ecology, foregrounding colonized, racialized, and disabled voices."
—Peter Drucker, author of *Warped: Gay Normality and Queer Anti-Capitalism*

"Alan Sears meticulously outlines how capitalism shapes human intimacy. *Eros and Alienation* offers a sweeping, original analysis that challenges how we think about sexuality, life-making, and building a better world."
—Holly Lewis, author of *The Politics of Everybody: Feminism, Queer Theory, and Marxism at the Intersection*

"With careful attention to our embodied, historically evolving, socially imbricated, and ecologically situated ways of laboring and seeking fulfillment in the midst of capitalist alienation, Sears' de-reifying tour-de-force moves with revolutionary passion towards the liberation of our erotic lives."
—Aaron Jaffe, author of *Social Reproduction Theory and the Socialist Horizon: Work, Power and Political Strategy*

"*Eros and Alienation* brings into focus how profoundly the alienating logic of capitalism shapes needs and desires, labor, and wellbeing. Expanding on Queer Marxism and Social Reproduction Theory, Alan Sears lucidly explains how capitalist alienation constrains human capacities, undermines the ecology of intimacy, and limits agency for alternative world-making. This call for an eco-socialism of life-sustaining practice will transform how you think about sexual liberation, queer politics, and love."
—Rosemary Hennessy, author of *In the Company of Radical Women Writers*

"Alan Sears offers a compelling argument on the pervasive alienation of capitalist society that truncates and distorts our capacities for creative expression, love, and human flourishing. He maps erotics as a terrain of struggle, both captured by profit and the state, as well as a means of resistance and collective emancipation. Sears shows the vitality and necessity of queer Marxism, deftly synthesized with Black feminism, family abolitionism, Social Reproduction Theory, utopian speculation, and critical theory. This book is a powerful tool towards the reclaiming of ourselves as sexual beings in a revolutionary transformation of society."
—M.E. O'Brien, author of *Family Abolition: Capitalism and the Communizing of Care*

'A major contribution to queering and extending Marxism. This broad ranging exploration makes clear how the alienating racial capitalist exploitation of unwaged and waged labour is also the de-eroticization of bodies making them productive for capital. The permanent sexual and gender revolution that Sears calls for is based on expanding eroticization of bodies; working against productivity for capital; for queer and trans life-making; and expanding sexual time and control over our bodies and lives'
Gary Kinsman, author of *The Regulation of Desire: Queer Histories, Queer Struggles*

Mapping Social Reproduction Theory

Series editors Tithi Bhattacharya, Professor of South Asian History and Susan Ferguson, Associate Professor Emerita, Wilfrid Laurier University

Capitalism is a system of exploitation and oppression. This series uses the insights of social reproduction theory to deepen our understanding of the intimacy of that relationship, and the contradictions within it, past and present. The books include empirical investigations of the ways in which social oppressions of race, sexuality, ability, gender and more inhabit, shape and are shaped by the processes of creating labour power for capital. The books engage a critical exploration of social reproduction, enjoining debates about the theoretical and political tools required to challenge capitalism today.

Also available

Social Reproduction Theory:
Remapping Class, Recentering Oppression
Edited by Tithi Bhattacharya

A Feminist Reading of Debt
Luci Cavallero and Verónica Gago

Women and Work:
Feminism, Labour, and Social Reproduction
Susan Ferguson

Going Into Labour:
Childbirth in Capitalism
Anna Fielder

Disasters and Social Reproduction:
Crisis Response between the State and Community
Peer Illner

Social Reproduction Theory and the Socialist Horizon:
Work, Power and Political Strategy
Aaron Jaffe

Eros and Alienation

Capitalism and the Making of Gendered Sexualities

Alan Sears

First published 2025 by Pluto Press
New Wing, Somerset House, Strand, London WC2R 1LA
and Pluto Press, Inc.
1930 Village Center Circle, 3-834, Las Vegas, NV 89134

www.plutobooks.com

British Library Cataloguing in Publication Data
A catalogue record for this book is available from the British Library

ISBN   978 0 7453 4943 5   Paperback
ISBN   978 0 7453 4945 9   PDF
ISBN   978 0 7453 4944 2   EPUB

This book is printed on paper suitable for recycling and made from fully managed
and sustained forest sources. Logging, pulping and manufacturing processes are
expected to conform to the environmental standards of the country of origin.

Typeset by Stanford DTP Services, Northampton, England

Simultaneously printed in the United Kingdom and United States of America

Printed and bound by CPI Group (UK) Ltd, Croydon CR0 4YY

Contents

To Rafeef Ziadah, inspiring activist, thinker, writer and creator. I have learned so much about Palestine specifically and effective mobilization more generally from you. Further, you are a brilliant theorist who has patiently guided me towards a broader view of queer feminist anti-racist and anti-colonial marxism. I hope it shows in this book.

Acknowledgements

It is so important to honor the ways that knowledge production is a collective activity, which is just one of the reasons we need effective organization on the left. This book benefited from feedback and informal discussion with comrades and friends. Sue Ferguson provided intellectual inspiration and rich feedback in every phase of this project, along with lovely friendship. David Shulman is a visionary editor, who nurtured the development of this book from the early phases. The book benefited from conversation with and/or written feedback from: James Cairns, Peter Drucker, Sue Ferguson, Aaron Jaffe, Gary Kinsman, Melanie Knight, Xavier LaFrance, Holly Lewis, David McNally, Colin Mooers, Jacqueline Murray, M.E. O'Brien, Charlene Senn and Rafeef Ziadah. I was fortunate to work with Markus Harwood-Jones, Kyle Rubini, Kris Sayer and Abarnan Vasanthan, who provided thoughtful and insightful research assistance. Thanks to the Faculty of Arts at Toronto Metropolitan University for their support of this project. The Historical Materialism Conferences in London, Montreal and Toronto provided crucial venues for learning from others working in the field of queer marxism and workshopping core ideas from this book. Finally, this work would not have been possible without the comrades who everyday build activist knowledge through their organizing activities in struggles to make a better world.

1
Introduction: Eros and Alienation

The lesbian, gay, bisexual, trans and queer (LGBTQ+) advocacy organization Stonewall named the spy agency MI5 as Britain's most gay-friendly employer in 2016.[1] That designation marked an astonishing change, given that MI5 had barred LGBTQ+ people from employment in the agency until 1991, on the basis that they constituted a security threat. Indeed, MI5 along with similar security agencies in a number of Western countries hounded people perceived as queer throughout the period of the Cold War, attempting to bar them from government employment and engaging in active harassment, up to and including prosecution.

Computer science trailblazer Alan Turing was one of the most famous victims of this state-organized persecution. Turing was a British computer scientist and mathematician renowned for his code-breaking role during World War II. He died at the age of 41 in 1954, two years after undergoing chemical castration to avoid a prison sentence after being charged with gross indecency. Officials ruled his death a suicide. Turing is just one of many thousands of people who lost their jobs, freedom and at times their lives due to the active harassment waged by the security agencies of Britain, Canada, the United States and other Western powers. Gary Kinsman and Patrizia Gentile refer to this regime of torment as the "war on queers."[2]

It is remarkable that in a matter of decades MI5 went from coordinating the war on queers to being named a model employer of LGBTQ+ people. The significance of this transformation goes well beyond the employment practices of one government spy agency. LGBTQ+ people, who not long ago were classified as dangerous outsiders, are now welcome into the apparatus that labels, punishes, excludes and spies on others in the name of national security. Indeed, the governments who quite recently terrorized queer people now use claims of LGBTQ+ inclusion to justify the so-called "war on terror" since September 11, 2001. Governments in North America and Europe hold up the legal status of LGBTQ+ people in their countries as a marker of a superior human rights regime that legitimates wars of aggression in the

Middle East, South Asia and North Africa, as well as Islamophobic attacks on the rights of citizens and migrants perceived to be Muslim.

The change in employment practices at MI5 is but one dimension of a dramatic shift in the position of LGBTQ+ people in many places in the world since the 1960s, particularly in certain parts of the Global North (much of Western Europe and North America) as well as in specific locations in the Global South (among layers of the urban population in Brazil and South Africa, for example). In Canada where I live, LGBTQ+ people have won formal legal equality including state and employment benefits for same-gender partners, the right to marry, recognition of certain trans rights, and the ability to adopt children. These rights have led to a certain optimism about lesbian and gay acceptance. We can even aspire to be spies!

The more radical, queer wing of the LGBTQ+ movement argues that winning the right to be a gay, lesbian or trans James Bond is not sufficient. It is not enough for some queers, particularly cis-gendered middle-class white lesbians and gays in sustained couple relationships, to gain conditional status recognizing them as "normal." Legal equality rights fall far short of genuine liberation in the realms of gender and sexuality. The queer wing of LGBTQ+ mobilizing took form in the late 1980s, when AIDS activist mobilizations led by groups like ACT UP and AIDS Action NOW! challenged the mainstream gay and AIDS organizations that were oriented around respectability and gaining access to the existing corridors of power. Queer activists mobilized around the promise of queer liberation extending far beyond opening up limited spaces within the dominant relations of gender and sexuality for those who can squeeze into them. "The present is not enough," wrote critical queer theorist José Muñoz.[3]

Even this insufficient present has proven to be fragile and embattled, particularly with the rise of the far right in the early twenty-first century, with their specifically anti-trans and more broadly anti-LGBTQ+ agenda, whether in Poland, Uganda, Britain, Canada or the United States. Indeed, the right-wing offensive against trans lives is spreading rapidly as this book goes to press, demonstrating the fragility of queer normality in contemporary capitalist societies. The far right seeks to misdirect the very real insecurities that many feel as they try to get by in increasingly precarious conditions, blaming this instability on the erosion of the supposedly natural gender order. People who daily negotiate limited access to housing, food, health care and other necessities due to contingent employment, poverty wages, decaying social programs and eroding migrants' rights experience very real insecurities. The far right builds on these insecurities, blaming migration, anti-racist measures and trans rights for undermining the social order we could count on, founded on the supposedly natural or god-given bedrock of gender relations and national belonging.[4]

In the face of the current anti-trans offensive, it is necessary to defend trans and lesbian/gay rights and full personhood in a way that opens up wider perspectives for liberation. Muñoz argues that queerness must be transformative, pointing to a better world beyond the frame of the present: "we are not yet queer. We may never touch queerness, but we can feel it as the warm illumination of a horizon imbued with potentiality."[5] Queerness in this political sense is a struggle for the liberation of gender and sexuality, opening up the bounds of human possibility by removing the strictures of everyday compulsion and violence.

Queer marxism contributes to this transformative project by locating the everyday compulsion and violence shaping the contemporary organization of gender and sexuality within the broader frame of capitalist social relations. The war on queers was not simply a historical aberration resulting from the overenthusiastic actions of state security agencies in conditions of Cold War anti-communism, but rather the actualization of the anti-queer logic set deep in the foundations of capitalist societies. The successful struggle of LGBTQ+ people for basic rights in some capitalist societies does not undo this anti-queer logic, even with government apologies for past wrongdoings. Certainly, LGBTQ+ and feminist movements have fought for, and won, an expansion of the acceptable forms of intimate relationship and gender expression within an always contested conception of normal. This expansion of the normative has been limited, however, to ways of living that are sustainable within the capitalist organization of monetized work and caregiving labor around class relations formed along the lines of gender, sexuality, racialization and colonialism.

I argue in this book that the anti-queer logic of capitalism derives from the alienation of labor at the heart of the system. The alienation of labor, understood broadly as human life-making activity, is founded on relations of compulsion and subordination that require the containment of eroticism. Humans are fundamentally makers, creatively transforming the world around us to meet our wants and needs. People realize their passions through life-making activity, at once fulfilling hungers and developing tastes. The open-ended making that characterizes human social life drives the dynamism of human erotic practices, which take very different forms through history. The project of this book is to locate making love within the broader panoply of human making, examining the impact of the alienation of labor on the erotic realm. My title here acknowledges the influence of Herbert Marcuse, who explored the role of alienation in sexual repression in his path-breaking book *Eros and Civilization*.[6]

Alienation undermines creative self-realization through life-making activity, as capitalists lever their control over the key productive resources in society to organize production around the generation of profits rather than the fulfillment of our wants and needs. People making lives in relations of alienation are compelled to produce in conditions of dehumanizing subordination under the control of capitalists, in order to gain access to the resources required to sustain themselves and each other. Members of the working class are denied the self-realization of creative life-making to meet their individually and collectively defined wants and needs. In these conditions, the playful and inherently fulfilling eroticism of human life-making is contained, pushing people to direct their life-energies first and foremost towards activities deemed "productive," oriented around making profits for capitalists.

The realization of queerness requires the emancipation of human making, overcoming alienation through a liberatory process in which the laboring population takes control of the key productive resources required to fulfill our practical, aesthetic and erotic wants and needs. Queer marxism maps the particular dynamics of gender and sexual formation in capitalist societies to provide tools to help envision and mobilize towards a liberated future.[7] My goal here is to contribute to queer marxism by locating compulsion in the realm of gender and sexuality within a broader set of capitalist relations organized around the alienation of labor.

CAPITALISM AND ALIENATED MAKING

I recognize that this argument about the relationship between alienation and queerness may at first sight seem a bit of a stretch. The Marxist conception of alienation has often been conceived rather narrowly, focusing almost exclusively on the dehumanizing labor of workers in capitalist employment. I am drawing on social reproduction theory here, arguing that capitalist alienation shapes not only the paid labor in employment (or monetized equivalents), but also the unpaid or poorly paid reproductive labor through which members of the working class sustain their households, including such activities as caregiving, cleaning and cooking. Further, I am arguing that labor needs to be understood broadly as human life-making, the creative transformation of the world around us to meet our needs and realize our passions. Capitalist alienation undermines this multidimensional material, aesthetic and erotic self-realization through life-making activity.

In conditions of alienation, people do not realize themselves by engaging in transformative life-making as a fulfilling end in itself, but rather must perform subordinated labor, whether in employment or in the household, as the means to an end, to attain access to the resources required for survival. Members of the working class must treat their fundamental human transformative capacities as property, to be exchanged for access to the resources required to meet their wants and needs. Workers in conditions of alienation do not experience inherent fulfillment through their own creative making, and so the "realisation of labour appears as loss of realisation for the workers."[8] In conditions of employment, workers neither realize themselves through fulfilling life-making activity, nor own the products of their labor at the end of the day. Rather, they must perform subordinated labor under the control of capitalists, who direct the process of production and own the ultimate product as a result of their command over the key productive resources of society, including the land and its yield, workplaces, technical knowledge and other resources. The impact of alienation in the private realm of unpaid or poorly paid reproductive labor does not result from direct capitalist control, but rather from the need to trade on one's human capacities and to perform subordinated labor to attain access to the resources for life-making.

This conception of alienation is founded on an understanding of people as creative makers who fulfill their wants and needs by engaging socially in labor to transform the world around them, shaping and fulfilling desires through their own life-making activity. Sue Ferguson described this sense of labor as "expansive": "It includes the things people do to create their entire worlds – not just their labour for lords or capitalists."[9] People make their individual and collective mark on the world through transformative life-making activity, not only meeting subsistence needs but also realizing themselves as purposive world-makers who craft themselves, each other, and their milieux. In the words of Marx: "Through this production, nature appears, as *his* work and his reality ... he duplicates himself not only, as in consciousness, intellectually, but also actively, in reality, and therefore he sees himself in a world he has created."[10]

People living and working in conditions of alienation experience their own humanity, and that of others, in a stunted form. They underdevelop their creative agency as transformative world-makers through lack of practice in the absence of opportunity, as they must focus their life-energy on unrewarding work (including both monetized and household labor) required to attain access to resources to meet their wants and needs. People who live and work under conditions of alienation are deprived of control over key aspects of their human life-making activity, which has a deep impact on erotic practices and gender expression. In these conditions, sexual activity tends to be confined to the unseen private realm, often under cover of darkness, fueled by only the depleted energy left over after completing the work required to sustain survival.[11] People tend to organize their personal lives around sustainability in conditions of alienation, building relationships structured around dominant divisions of labor in monetized and household work as well as the discipline of state regulation which sanctions certain forms of relationship while proscribing others. The alienation of labor in capitalist societies is fundamental to the formation of regimes of gendered sexualities organized around necessity and governed by regulation.

Erotic practice, an eternal feature of human life, has been forged into historically specific relationship forms in the context of particular ways of making lives throughout human history. Specific forms of gendered sexuality have developed in the context of capitalist society and conditions of alienation, as people organize desires within horizons of possibility framed by dominant divisions of labor, the necessity of monetized labor and the requirement to trade on our most human capacities to attain the requirement of life through exchange. Erotic practice is an ever-present condition of human existence grounded in biological urges we share with other species, but it is much more than that. For Ellen Ross and Rayna Rapp, "The bare biological facts of sexuality do not speak for themselves; they must be expressed socially. Sex feels individual, or at least private, but those feelings always incorporate the roles, definitions, symbols and meanings of the worlds in which they are constructed."[12] This is not to deny the importance of biology, but to argue that our experience of embodiment is organized socially through our life practices in the context of particular ways of organizing society. It is necessary but not sufficient to understand eroticism as an ever-present condition of human existence grounded in biological urges we share with other species, for it is precisely the combination of biology and culture that makes human sexuality what it is and what it could be.

Erotic self-realization is separated from transformative life-making in conditions of alienation, organizing work and sex into purportedly distinct realms of existence and directing energies primarily towards subordinated labor. This formal separation between labor and erotic fulfillment in conditions of alienation tends to cast sexual activity, as all other areas of human life-making activity, as a means to an end, the way to gain access to required resources to meet wants and needs rather than inherently fulfilling in itself. Labor separated from inherent fulfillment ends up as drudge work marked by compulsion. Erotic practice, separated from creative life-making, often gets channeled towards the narrow normative realm of the sexual, focused on specific forms of relationship organized around gendered sexualities and particular practices centered around those body parts (e.g. genitals) deemed erogenous.[13] Sexuality under conditions of alienation tends to become transactional as people face relentless pressure to offer up their core human capacities in exchange for access to resources to meet their wants and needs.

People both generate and fulfill erotic desires through their social engagement in transformative labor. I am using erotic here in the expansive sense of embodied aesthetic fulfillment grounded in social connection, in line with the expansive understanding of labor as transformative life-making activity. Freud defined eros most broadly as the instinct "to establish ever greater unities and preserve them – thus in short to bind together ..."[14] Freud wrote there was no question that the erotic energy that he labeled libido "has somatic sources, that it streams into the ego from various organs and parts of the body."[15] While in contemporary Western society we tend to associate the erotic with very specific body parts (such as genitals and breasts), Freud argued, "strictly speaking the whole body is an erotogenic zone."[16] R. Danielle Egan, following Freud, understands eroticism broadly as "the result of a complex amalgamation of aims, objects, bodily pleasures, scopic registers, sexual curiosity ... as well as the desire for mastery and surrender."[17]

In conditions of alienation in contemporary capitalist societies, the erotic tends to be separated from labor in the expansive sense of transformative activity, hived off and confined to private sexual engagement narrowly understood as a set of specific genital-oriented activities organized primarily around coupling. Particular patterns of human sexual life may seem natural and eternal, but in reality people have organized erotic fulfillment and household formation in very different ways across time and place. In the contemporary capitalist societies of the Global North, coupling has been increasingly structured around sexualities, identities defined by the gendered orientation of desire – the preference for other (heterosexual) or same-gender (lesbian and gay) partners or both (bi). The normalization of gendered sexualities in contemporary capitalist societies leads people to orient their passions in particular ways, and to develop historically specific erotic sensibilities. Erotic desire, like hunger, is natural, but it gets directed towards particular forms of satiation through a variety of social processes.

Our desires are open-ended in the sense that they are products of particular social experiences, and are therefore subject to change. We commonly assume our desires are fixed by nature as they seem to emanate from our bodies without, or indeed despite, conscious direction. Sexual desire, for example, seems to be a natural phenomenon in which our bodies are hard-wired to generate longings and orient us towards particular objects of satisfaction (e.g. same or other gender). When our body responds definitively to particular forms of stimulation rather than others, it is easy to assume we were born that way. Jeffrey Weeks maintains that people often assume "that our sexuality is the most spontaneously natural thing about us."[18] Of course, erotic desire like hunger or thirst is natural and grounded in bodily needs, but the means we mobilize to satisfy those needs reflects the very specific social and historical circumstances in which we make our lives.

The historical materialist approach to eroticism grounded in life-making activity challenges the conception that we should understand sexuality either through the lens of nature or nurture, biology or culture. This is not to deny the importance of biology, but to argue that our experience of embodiment is organized socially through our life practices. The confinement of erotic practice to sexual activity in the private realm in conditions of alienation is a social and historical process. This confinement of erotic practice has been accompanied by the generalization of disembodied erotic charge in the form of the sexualization of commodities, products exchanged on the market. Allison Moore and Paul Reynolds described the paradoxical situation in which "supposedly private practices and relationships are simultaneously everywhere in the public domain, often in fetishised forms: in advertisements; in the media, in film, television, magazine and social media; in pornography, sex work and sexual commerce..."[19] People have trouble expressing their most basic desires even to intimate partners, yet at the same time sexualization charges everyday commodities with allure, so that products ranging from beer and cars to fashion and food, beckon us with the promise of erotic fulfillment that is ultimately broken, again and again.

In the context of alienation and the separation of erotic fulfillment from transformative labor, people tend to lose touch with their own creative world-making, at both the individual and societal levels. Contemporary gendered sexualities have been produced through historical contestation, as people have actively made lives in the context of capitalist social relations. From below, people have audaciously created new ways of living gender and sexuality, in the context of the limited and contradictory freedom of members of the working class who own their own bodies yet are compelled to sell their capacities to work. From above, employers and state policy-makers have sought to regulate sexual activity, orienting private life around productivity, so that so as to create a reliable source of exploitable labor for employers.

In conditions of alienation, we lose touch with our own biographical and historical role in the construction of desire. In the technical sense, our desire is reified, obscuring the transformative role of human activity, including our own, in organizing our passions in particular ways. The reification of desire in the context of capitalist alienation means that we take for granted a particular regime of gendered sexualities, assuming natural forces beyond our control orient our desire towards the same gender, or another, or both.[20] People tend to casually assume we are born this way, hard wired for a specific orientation of desire.

Social relations get right inside us, developing our passions to the extent that they can feel that they emanate from our bodies. For Ross and Rapp, power relations "are more than "sociological." They are also internalized at the most intimate level of sexual fantasies and feelings and become part of human personality itself."[21] Humans form their desire through the communal and embodied experience of life practices framed by specific social relations. Desire may feel as if it emanates from our body as a drive, but we participate in its production. For Gary Kinsman, "We see our sexualities as a personal essence defining who we are rather than as constituted through social practices that we ourselves have been active in through which our sexualities have been made."[22]

Reification means that we misattribute human agency to impersonal forces, and thus experience the outcome of our own individual and social world-making as the unalterable product of conditions beyond our control. The reification of desire means our unbounded wants and needs for each other get directed, on the one hand, into the narrow realm of private coupling organized around gendered sexualities, and, on the other hand, towards the sexualization of commodities. We are deeply dependent on each other to meet material, cultural and personal needs. In the context of alienation, our integral connection with others as we engage in the shared work of realizing ourselves through world-making is undermined. As we lose control over our labor in the expansive sense of creative transformative life-making activity, we lose the sense that we are bound together by shared projects and communal outcomes. In the context of alienation, we experience our broad spectrum wants and needs for human connection as desire

to be satiated through sexual coupling and/or the consumption of sexualized commodities.

THE SOCIAL REPRODUCTION OF SEXUALITIES

The connection between sexuality and alienation I am making here is
founded on the broad conception of life-making labor developed through
social reproduction theory, which emerged as a Marxist-feminist corrective
to Marxist traditions that focused on the analysis of production at the site of
capitalist employment but did not examine the conditions for the sustenance
and generational reproduction of the working class.[23] The social reproduction frame is grounded in a more holistic view of life-making, understanding
that members of the working class sustain themselves through paid labor,
the sale of their capacity to work as a commodity to employers (or monetized equivalent), and through unpaid or poorly paid reproductive labor
performed mainly by women, with low-pay reproductive labor falling disproportionately on the shoulders of racialized women. Social reproduction
theory takes a broad view on who is included as members of the working
class, which is made up of all who have no alternative but to rely on wages
(or equivalent) to meet their wants and needs, including not only employees, but also their household members and family or community networks
as well as those who are unemployed or unable to work.

My goal here is to contribute to social reproduction theory by exploring
the specifically erotic dimensions of life-making labor, which thus far have
been underexamined. We gain new perspectives on both monetized and
reproductive labor when considering the role of erotic fulfillment and its
repression in human life-making. The alienation of labor, crucially including erotic containment, undermines the agency and human connection of
those engaged in both monetized and reproductive labor. The containment
of sexuality has played a crucial role in shaping contemporary relationships
of social reproduction, which have increasingly been organized around
sexual attraction as a core dynamic of relationship-formation. It is a relatively
recent historical phenomenon, largely dating to the twentieth century, that
people have primarily organized these relationships on the basis of sexual
attraction, though this pattern varies tremendously depending on one's
social location, self-defined needs and access to resources. Sexual attraction has come to be defined as a central fulcrum around which relationships
foundational to survival projects are built. The remit of these relationships
organized around sexual attraction stretches far beyond erotic fulfillment to

include companionship, caregiving in many forms, sharing economic and social resources, raising children, engaging with wider kin and companionship networks, co-residence and shared involvement in various forms of leisure activity.

The social reproduction frame has a strong focus on human agency as makers, focusing our attention on the ways members of the working class actively make lives, engaging in what Johanna Brenner refers to as "survival projects."[24] People engage purposively in survival projects to meet their wants and needs within the constraints of the dominant social relations, organizing their monetized and unpaid labor as well as leisure and restorative activities through the formation of households and communities in various configurations.

People engage in survival projects, creative life-making from below, yet in conditions not of their own choosing that severely limit the field of play due to the need to engage in particular forms of monetized and reproductive labor to sustain themselves and their household or community. It is crucial to recognize the world-making agency exercised from below, despite privation, violence and dehumanization. As described by Saidiya Hartman, for example, Black women living in the slums of certain cities in the United States created new ways of living in the early twentieth century grounded in "waywardness and the refusal to be governed."[25] People have creative capacities for making gender and sexuality, but must do so within the constraints of social-ecological niches oriented around the reproduction of capitalist relations that create real barriers to transgressive practices, for example, in the exclusion from employment often experienced by trans people and particularly racialized trans people.[26]

People forge caregiving relationships to aggregate capacities and resources as a key dimension of their survival projects to meet wants and needs. Human life-making is a communal project, even in the context of the individuation associated with capitalist societies. The specific form of caregiving relationships people build, which might include officially sanctioned family forms as well as various other configurations of household and community, depends on both participants' own self-defined desires and the options available given the circumstances of their life-making. Members of the working class negotiate their survival projects from specific locations within dominant social relations, on the basis of gender, sexuality, racialization, citizenship and/or colonial status and classification as disabled.

At the same time, states and employers have sought from above to regulate these survival projects so as to orient them around the reproduction of the required labor force for capital with appropriate capacities and expectations. As we shall explore in Chapter 5, state policy-makers have developed welfare and health care systems, immigration regimes, carceral practices and educational institutions to regulate working-class survival projects, in part in response to demands from below for improved conditions of work and life. Gender discipline and sexual regulation feature prominently in this project of regulating the social reproduction of the population to create the working class required to sustain capitalist relations.

The social reproduction frame has been limited by a tendency to generalize the analysis of family and household formation from the normative conditions of life of specific layers of the working class (predominantly white, heterosexual and employed in more lucrative and secure working-class jobs) in particular locations in the Global North. The frame must be "stretched" to capture the different forms of community and household that have been created from below, for example, by racialized trans people or by migrants who are negotiating the geographic separation of households exacerbated by the brutal impact of state-assigned statuses.[27] Queer people have built survival strategies oriented around the formation of communities in specific spaces (ranging from cruising sites to bars to shared housing) that have provided crucial support and resources in sustaining ways of living that run counter to the normative. Informal trans communities have played a crucial role in the construction of ways of living that support transition and sustain trans lives, such as "new language, lifestyle developments, and culture."[28] Mutual support to sustain life and activism to change the world were intertwined in racialized trans community formation such as the important example of STAR (Street Transvestites Action Revolutionaries) in New York City.[29] Gay bars played a fundamental role in the formation of communities that made particular kinds of queer life possible for much of the twentieth century, even if their role has shifted with the development of new forms of homonormativity.[30]

ALIENATION OF THE PASSIONS

In conditions of alienation, labor is motivated more by necessity than realization of passions. People become estranged from their fundamental character as makers who are passionate for transformative activity that is inherently fulfilling as it is creative, social, charged with eroticism and open-ended. Under conditions of alienation, we face pressure to treat our most human capacities in a transactional manner. Members of the working class must monetize their capacity to work, commonly by selling it to an employer. Similarly, we feel the need to trade on our erotic capacities to attract mates, build caregiving partnerships, overcome loneliness, attain financial security, obtain housing, enhance self-esteem, engage in shared leisure, or for other outcomes as we shall discuss below.

Alienation profoundly shapes the way we experience our needs and desires. Richard Seymour states that Marx defines human needs "not in instinctual or biological terms, but in terms of the *passions*."[31] People suffer, in the sense that we need things outside ourselves to sustain our being. The human is "a *suffering* being – and because he feels he suffers, a *passionate* being. Passion is the essential power of man energetically bent on its object."[32] People realize their passions through their life-making labor to attain the external objects that meet their wants and needs, expressing themselves individually and collectively in their work on the world.

People not only satisfy their hungers through their transformative labor, but also develop tastes and meanings as they forge ways of meeting needs and fulfilling desires that define them as individuals and as communities. We both satisfy and generate needs through our life-making work on the world: "the satisfaction of the first need, the act of satisfying and the instrument of satisfaction which has been acquired, leads to new needs; and this creation of new needs is the first historical act."[33] The generation of new needs is a defining characteristic of human experience, as the ways we sustain biological life are always woven in with the ways we express ourselves as individuals and communities. While humans have a biological need for nourishment, they meet these needs according to tastes they have developed in the light of ecological location and community practices.

Transformative labor, in the expansive sense of life-making activity, is not only our means of practical survival through meeting basic biological needs, but is also central to our fulfillment, our understanding of ourselves, and the generation of cultural meanings. Labor in this expansive sense is not simply about staying alive and raising the next generation, but also forming ourselves individually and collectively through our activity on the world. People distinguish themselves in the specific ways they overcome suffering and affirm their passions: "the distinct character of their existence, of their life, is constituted by the distinct mode of their affirmation."[34]

People develop distinct modes of affirmation for their passions as they negotiate particular cultural, ecological and social circumstances. The configuration of desires around specific historical conditions is both passive and active. The shaping of wants and needs is passive in the sense that people frame their expectations around what is possible within the limitations of a particular social order. It is common in contemporary capitalist societies, for example, for people to develop tastes for the highly processed food that is often the only affordable means to sate hunger. The education of desire is also active. From below, people explore and innovate, forging community around developing and fulfilling passions. From above, the powerful attempt to train the desires of the subordinated population. Capitalist states, for example, use social policy in the form of health programs, compulsory education, immigration controls, penal laws and other interventions to form a population oriented around meeting their wants and needs within the parameters of a specific normative regime. As we explore in detail in Chapter 5, state social policy-makers craft modes of regulation that actively teach people how to live in a variety of ways, whether that is learning to silence yourself unless your raised hand is called upon by the teacher, disqualification from benefits on the basis of a job search deemed inadequate, or the visit of a social worker to investigate household practices.

Queerness in the utopian sense is subversive in that it opens up the horizons of desire beyond the constraints of what is possible under existing conditions. One of the key features of radical utopianism is that it cultivates the passions to hunger for more. E.P. Thompson powerfully described the perspective of artist and activist William Morris on the importance of utopian visioning in accomplishing the goal of socialist transformation:

> The end itself was unobtainable without the prior education of desire or "need". And science cannot tell us what to desire or how to desire. Morris saw it as a task of Socialists (his own first task) to help people to find out their wants, to encourage them to want more, to challenge them to want differently, and to envisage a society of the future in which people, freed at last of necessity, might choose between different wants.[35]

ALIENATION AND MARKET EXCHANGE

In capitalist societies, members of the working class cannot directly realize their passions through labor as they are dispossessed of control over the key productive resources of society, such as the land and its yield, technologies and core sites of production, which are appropriated by capitalists. Deprived of access to these resources of life-making, members of the working class must alienate their capacities for transformative activity as property for exchange, to be sold to employers (or monetized in equivalent ways) in order to sustain themselves through buying goods and services on the market. Rather than realizing their passions through their own transformative life-making, people in capitalist societies meet their wants and needs through market exchange, trading on their human capacities to gain access to the necessities of life, sources of pleasure and to build caregiving relationships.

The market model has penetrated deeper into everyday life throughout the history of capitalist development. People increasingly meet their wants and needs through the sale of their human capacities to purchase goods and services. This intensification of the exchange logic of capitalism has had a profound impact on the sphere of interpersonal and sexual relations. Exchange transactions now influence human engagement across the whole range of social and ecological relationships. People often feel the need, for example, to trade on their sexual allure by deploying eroticism in transactional ways; using sex not for inherent fulfillment but as a means to develop relationships that help them meet their material and emotional needs.

The transactional mode of erotic engagement is at the core of the regime of sexual liberalism, which developed through the twentieth century as state policy-makers and social reformers responded to struggles from below for personal and erotic freedom.[36] In conditions of sexual liberalism, sexuality is increasingly regulated by a market model of intimate relations, organized along the lines of commodity exchange. Thus, sexual engagement has increasingly been regulated by contract, the agreement between formally equal parties to pursue a particular transaction. Contract is the primary form of governance of market exchange relations, ranging from the buying and selling of particular goods and services through to the labor contract governing employment relations. Marriage, common-law relationships and sexual hook-ups are regulated by various forms of implicit or explicit contract. The alienating logic of capitalism tends to push relationships towards a transactional exchange mode, though this does not reduce all interpersonal connections to market exchange. People do express passion, practice love for each other and explore erotic fulfillment in many forms, even in conditions of alienation. In practice, we negotiate the contradictions that derive from our attempts to realize our authentic passions within relationships structured on a transactional contract basis.

The market model of interpersonal engagement is founded on the centrality of property relations to the experience of bodily autonomy in capitalist societies. Free workers in capitalist societies are distinguished historically as an exploited class by the fact that they own their bodies, even if this is inseparable from the need to alienate their human capacities to survive. Members of the working class have a very real, if contradictory, bodily autonomy that is the basis of practices of freedom based on self-ownership and the existence of a private realm not under the direct control of the ruling classes. This bodily autonomy is central to struggles for sexual freedom in capitalist societies, as reflected in crucial slogans like "my body, my choice." Working-class self-ownership is central to the construction of a right to privacy in capitalist societies, and to certain degrees of freedom in one's personal life. Yet, this private realm of bodily autonomy is constrained by the need to engage in necessary monetized or household labor to sustain yourself and others in your household/family in the absence of control over the key productive resources in society.

People thus become accustomed to a limited and contradictory bodily autonomy grounded in property ownership, in which freedom is inseparable from compulsion to alienate their human capacities. The model of property exchange penetrates ever more deeply into the configuration of interpersonal relations, as erotic engagement is increasingly organized around market forms in which people mobilize allure to attract mates for contractually regulated engagements, whether in the form of sustained relationships or short-term sexual encounters. In these conditions, people often deploy their eroticism in transactional ways, using sex as a means to develop relationships with such goals as economic security, self-esteem or care in times of need.

The transactional model is reflected in the orientation of the most important interpersonal relationships (marriage, common law) around a single bonding element, the magnetism of sexual allure. The organization of interpersonal relationships around sexual attraction is a very recent historical development, as we discuss in Chapter 4. In this situation, people tend to read each other through the lens of sexual allure, measuring each other by erotic standards of apparent fitness, bodily features, comportment, fashion sense and/or sexual repertoire. People in this sexual marketplace face tremendous pressures to hone their allure through diet, training, fashion, makeup, online presence and the development of an engaging personality. These pressures have been particularly high for women, given the dominant gendered divisions of labor that tended to render women dependent on men to thrive, as a result of lower pay and/or employment exclusions as well as expectations in terms of reproductive labor and multigenerational caregiving.

This exchange model is founded on massive inequalities, as large layers of the laboring population have diminished bodily autonomy due to conditions of unfreedom on the basis of enslavement, incarceration, gendered abjection, colonization, presence or absence of national status and/or classification as disabled. Specific bodies are marked by abjection, a dehumanized status accorded on the basis of gender, sexuality, racialization, colonization, national status or designation as disabled, that leads to devaluation in such forms as lower pay, exposure to greater risks to health and safety, compulsory deference and undermined bodily autonomy.[37]

Unfree members of the working class are denied full self-ownership and therefore have a limited experience of even the bounded autonomy accorded free workers. As we shall explore in Chapter 4, this unfreedom undermines even the contradictory and bounded sexual agency grounded in formal self-ownership, leaving people (e.g. enslaved, incarcerated, undocumented or categorized as disabled) vulnerable to systemic sexual assault and violence while facing a lack of recognition of full personhood including erotic rights.

People have mobilized around practices and visions of sexual freedom grounded in enhanced bodily autonomy and the right to privacy in struggles for gay and lesbian rights, the recognition of women's sexual agency and the ongoing battle against sexual assault. These movements produced real gains, yet have often been caught up within the limits of the property exchange model of interaction. The consent frame for sexual relationships, for example, is contradictory. The consent frame developed out of crucial struggles from below (particularly those of racialized women) to protect the bodily autonomy of women, racialized and Indigenous people and others made vulnerable to violence and rape and by the dominant power relations that denied them the right to say no.[38] Yet, consent is necessarily limited as a tool for justice in erotic relations, as it is built on the model of contractually regulated property exchange between formally equal parties rather than the fulfillment of human needs in erotic engagement.[39] In market model exchange, a contract is only valid if the parties freely consented to it. While this does offer crucial protections against coercion, the complex emotional and interpersonal realm of sexual engagement does not necessarily follow the same logic as the purchase and sale of market goods and services. Further, the formal equality of sexual exchange relationships is underlaid with deep, substantive inequalities along the integrally connected lines of gender, racialization, colonization, migration status, sexuality and categorization as disabled, as well as social class.

SEXUALITY AND ECOLOGY

The transactional market mode grounded in alienation and dispossession reshapes ecological relations, as people treat the social and natural environment as resources for exploitation and property for exchange. People are estranged from nature, both externally in their relations with the environment and internally in relations with their own body. This estrangement underlies the ecological crisis of our times, as people relate to their own bodies and the external environment transactionally, as property and resources, undermining the commitment to mutuality based on the recognition that sustaining ourselves, each other, other species and the natural environment is the fundamental basis for our wellbeing over generations.

Unsustainable profit-making practices disrupt the ongoing interchanges between people and their environment, creating "the material estrangement of human beings in capitalist societies from the natural conditions of their existence."[40] People make sexual lives in the context of this destruction of mutuality in the interchange with nature, within (their own bodies) and without. Extraction from nature in capitalist societies is generally seen as a right of ownership rather than an ongoing interchange in which harvest is associated with responsibilities for sowing to ensure sustainability.

Alienation and dispossession rupture relations of mutuality and reciprocity with other people (individuals and communities), other species, the land and the natural environment. Indigenous theorist Leanne Simpson described her nation as "an ecology of intimacy" grounded in "connectivity based on the sanctity of the land, the love we have for our families, our language, our way of life. It is relationships based on deep reciprocity, respect, noninterference, self-determination and freedom."[41] Capitalism undermines this ecology of intimacy, replacing connectivity, reciprocity and mutuality with transaction, exploitation and colonization. This is not to flatten or idealize non-capitalist societies, but to argue that the globalization of alienation and dispossession through imperialism and colonialism created a quantitative and qualitative shift in the interchange with the earth, other species, other peoples and each other.

Under these conditions, people come to understand nature and our own bodies as resources, valued only for their potential role in processes of production, not for themselves in their unimproved state. The untrained body that is not made up to the current standards of fashion and fitness is reviled, not only condemned as unattractive but treated as an indicator of the moral failure of its owner. People orient their desires towards cultivated bodies and sexualized commodities as part of what Rosemary Hennessy described as the "aestheticization of everyday life."[42] In conditions of alienation, where erotic fulfillment is channeled away from transformative life activity, commodities are sexualized, imbued with allure to fulfill desires. This is a dimension of what Marx referred to as "commodity fetishism," in which people misattribute the agency of human makers to commodities, the products of their labor in circulation on the market.[43] Commodities seem to have a real impersonal power, setting the terms of our access to them, for example, by naming a price. The rise in food prices, which drive many into hunger, seems to be driven by the commodities themselves as they circulate on the market.

People attempt to sexualize themselves by mimicking commodities, entering into the realm of circulation, freeing themselves from the earthly burden of actual bodies and making themselves up as images, through training, fashion, diet, selfies and other means. In Chapter 6, I argue that eco-socialism requires a transformation not only towards more sustainable relations with external nature based on reciprocity and mutuality, but also a new frame for relating to each other and our own bodies. Queer liberation in the utopian sense requires a revolutionary change in our ecological relations.

SEXUAL REVOLUTION: THE REALIZATION OF QUEERNESS

Queerness in the utopian sense can be realized only through a revolutionary process of overcoming alienation as the dispossessed take democratic and collective control over the means of life-making to establish relations of mutuality and reciprocity with each other, other species and the natural world. Sexual revolution is woven into the fabric of this broader revolutionary process, as erotic containment is a fundamental feature of capitalist alienation. Over the history of capitalist societies, people have made sexual revolutions that have produced the contemporary regime of gendered sexualities. From below, people have used the limited and contradictory bodily autonomy associated with self-ownership to develop new ways of living through innovation in the realms of gender and sexuality. From above, state policy-makers developed modes of regulation to organize emergent modes of sexuality around the requirements for capitalist social reproduction, most importantly the supply of a labor force willing and able to work under existing conditions.

Capitalist dispossession and alienation created the conditions for these sexual revolutions through the deliberate destruction of existing communities and nations: stripping people of their communities and their ecological relations; blocking their access to key resources for living; and subjecting them to various degrees of dehumanization associated with colonization, racialization, gender, sexuality, classification as disabled and assigned national status (citizen, Indigenous, migrant). At the same time, it opened up certain possibilities for collective world-making in the ruins, which people took up in a variety of ways through creative and resilient life-making from below. Sexuality in the sense that we use the word today is a product of this capitalist sexual revolution.

In non-capitalist societies, sexual desire did not tend to be considered a personal taste or source of identity. Rather it was organized through the system of relations which provided social criteria for erotic engagement and household formation, for example, guiding marriage towards partners within or outside one's own community depending on the dominant societal frame. In some cultures, people married cousins or other kin to intensify the network of social connections that was central to their lives, so that every member of the community was linked to each other through a number of ties. These patterns of relationship formation tend to weaken when capitalist market relations become important in a region. Shenk, Towner, Voss and Alam found that women in rural Matlab in Bangladesh, an area where market relations were becoming more important, explained their preference to marry outside of their immediate kin in terms of increasing freedom from family expectations: "Women said that with new relatives, it was easier to state one's grievances or make demands without 'breaking' the family relationship ..."[44] Marrying outside immediate kin broadened, rather than intensified, their kin networks which they felt improved their economic prospects. "New relatives were ... seen as useful in increasing a family's social status and providing valuable connections for gaining school admissions, jobs, help in sending a son abroad, or other forms of aid typically sought through social networks."[45]

Capitalist development weakened the bonds of kinship and community, leaving individuals to forge their own relationships.[46] In these conditions, people began to develop erotic sensibilities organized around an understanding of sexuality as personal expression. Weeks posits that sexuality "developed its modern meaning in the second half of the nineteenth century, and came to mean the personalized sexual feelings that distinguished one person from another (*my* sexuality), while hinting at that mysterious essence that attracts us to each other."[47]

Capitalism created the conditions for the sexual revolutions that organized sexuality as a distinctly defined realm of experience. But capitalist regimes of gender and sexual formation have not developed along a single linear historical path. The changes associated with the rise of capitalism, including the spread of colonialism, the movement of larger portions of the population into cities, global migration connected to dispossession and dislocation, and the rise of large-scale industrial production, framed a global process that Peter Drucker described as combined and uneven sexual formation.[48] People created new ways of living that were local and culturally specific, and at the same time part of a global process marked by colonial imposition, subordination in new labor regimes, mass displacement and migration, and the flow of cultural influences.

These capitalist sexual revolutions are an important reminder of the mutability of relations of gender and sexuality. These sexual revolutions have fueled a hunger for sexual emancipation that points far beyond the limits of capitalist alienation. This requires a vision of social revolution that builds on and goes beyond transgressions against the dominant normative order.[49] Transgression has been crucial in forging new ways of living, as individuals find ways to meet their wants and needs despite huge economic, social and legal costs. But liberation needs to go beyond transgression to transformation, eliminating the barriers to free gender and sexual expression by overcoming alienation and dispossession.

People forge collectivity from below to achieve such emancipation, and there are fundamental erotic dimensions to the process of coming together to remake the world. The erotic elements of collectivity are a component of what Bhandar and Ziadah describe as "shared forms of leisure, pleasure and joy that are also sources of our collective resilience."[50] The erotic dimensions of revolutionary collectivity bestow certain responsibilities on activists, as that can and does produce abuse. People negotiate a contradictory path as they forge relationships to change the world. These relationships combine elements of this existing world (its hierarchies and transactional modality) with possibilities, hopes and dreams for better ways of living. There is a long history of sexual abuse and violence within movements and organizations focused on radical change. Addressing the erotic elements of collective energies is a reminder of the responsibilities of our movements, and at the same time, a reminder of the fundamental role of sexual revolution in the process of revolutionary transformation.

2

Alienation and the Making of Sexualities

Human erotic life is shaped by our characteristic activity as makers. We transform nature to satisfy our hungers, quench our thirsts, care for each other, and fulfill our potential. People create deliberately through our life-making activity, making our individual and communal mark on the world through transforming the world around us physically and mentally to collectively produce what we want and need. Marx emphasized the centrality of purposive agency to human life-making activity: "Labour is, first of all, a process by which man, through his own actions, mediates, regulates and controls the metabolism between himself and nature."[1]

This broad definition of labor as life-making activity extends far beyond the realm of "work" in the everyday sense that is generally associated with paid employment or equivalent monetized activity.[2] Labor as life-making includes a range of transformative activities that we associate with work, caring, aesthetic expression, physical performance and social belonging. One of the defining features of the human experience is that people make deliberate choices about their life-making activity. The human "makes his life activity the object of his will and his consciousness."[3] Humans incorporate aesthetic standards into our life activity of making, and work to satisfy even our most basic needs "in accordance with the laws of beauty."[4] Human eroticism is woven into these creative, deliberate, sensual and aesthetic dimensions of self-realization.

Those who do not own or control the means of production in capitalist societies must alienate their capacity to work by selling it to employers for a specific period of time in exchange for a wage, or must engage in equivalent forms of money-making activity. In these situations, workers control neither the process of production nor the product of their labor at the end of the day. Marx wrote of the worker in capitalist societies: "His labour is therefore not voluntary, but coerced; it is *forced labour*. It is therefore not the satisfaction of a need; it is merely a *means* to satisfy needs external to it."[5] In these conditions, life-making activity is not self-realization but "it is the loss of his self."[6] Life-making activity under conditions of alienation in capitalist societies becomes the means to an end (access to resources to meet wants and needs) rather than an inherently fulfilling end in itself.

As a result, workers do not realize themselves through their labors: "in his work, therefore, he does not affirm himself but denies himself, does not feel content but unhappy, does not develop freely his physical and mental energy but mortifies his body and ruins his mind."[7] Alienated work is exhausting, boring and often harmful mentally or physically. We are dehumanized, developing only the most stunted sense of our individual and collective world-making agency. As we discuss below, the alienation of labor is not limited to paid employment and other monetized life-making activities, but also has a dramatic impact on unpaid reproductive work people do in their private lives in their own time.

Other species produce objects of breathtaking beauty, often far surpassing the aesthetic standards of human work. Bee hives may be far more elegant than many bland institutional hospital rooms, but even the most unsightly human construction reflects an intentional process. In the words of Marx, "what distinguishes the worst architect from the best of bees is that the architect builds the cell in his mind before he constructs it in wax."[8] Humans make deliberately, coordinating minds and bodies to produce food, housing, care-taking, music, erotic fulfillment, and indeed cultured bodies that both reflect and shape who we are. The dynamism of erotic expression in human cultures is an important dimension of this deliberate life-making, articulating mental and physical dimensions of creative processes.

The erotic dimensions of life-making labor are connected to the communal character of our world-making. People express their individuality as we make our mark by transforming the world around us; and we also express connectivity as the activity of making is necessarily social. People engage socially in the life-making activities of production and reproduction, organized around fundamentally collective capacities, including the learning and teaching of skills (such as tool use) and language development. Humans develop skills collectively and reproduce these capacities over generations through language (both gestural and spoken). For Peter C. Reynolds, "The human proclivity to assume intentionality in the behavior of others (the intentionality axiom) and the human capacity to infer the intention of others from their action (the intentionality capacity) underlies human skill acquisition in general and human linguistic ability in particular."[9]

Human labor is characterized by shared intentionality, the collective ability to define shared goals and to work together to direct our life-making activity towards realizing ourselves by fulfilling our wants and needs in particular ways. People develop shared intentionality through the characteristic organization of our life-making labor, perhaps most importantly through the social organization of child-rearing in the form of cooperative breeding in which non-parental members of the community work with the mother to sustain children, in contrast with other great apes.[10] The cooperative organization of child-rearing includes the involvement of non-parental community members in caregiving and food provision (allo-parenting).[11] People develop capacities for shared intentionality, deliberate collective formation grounded in cooperative breeding and intensive communal relations, including extensive food sharing: "Among human foragers, the reliance on sharing, with its manifold benefits, is greater than in any other primate species."[12] In this context, people develop an orientation towards mutuality, "a prosocial motivational disposition that involves an interest in sharing psychological states with others."[13]

Humans engage in communal meaning-making, defining themselves as individuals and collectives through shared intentionality in life-making activity. Our erotic sense is soaked in shared intentionality, the recognition of each other's wants and needs. In conditions of alienation, we lose touch with our agency in collective world-making. Rather than realizing ourselves as part of a communal life-making project, we spend ourselves in subordinated labor. We engage with the products of our collective work only through the mediation of the market, rather than directly as the fulfillment derived from our life-making activity. Rather than creating what we want and need, we make money for capitalists by producing what is profitable.

ALIENATION AND SOCIAL REPRODUCTION

Alienated work does not cease at the end of the "working day," the period of paid employment or equivalent earning. Self-owning members of the working class in capitalist societies bear private responsibility for sustaining themselves, caring for vulnerable kin and raising the next generation. At least some members of working-class households must engage in unpaid or poorly paid reproductive labor processes, shopping for food and other needs, preparing meals and cleaning up, caring for children and vulnerable kin or community members, maintaining the place of residence, etc. This labor falls disproportionately on the shoulders of women and people who are racialized.

The social reproduction frame contributes to the development of a holistic understanding of the two-sided character of alienated labor for working-class households, including both capitalist employment or equivalent and private (unpaid or poorly paid) reproductive labor. The capitalist system must attend to the life-making processes that sustain and generationally reproduce (or replace) the laboring population, as workers must be alive in order to be exploited. The lives of the laboring population must be replenished through nourishment, rest and/or leisure after energies have been dissipated in the activity of production; and new generations of humans must be raised and/or recruited.[14]

Yet, capitalists do not have a straightforward interest in meeting the requirements for the reproduction of a healthy laboring population, as they are driven to maximize profits in a competitive environment. Sue Ferguson describes the contradictory interests of capitalists in social reproduction: "Because competition compels capitalists to keep wages and taxes as low as possible, the social reproduction of labour presents them with a dilemma: they require human labour power but must constrain the conditions of life that generate it."[15] The social reproduction of the working class is at once an "essential condition for capitalism" and at the same time "stands in the way of capitalism's drive for profit."[16]

Capitalists need to purchase labor power, the human capacity to work. However, the capacity to work cannot be separated from the intentional human beings (mind and body) who must submit to the temporary alienation of their capacities. As suggested by Sue Fergusons, "labour power necessarily comes with a body attached to it."[17] Self-owning members of the working class do not simply reproduce themselves as potential sources of labor power for employers, but as creative, self-realizing human beings.[18]

Workers act in their own interests, developing strategies for sustainability and self-realization that challenge employers' efforts to get these laboring bodies to work, in ways that range from absenteeism to active resistance. David McNally argues: "Capital's drive to fully subsume labour, to instrumentalise it, to strip it of all embodiment and subjectivity, runs up against its dependence on concrete, living labour – sentient, embodied, thinking, self-conscious labour."[19] Members of the working class, then, are not alienated from their human being, but must alienate their own human capacities as property to attain the resources required to realize themselves.

The compulsion to alienate human capacities does not finish when the shift ends, but continues in the realm of reproductive labor which cannot be seen simply as unalienated labor performed for inherent fulfillment. in her path-breaking analysis *More than a Labour of Love,* Meg Luxton writes that reproductive labor "is profoundly determined by capitalist production and functions at the heart of the social relations integral to the capitalist mode of production."[20] Reproductive labor is necessarily oriented around the present or future participation of household members in monetized labor as a survival project.

While reproductive labor does take place outside of direct capitalist control, it is policed by the state, through child protection bureaucracies, compulsory education, public health interventions, housing policy, immigration controls and welfare benefits requirements. State policy-makers have attempted to develop programs to shape the domestic realm to yield an appropriate working population without lifting the impossible burden of private responsibility from the shoulders of working-class households. In Chapter 5 we will explore this state regulation, focusing specifically on the delicate balance between reinforcing private responsibility and policing through state regulation.

Since the 1980s, state social policies have been reoriented around the neoliberal project of undermining the broad welfare state, which was inadequate and bureaucratic even at its most expansive, has increased the pressures on the private family. Griffiths and Gleeson argue that the role of the family in hegemony has increased through the neoliberal era: "Increasingly in the face of global austerity, the family is ideologically and structurally emphasized to such an extent that it is posed as natural and timeless while simultaneously capable of accommodating and facilitating changes in the labor market."[21] In this situation, the family is at once a crucial lifeline and a central means of regulation and subordination: "The family, therefore, takes a contradictory form in our world, both the means of love in the midst of a harsh and dangerous world, and a space of private dependency with little protection from the risk of internal abuse, violence, and heteronormativity."[22] The private realm of the family is grounded in power relations of domination that often create violence and abuse. In the words of M.E. O'Brien, "The family's horrors are vast, its abuses widespread, its logic coercive."[23]

Yet, the privatized realm of reproduction also offers some space for self-realization through creative and transformative life-making. In the early twentieth century, the domestic realm offered Black women in the United States a certain space of self-making, as they migrated north to particular urban centers to attempt to realize the promise of freedom after formal emancipation from enslavement in the face of persistent dehumanizing racism. Saidiya Hartman notes, "What took place behind the closed doors of a rented room in a lodging house was a moment, *an iteration of the revolution of black intimate life* that was taking place in New York, Philadelphia and Chicago in the first decades of the twentieth century."[24] The domestic realm provided potential spaces for experimentation in self-realization, though always precarious given the lack of resources and the pervasive threat of violence.

In the private realm, people build community to sustain themselves. This includes the development of forms of mutual support outside of dominant family forms, ranging from informal networks among mother-led families living in the same building to queer community in gay bars or other sites. These communities are crucial both in the development of counter-hegemonic ways of knowing and the provision of practical support to sustain life in the face of exclusion, privation and violence. Hugh Ryan describes that in the early twentieth century, the formation of queer Brooklyn took a new step when the "scattered moments of queer sexuality that had existed in earlier decades had begun to coalesce into a critical mass."[25] The self-making of new ways of living gender and sexuality built up from very small-scale personal endeavors to reach the threshold of "a more robust and self-organized queer world" by the 1920s and 1930s.[26]

The social reproduction frame needs to be expanded to capture the important work of building queer, trans and other counter-normative communities, whether in bars, homes, performance spaces or meeting rooms, that collectively develop new capacities for self-understanding, self-expression, political action and functional support.[27] The mobilization of queer communities to confront the impact of HIV/AIDS in the face of official obstruction and inaction from the state, much of the health care system and many families of origin provide important examples of counter-normative social reproduction, which includes building care for those who are ill, developing appropriate rituals of grieving, and the production of resources for sustaining health from below, such as safer sex education.[28] M.E. O'Brien discusses this broader conception of caregiving as communist social reproduction associated with family abolition: "In place of the coercive system of atomized family units, the abolition of the family would generalize what we now call care. Care of mutual love and support; care of the labor of raising children and caring for the ill; care of erotic connection and pleasure; care of aiding each other in fulfilling the vast possibilities of our humanity, expressed in countless ways, including forms of self-expression we now call gender."[29]

This expanded understanding of social reproduction helps us understand not only the potential for a post-revolutionary future, but also the insurgent practices of queer and counter-normative communities making lives while negotiating heteronormativity and racialized oppression under conditions of alienation and dispossession. Nat Raha pointed to the crucial role of reproductive labor in practices of racialized trans and queer communities, noting, for example, the Street Transvestites Action Revolutionaries (STAR) commune as a combination of "caring labour, sex work, prison solidarity and political activism."[30] The goal was not only to aggregate resources for subsistence, but also to develop and share practices of emancipation.

LABOR, EROS AND ALIENATION

People realize themselves through life-making activity grounded in shared intentionality that is suffused with eroticism. The aesthetic, material, social and sensuous pleasures of making our mark on the world are inseparable from erotic fulfillment, as our wants and needs intermingle. Given that people are engaged in an ongoing transformative process of making, human nature, including the organization of desire, is necessarily dynamic and open-ended. Marx wrote that through labor, the human "acts on external nature and changes it, and in this way he simultaneously changes his own nature."[31] People transform themselves as they act on the world around them, so that labor is a central dimension of individual and collective self-making.

Marx defined labor power, the capacity to work, as "the aggregate of those mental and physical capacities existing in the physical form, the living personality, of a human being ..."[32] The living personality is oriented towards the realization of actualization of passions through the individual and collective transformation of the world around them. Human labor is not simply the drudge work required to obtain the necessities of life. Marx argued that the human being "produces even when he is free from physical need and only truly produces in freedom therefrom."[33]

The living personality is thus characterized by deliberate world-making that produces an open-endedness, an unrealized transformative potential, a "freedom to do and be otherwise."[34] Capitalist alienation blocks the realization of the potential powers of the living personality. Aaron Jaffe puts the freedom to actualize these potentials at the core of the project of human liberation: "For Marx, this love of freedom, and then what flows from it, is a deep part of every living personality."[35]

The erotic desires of the living personality are an integral dimension of individual and collective life-making, fulfilled not only through sexual activity narrowly defined, but a whole range of physical, mental and spiritual activities in which we realize ourselves and connect to each other. The alienation of our life-making activity undermines human self-realization, creating conditions in which we must trade on our human capacities as the means to an end: "Life itself appears only as a means to life."[36] People may need to trade on sexual allure, for example, to attain access to the necessities of life. As their own humanness is undermined by alienation, people tend to treat each other instrumentally, using each other to meet their own needs: "An immediate consequence of the fact that man is estranged from the product of his labour, from his life activity, from his species-being is the estrangement of man from man."[37]

Yet, at the same time, sexuality can provide tastes of freedom, elements of unalienated life-making. John Rechy provided a sense of this in his 1977 chronicle of the gay erotic underground, *The Sexual Outlaw*: "In the sex moments pressurized into high intensity by life-crushing strictures challenged, the sexual outlaw experiences to the utmost the rush of soul, blood, cum through every channel of his being to the physical and psychical discharge of the fully awakened, living, *defiant* body."[38] The specific masculinity of this sexual underground may tell us something about who is more likely to experience sex as a taste of freedom given dominant power relations of gender and racialization, which tend to undermine the bodily autonomy and sexual agency of women and people who are colonized and racialized.

Erotic expression in capitalist societies is therefore profoundly contradictory, at once deeply formed by alienation and at the same time offering a taste of self-realization and human connection. For Bertell Ollman, alienated sexuality is characterized by loss of control over one's own erotic fulfillment, "the split between the individual and his natural sexual activity …"[39] As humans lose touch with their own erotic subjectivity, they also misrecognize the subjectivity of others, and thus tend to treat each other as means to an end. This produces a transactional approach to sexuality, reflected in "people's treatment of one another as sexual objects and the dissatisfaction this breeds."[40]

Queer revolutionary Mario Mieli, in his pathbreaking *Towards a Gay Communism*, maintains that sexual repression was fundamental to capitalist alienation. The capitalist system "rests on the masculinist and heterosexual

foundations of society and on the repression of Eros that together guaran-
tee the perpetuation of alienated labour and hence the rule of capital."[41] The
repression of the erotic is part of the fragmentation of life-making in conditions of alienation. For John Holloway, in conditions of capitalist alienation:
"Labour is constituted by its separation or abstraction from life-activity.
This separation is supported by a radical subordination of life-activity to the
requirements of labour."[42] The rest of our life-making activity is organized
around alienated labor which is necessary for the survival of workers (their
only way of accessing the means of subsistence) and the profits of capitalists.
This fragmentation and subordination also produces sexuality as a distinct
realm of life-activity:

> This fragmentation of our life-activity is a fragmentation of our lives in
> every aspect. The separation of sexuality from the body as a whole and
> its concentration in the genitals was imposed historically at the same
> time as the abstraction of labour, made a fundamental contribution to
> the creation of the body as a machine for labour and is part of the general
> process of abstraction or separation, the process of limitation, classifica-
> tion and identification.[43]

Alienation fragments life-making activity, undermining the direct connection between labor, self-realization and the inherent fulfillment of wants
and needs. The laboring body is largely desexualized (in terms of the erotic
fulfillment of the worker) to conserve life-energy for the completion of tasks
deemed productive by employers, and sexual activity is confined spatially
and temporally to private locations outside of the time dedicated to alienated work. Certainly, paid labor ranging from fashion sales to waiting tables
may involve elements of sexualized objectification, but that is a dimension of
the labor process distinct from one's own erotic fulfillment.

In the realm of reproductive labor, the alienation of sexuality is more contradictory. On the one hand, there are also important elements of sexual
repression in this realm. In the absence of direct access to the productive
resources to meet wants and needs, reproductive labor tends to become a
privatized responsibility (disproportionately for women) to do the necessary
work to sustain members of the household and connected kin networks,
separated from inherent self-realization and erotic fulfillment. In these conditions, sex tends to take on a transactional dimension as people need to
trade on their sexuality as the means to meet such ends as economic sustenance, being cared for, a sense of self-worth and/or companionship. Yet,

at the same time, sexuality can also take on the taste of freedom, offering elements of genuine connection and fulfillment.

Sexual repression to promote productivity is naturalized under conditions of alienation, where labor and sexuality seem to be distinct and indeed opposed. Freud argued that sexual repression was necessary to orient life-energy productively, as productive work was powered by life-energy redirected from the sexual sphere: "civilization is obeying the laws of economic necessity, since a large part of the psychical energy which it uses for its own purposes has to be withdrawn from sexuality."[44] Herbert Marcuse drew on Freud's analysis of sexual repression, combining it with a Marxist analysis of power in capitalist societies. to argue that the repression of eroticism in capitalist society went beyond what might be necessary to develop the degree of self-regulation required to live in community.

Marcuse accepted that any form of social organization will require some degree of basic repression, "the 'modifications' of the instincts necessary for the perpetuation of the human race in civilization."[45] As social beings, human individuals must develop certain abilities to defer gratification and engage with others. Marcuse suggested that capitalist society was characterized by surplus repression that went well beyond the basic requirements of social engagement, comprising "the restrictions necessitated by social domination."[46]

Alienated labor requires surplus repression to direct life-energy to subordinated drudge work rather than self-realization through creative transformation: "body and mind are made into instruments of alienated labor; they can function as such instruments only if they renounce the freedom of the libidinal subject-object which the human organism primarily is and desires."[47] Freud argued such repression was "normal" development, but Marcuse understood it as a product of specifically capitalist conditions. These constraints on sexuality, "enforced by the need for sustaining a large quantum of energy and time for non-gratifying labour, perpetuate the desexualization of the body in order to make the organism into a subject-object of socially useful performances."[48]

Surplus repression is built on the temporal containment of erotic fulfillment, to the limited free time bounded by subordinated labor: "This happiness which take place part-time during the few hours of leisure between the working days or working nights, but sometimes also during work, enables him to continue his performance, which in turn perpetuates his labor and that of others."[49] This temporal organization of sexuality does not fit easily with the nature of desire, as "the pleasure principle which governs the id is 'timeless' also in the sense that it militates against the temporal dismemberment of pleasure, against its distribution in small sep-arated doses."[50]

Genuine sexual liberation offers the promise of a reintegration of sexuality and labor: "the free development of transformed libido within transformed institutions, while eroticizing previously tabooed zones, times and rela-tions, would minimize the manifestations of mere sexuality by integrating them into a far larger order, including the order of work."[51] This liberation requires "a *transformation* of the libido: from sexuality constrained under genital supremacy to the erotization of the entire personality."[52] In this situ-ation, liberated sexuality "ceases to be a threat to culture and can itself lead to culture-building if the organism exists not as an instrument of alienated labor but as a subject of self-realization – in other words, if socially useful work is at the same time the transparent satisfaction of an individual need."[53] The ultimate result is the "transformation of work into play," the erosion of the boundary between necessary labor and self-realization.[54]

For Audre Lorde, de-eroticization was a central feature of the dominant power structure, reinforcing the gendered and racialized class domination and making our life-making activity into drudgery:

> The principal horror of any system which defines the good in terms of profit rather than in terms of human need, or which defines human need to the exclusion of the psychic and emotional components of that need – the principal horror of such a system is that it robs our work of its erotic value, its erotic power and life appeal and fulfillment. Such a system reduces work to a travesty of necessities, a duty by which we earn bread or oblivion for ourselves and those we love.[55]

Lorde argues that the suppression of the erotic undermines power from below and weakens the bonds of human community as people use each other instrumentally rather than engaging around bonds of mutuality and reciprocity:

> When we look away from the importance of the erotic in the develop-ment and sustenance of our power, or when we look away from ourselves as we satisfy our erotic needs in concert with others, we use each other as objects of satisfaction rather than share our joy in the satisfying, rather than make connection with our similarities and our differences.[56]

Lorde posits that the suppression of erotic fulfillment was a central feature in the organization of subordination:

> When we live outside ourselves, and by that I mean on external directives only rather than from our internal knowledge and needs, when we live away from those erotic guides from within ourselves, then our lives are limited by external and alien forms, and we conform to the needs of a structure that is not based on human need, let alone an individual's.[57]

The struggle to overcome alienation is not only about improving working conditions, but also about opening up the freedom to express and realize ourselves, individually and collectively. Kay Gabriel argues that struggle against alienation is a fundamental feature of trans liberation, which "looks to the aesthetic and sensuous qualities of gender as a dimension of bodily autonomy ..."[58] Overcoming alienation is fundamental to realizing the potential of our bodies and minds: "The point of this politics is to attend to the body as a site of struggle over the intensive disalienation of mental and manual labour."[59]

REIFICATION AND SEXUALITY

People who make lives in conditions of capitalist alienation develop an atrophied sense of their individual and collective generative capacities. They misattribute the outcomes of their own world-making to external forces that seem to operate independently of their will. This is the process of reification, in which our own purposive making is obscured and the historical products of human action take on a life of their own.

People experience reification in the sexual realm in conditions of alienation, where we neither directly inherently sate our desires through our transformative labor nor realize the powers of collectivity through our social world-making. In these conditions, we see our erotic longings as a magnetic force of attraction and repulsion beyond our control. This force seems to be oriented around gender, so that we begin to identify ourselves as primarily lesbian/gay, straight or bi. We misrecognize this historically specific organization of erotic practice as the eternal and natural expression of human desire hard-wired into our being.

Georg Lukacs argues that reification has become a defining feature of human experience in capitalist societies: "man in capitalist society confronts a reality 'made' by himself (as a class) which appears to be a natural phenom enon alien to himself; he is wholly at the mercy of its 'laws', his activity is confined to the exploitation of certain individual laws for his own (egoistic) interests."[60] People develop a sense of their own agency that is largely limited to meeting their own needs within the constraints of capitalism, a social system that seems to be beyond our control – the product of natural laws. While people are indeed subject to the laws of nature, it is a fundamental characteristic of processes of reification to naturalize phenomena that are historical outcomes of human action.

Kevin Floyd, in his path-breaking *Reification of Desire*, maintains that desire itself was reified through the historical development of capitalist societies. People lose touch with their history-making capacities through processes of reification, seeing their life conditions as the unfolding of forces they cannot shape: "Reification enforces an objective but false, 'frozen' immediacy that causes human beings to experience historical processes as natural laws that govern human life and elude human control."[61]

Through the reification of sexual desire, "a bodily capacity is epistemologically abstracted in the form, for example, of qualitatively new heterosexual and homosexual subjectivities."[62] The historical and biographical making of sexuality as a way of organizing the erotic dimensions of life-making disappears from view, constructing the end product of this social process as an independent force shaping human existence rather than as a set of relations that people participate in producing. For Gary Kinsman, "sexuality has come to be fetishized as something individual, "natural" and essential in which social relations and practices disappear."[63]

People experience their own desire as a natural force that drives them, rather than the biographical and historical product of human making in particular circumstances. Sexuality is a reified form of eroticism, naturalized and eternalized so that the historical process of sexual formation is read as the unleashing of in-built tendencies. Thus, for example, the bifurcation of normative sexuality as either queer (LGBTQ) or straight is taken as a foundational feature of human experience. Coming out is characterized as the revelation of an inner truth, but also an eternal one that has been hidden for much of human history by relations of domination.

Reification detaches the present moment from the ongoing process of social formation, and therefore erases the deliberate activity of making that produced the social world we inhabit. Horkheimer and Adorno write in *Dialectic of Enlightenment*, "All reification is forgetting."[64] The erasure of processes of formation naturalizes things as they are at the present moment, so that relations that were built over time are experienced as if they were products of the inevitable working out of immutable natural forces.

David McNally posits that reification specifically produces a forgetting of the laboring body. Reification in capitalist societies produces "a unique kind of fetishistic thinking which 'forgets' the concrete labors that go into producing things."[65] Meat, clothing or electronic tablets beckon from the store shelves, detached from their back stories of gruelling labor, cruelty to animals and imperialist dispossession. People experience their own work (whether for a capitalist employer or in the household) as exhausting and degrading, something to flee. As a result, people learn to idealize the body that "does not experience the ardors of labor, be they those of childbirth or manual work."[66] Bodies are degraded by their association with labor. Given the dominant divisions of labor in capitalist society, this means that the bodies of women and people who are racialized are cast as lesser: "Ideal bodies are white, male, non-laboring and non-libidinal; real bodies are nonwhite, female things, beastly objects of labor and erotic desire."[67] People make sexual lives in the context of this differentiating degradation of the laboring body.

Reification is not simply an illusion, but a lived reality in the context of capitalist alienation where labor is subordinated and human engagement is mediated by commodity exchange. The universalization of commodity exchange is grounded in processes of alienation and dispossession which transform human capacities, land and products into property for exchange. Marx discussed in detail the way people come to fetishize commodities, attributing subjective powers to the products of their own collective labor. He offers the example of a table, at the obvious level an object made from wood for particular use, "an ordinary, sensuous thing."[68] Once that table goes into circulation as a commodity for exchange on the market, it seems to become endowed with its own subjective powers: "It not only stands with its feet on the ground, but in relation to all other commodities, it stands on its head and evolves out of its wooden brain grotesque ideas, far more than if it were to begin dancing of its own free will."[69] In circulation as a commodity for market exchange, the table seems to develop a will of its own and to escape from the grasp of human makers. The relations between makers and products are reversed, so that the things seem to set the terms of engagement. The table, like other commodities ranging from food to clothing to housing, persuades us we need it and establishes (in negotiation with other commodities in circulation) the price it will command for access.

Through processes of reification, particular regimes of sex and gender formation developed in specifically capitalist conditions become naturalized. Sexuality can seem to be among the most natural dimensions of contemporary social life, desire welling up from the body and seizing control of our being. One of the important contributions of queer marxism to our understanding of sexual liberation is in demystifying this process of the naturalization of sexuality, clarifying the ways historically specific forms of sexual practice come to be understood, through processes of reification, as biologically determined natural and eternal dimensions of human life. Queer marxism provides tools to unpack the process of social formation, allowing us to understand the historical character of contemporary configurations of gender and sexuality, and thereby affirming possibilities for change. Unalienated life-making oriented around creative life-making to fulfill our needs and wants opens up the possibilities for new ways of organizing human erotic life beyond contemporary regimes of sexuality and gender expression, opening up possibilities for the realization of our passions and satiation of our hungers.

3

Sexualities at Work

We experience our own bodies, and those of other people, largely through the work practices that take up so much of our waking time. We know the world through our bodily engagement with the world, and different forms of life-making activity habituate us to particular ways of doing and knowing. Carolyn Steedman reflected on the ways her work as a teacher affected her erotic sensibility: "My body died during those years, the little fingers that caught my hand, the warmth of a child leaning and reading her book to me somehow prevented all other meetings of bodies."[1] The emergency room nurse, autoworker on an assembly line, agricultural worker, parent of a newborn, professional football player, porn worker and cosmetics sales person have very different daily experiences of touch, sound, sight, smell, interpersonal interaction, pain and fulfillment. The making of gendered sexualities is organized in part around these everyday life practices that shape the experience of body, self and others.

People spend vast amounts of time immersed in work activities that frame the experience of their bodies in particular ways. Our daily work practices create particular expectations in such areas as hygiene, appearance, dexterity and human touch. The experience of our own bodies and those of others in our work practices contribute to patterns of sexual being. Tamsin Wilton reports that heterosexual women often had limited erotic expectations for their male partners: "Expectations of male sexual proficiency were also low for many women, and there seemed to be a tendency to accept that men's physical presence – their bodies, hygiene and personal habits – were unlikely to be a source of pleasure."[2] It is not surprising that women and men might tend to bring different repertoires of bodily and interpersonal practice to erotic engagement, given their divergent everyday experiences of their bodies at work. Calming a young child with a gentle kiss after a fall in the playground is a very different experience than installing drywall or filling orders in a warehouse. Gender is not only a regime of norms people are taught, but a set of practices they engage in. *Men's Health* magazine was drawing on a specific repertoire of experiences when it referred to sexual activity as "grunt work you'll enjoy."[3]

The everyday experience of embodiment through work is not the only factor that forms gender and shapes practices of desire, but it is a telling factor that is underexplored. Dorothy Smith argues that given the dominant divisions of labor in capitalist societies, there is a tendency to reproduce a gendered organization in ways of knowing the world grounded in everyday life practices: "A bifurcated consciousness is an effect of the actual social relations in which we participate as part of a daily work life."[4] The daily labor of caregiving, which tends to be disproportionately the responsibility of women, leads to a particular experience of the world, a gendered perspective: "The standpoint of women situates the inquirer in the site of her bodily existence and in the local actualities of her working world." Men's work in these divisions of labor tends to be less engaged in direct caregiving. Given this distance from caregiving practices, men's experiences tend to become associated with more abstract and conceptual ways of knowing: "It has been a condition of a man's being able to enter and become absorbed in the conceptual modes, and to forget the dependence of his being in that mode upon his bodily existence, that he does not have to focus his activities and interests upon his bodily existence."[5]

This abstracted conceptual way of living is only possible for a given man because of the reproductive work performed by a woman, "who keeps house for him, bears and cares for his children, washes his clothes, looks after him when he is sick, and generally provides for the logistics of his bodily existence."[6] Caregiving labor in capitalist societies is hidden in the private realm and freighted disproportionately onto the shoulders of women. This leaves the disproportionately masculine public realm emptied of the concrete concerns of sustaining life, allowing for an abstraction from embodiment. Smith maintains that men are positioned to engage in less concrete ways of knowing by their life practices: "Full participation in the abstract mode of action requires liberation from attending to needs in the concrete and particular."[7]

The embodied experience of particular sets of life practices organized around gendered and racialized divisions of labor contributes to forming our sense of self. Jack Halberstam notes that female masculinity is not necessarily an intentional transgression, but can also be constructed through work, so that: "some rural women may be considered masculine by urban standards, and their masculinity may simply have to do with the fact that they engage in more manual labor than other women or live within a community with very different gender standards."[8] A woman's gendered patterns can be "as much a product of her work as her desire."[9]

Knowing is not an exclusively mental activity, but a whole body experience that combines thought and action. For Maurice Merleau-Ponty, we make sense of the world through our bodily experiences: "the grasping of signification is accomplished by the body."[10] Embodied knowledge production maps together sense data and interpretation, as we make sense of the world through our work on it. Sexuality is one dimension of this process of signification through the body, "internally linked to the whole thinking and acting being."[11]

People have very different experiences of everyday labor depending on where they are inserted into complex production processes founded on hierarchical divisions of labor organized around gender, racialization, disability categorizations, migration status, etc. People engage in sexual self-realization in the context of bodily experience grounded in specific daily practices of work under particular conditions, depending on their location within these divisions of labor. Further, workers experience their bodies as sites of subordination, as management develops strategies to utilize divisions of labor and organize labor processes deliberately to undermine worker agency. This experience of subordination, driven deep into the body by everyday practices, has an impact on the formation of sexual selves.

EROTIC CONTAINMENT

The experience of subordination in alienated life-making is reinforced by erotic containment, the repression of inherent embodied and social fulfillment through labor. Chris Chitty suggests that this containment of sexual expression to the private realm was a form of enclosure, parallel to the construction of walls on the land to bound private property and eliminate the commons where all had rights:

> The establishment of bourgeois sexual hegemony – which facilitated both middle-class and working-class men's adjustment to developments in the mode of production by confining sexuality within private spaces and forms of intimacy revolving around the family – was tantamount to a kind of enclosure, forming one episode in a long history of accumulation by dispossession.[12]

One of the central features of erotic enclosure is the interruption of inherent erotic fulfillment through the whole spectrum of transformative labor. Erotic enclosure gets naturalized through the experience of labor in capitalist societies, so that people tend to take for granted the propriety of sexual privacy as if desire is inherently nurtured by silence and darkness.

Erotic enclosure is an important dimension of the productivist orientation in conditions of alienation, the direction of the life-energies of members of the working class away from wasteful (from the employer's point of view) self-gratification towards activities that contribute to capitalist profitability. In the nineteenth century, sexual regulation focused largely on the development of continence, conserving male energy, that might otherwise be misspent, to drive production and household reproduction: "Few forms of energy caused the nineteenth-century middle class more concern about its potential for 'waste' than the peculiar form of sexual energy that this normalized knowledge regime attributed to the male body, energy that was the apparent motor force of both labor and conjugality."[13]

The elimination of sexual practice from the workplace has been a foundational feature of the productivist orientation organized around continence to conserve life-energy for work that makes profits for capitalists or contributes more generally to sustaining the system. Gordon Burrell argues that the suppression of sexuality was a defining feature of bureaucratic and industrial forms of organization, dating back to the early nineteenth century: "the suppression of sexual relations is one of the initial tasks the early factory employers set themselves."[14] Sexuality and human feelings in general were expunged from the workplace and confined to the private realm of household and kin: "The desexualization of labour, for this is what is entailed, involves the repulsion and expulsion of many human feelings out of the organization and out of its sight."[15] Sexual objectification and harassment certainly remained part of the workplace, deeply connected to regimes of subordination, but erotic practice and human intimacy was eliminated as far as that was possible. The goal is not only the conservation of life-energy for labor, but also the increased subordination of the workers: "The control of sex becomes control of populations and control of individual bodies."[16]

The continence regime was focused primarily on producing male sexual temperance, as it was founded on a male-dominated conception of sexuality that understood "the male body as sexually autonomous and sexually active, as housing a potentially explosive sexual desire, and the female body as sexually dependent and *reproductively* active, as dominated by a maternal cycle."[17] This continence-oriented model of sexual regulation was supplanted through the sexual revolutions of the twentieth century, by the rise of sexual liberalism and a fully transactional model of sexuality that is associated with a more active conception of women's desires. These sexual revolutions produced an important reconfiguration of gender relations, challenging aspects of the male-centric model of sexuality by including women as sexual subjects. "The dissociation of sexual desire from male physiology then implicates male as well as female bodies in both sexual objectification and sexual subjectification."[18]

The sexual revolutions of the twentieth century reconfigured erotic containment from a continence-oriented model to a more permissive regulatory regime focused on the spatial and temporal confinement of sexual practice to private life. The temporal organization of erotic fulfillment through time-discipline was central to this regime. Employers and state institutions deployed time-discipline to configure everyday life around productivism and to actualize erotic enclosure. Time-discipline structures the day around the requirement that people be in particular places doing specific tasks during set hours.

E.P. Thompson documented the early resistance of English workers to time-discipline as it was being introduced, rejecting the compulsion to be somewhere simply because a bell had rung and it was Monday. Time-discipline is a dimension of dispossession that fragments the day into time belonging to the worker and that belonging to the employer. The organic rhythms of life, including production and reproduction, were interrupted by time-discipline and replaced by mechanical clock-time. Thompson describes this more organic approach to time and labor as "task orientation" and points out that "a community in which task orientation is common appears to show the least demarcation between 'work' and 'life.'"[19] In these communities, "[s]ocial intercourse and labour are intermingled – the work day lengthens or contracts according to the task – and there is no great sense of conflict between labour and the 'passing of the day.'"[20]

The shift to clock-time is part of the process of dispossession, where members of the working class literally lose control over parts of the day and the overall schedule. The development of compulsory schooling played an important part in that dispossession, habituating children to time-discipline: "Once inside the school gates, the child entered the new universe of disciplined time."[21] The historical resistance of workers to the introduction of time-discipline through absenteeism and refusals gave way to habituation to its rhythms and struggles within its frame: "In the first stage we find simple resistance. But in the next stage, as the new time-discipline is imposed, the workers begin to fight, not against time, but about it."[22]

People habituated to time discipline constantly negotiate the challenge between the abstract movement of the clock and the concrete rhythms of real-life activities, which have their own cycles of engagement and fulfillment. Martineau describes these real rhythms as the "lived temporalities ... of everyday life, the seasons, festivity, reproduction, recreation, emotions, bodies, birth and death ..."[23] People are driven to reconcile the concrete rhythms of erotic desire and fulfillment with the abstract regime of time-discipline. At a most basic level, students in school learn to organize their bodily functions around the rhythms of the clock, as special permission is required to access the toilets during class time and eating is generally prohibited. This means that our sense of our sexuality develops in a body already subordinated to the rhythms of time-discipline to the extent that we organize our hunger, fatigue, toilet time and personal appearance around a mapping of our time vs. theirs.

My comrade Paul Reynolds asked a bracing question from the floor at a Historical Materialism conference session, "Why is no one here talking about time to fuck?" Indeed, sex under capitalism tends to be confined to the margins of the day, when the best of our life-energies have already been spent on monetized and reproductive work. It is worth thinking about how sex might be different if we could take as long as we needed, in the full light of day, with the batteries of our life-energy fully loaded and without shame.

The temporal and spatial containment of erotic desire and fulfillment confronts limits. Firstly, the widespread sexualization of commodities, which has tended to increase over the history of capitalism, means that the sexual realm leaks out into public life in the form of advertisements, songs, films and other cultural artifacts; images and aspirations quite distinct from actual bodily erotic engagement. Secondly, many members of the working class do not have access to private space sufficient for the confinement of sexuality. People who share rooms or are unhoused, those whose work is organized around barracks in remote locations or residence in employer's households, and young people living in familial households lack access to spaces of privacy for sex. People in these situations must find cracks in public space in which to engage sexually, whether in parked cars or quiet woodlands or bars or university washrooms. The only privacy available in these situations is "paradoxically, to be had in public."[24]

MANAGING GENDER AND SEXUALITY

Employers built erotic containment combined with gender discipline into their strategies to enhance productivity. Beginning with the advent of the assembly line in early twentieth-century automotive production, employers developed scientific management strategies that separated the conception of tasks from their execution, so that workers repeat prescribed motions with minimal discretion or innovation. Antonio Gramsci argued that these management strategies required the development of a new sensibility among workers, which included erotic containment: "The truth is that the new type of man demanded by the rationalisation of production and work cannot be developed until the sexual instinct has been suitably regulated and until it too has been rationalized."[25] New scientific management strategies required "a rigorous discipline of the sexual instincts (at the level of the nervous system) and with it a strengthening of the 'family' in the wide sense (rather than a particular form of the familial system) and of the regulation and stability of sexual relations."[26]

This erotic containment was associated with new forms of gender discipline at work. Workers initially responded to the new work rhythms of rationalized mass production by walking away, creating high rates of absenteeism and turnover. The Ford Motor Company, a particularly forward-looking employer in the early twentieth century, began to develop new retention strategies which included an increase in wages for workers, but also the development of new forms of masculine consciousness compatible with the conditions of mass production. Before the development of mass production, masculinity in industrial work had been associated largely with pride in the mastery of a particular set of craft skills. Deskilling undermined this form of craft masculinity, leaving workers feeling demeaned and dehumanized.

Ford engaged the research of its internal sociology department to develop strategies that encouraged employees to associate masculinity with pride in their ability to provide for their family by enduring the pain, noise, dirt and monotony of their work. Wayne Lewchuk suggested that these strategies aimed to build a sense of masculine fulfillment around employment in an auto plant, despite the dehumanizing nature of the daily work,

Collectively, the campaign to glorify hard work and to generate pride in making useful articles, the promotion of a fraternal community through selective hiring policies, and the granting of a family wage that raised the status of men within their households and the community created a package intended to make monotonous and repetitive work manly and hence respectable, if not enjoyable, for Detroit men.[27]

These management strategies included a deliberate policy of hiring men and excluding women.[28] While deskilling had historically been associated with an increasing proportion of women in the workforce, this was not true of the American auto industry as mass production was generalized: "The automobile industry, despite major changes in technology, employed very few women in the United States,"[29] and indeed, by the beginning of World War II, "the purge of women from the plants of Detroit's major assemblers was almost total."[30] Management developed deliberate gendered strategies around the rationalization of labor processes associated with mass production that "tightened, indeed institutionalized, the modern sexual division of labour."[31] Employers have founded many of their management strategies on gender normativity, which, among other things, contributes to the exclusion of trans workers who are not assimilable to dominant divisions of labor.[32]

The centrality of gender discipline to management strategies was also present in Egypt in the early twentieth century, though it played out differently. Hanan Hammad mapped out gendered management strategies developed in Egypt to regulate a workforce of rural and urban origin who had not previously engaged in industrial production: "The construction and representation of masculinity was crucial in converting rural and urban men into industrial workers and involved a classed and gendered struggle over the normalization of the modern productive male subject."[33] Supervisors, for example, often used violence to establish their authority and reinforce labor discipline in the workplace, at times meeting a violent response from workers. Workers developed a sense of masculinity, "somewhere between the pride of securing an income and the defense of their dignity in a hostile work environment."[34] This was a wrenching process, and sometimes created responses of intensified violence against other vulnerable parties in men's lives. "The emotional pain inherent in the hard choice between keeping a job and resisting humiliation could be an important factor in explaining hypermasculine practices such as bullying."[35]

Employers folded in management strategies of racial formation with those of gender discipline and erotic containment. In the period before World War II, Ford stood out among automakers for its policies of hiring Black workers: "While other auto employers resisted integration until the labor shortages of World War II, Ford hired large numbers of black workers as early as 1918 and often put them in important positions, sometimes even supervising whites."[36] Black workers were paid the same amount as white workers, though they were often assigned to particularly difficult jobs, for example, in the foundries: "Though blacks were represented in most jobs at Ford, they were disproportionately assigned to the most distasteful jobs, such as those in the metal foundry, where workers were paid the same as co-workers who worked in less onerous jobs."[37] This pattern of employment reaffirmed dominant ideas of whiteness and blackness among Ford workers: "the strategy may have also reinforced existing stereotypes that black workers – who were entering northern labor markets in large numbers for the first time – were genetically suited for the hottest, dirtiest jobs."[38]

These strategies for racial formation also included the development of a whiteness focused around Americanization and the deliberate assimilation of immigrant workers, for example, through the imposition of a compulsory English-language course. For Clarence Hooker, this language education requirement was "the most readily observable sign of the cultural conversion of immigrant worker" which also included "marital status, home ownership, a savings account, and the purchase of life insurance" as "important indicators of a worker's desire and willingness to be transformed into the preferred type of employee."[39]

Along with gendered and racialized divisions of labor, certain kinds of work tend to be organized along the lines of sexuality, associated with queer or straight workers. Allan Bérubé notes three different characteristics that tended to demarcate work as queer. Firstly, some work is characterized as queer when "jobs are filled by people who are crossing gender roles: jobs where men do women's work and women do men's work, or where effeminate men and masculine women can make a living."[40] A second form is queer work which consists of: "jobs in same-sex environments, especially where women live with women and men live with men, like colleges, jails, and the military."[41] The third category of queer work is aesthetic or service-oriented work for men, including "both personal service jobs – like waiters – and work that focuses on the decorative, designing, and self-expressive arts."[42] Kade Doyle Griffiths contends that queers may develop the capacities to succeed in service-oriented work in part through their own negotiation of hostile heteronormative environments: "the skills to manage trans and queer existence on a social level lend themselves to exploitation as skilled labour in the spheres of social reproduction and hospitality."[43]

Of course, many queers work outside of these fields, often negotiating the challenges of gender discipline and sexual normativities. Anne Balay studied the experiences of lesbians, gays and transgendered workers in Indiana steel plants. She found that women working in those plants, traditionally a male domain, were expected to conduct themselves according to masculine norms: "To 'fit in' at work they need to be masculine, to talk about sex in ways that objectify women, and endure severe and hazardous working conditions without whining."[44] This created real tensions for some LGBTQ workers in these plants. On the one hand, the culture of masculinity did not create a comfortable setting to disclose same-sex relationships or gender non-conforming activities. On the other hand, part of the culture was to talk about life outside work both to create a sense of fellowship to help endure difficult and dangerous work, and to pass time when work was tedious. "Work traditions of gossip, small talk, and cooperation in basic steel mills serve to keep queers invisible, often marginalized and isolated."[45]

M.E. O'Brien maintains that it is the violation of gender discipline rather than sexual orientation that tends to label work as queer: "what makes jobs queer is not really about sexual object choice, but about gender expectations."[46] Particularly in the situations where recognition of lesbian and gay relationships is more widespread, cisgender queers may face only limited obstacles in negotiating employment structured around gendered expectations. In contrast, trans and non-binary workers face tremendous barriers. For O'Brien, "Employers, customers and co-workers have assumptions about the gendered nature of work itself, allowing gender-nonconforming queer people to find a limited and difficult niche." Indeed, the situation of gender-non-conforming people at work tends to be characterized by precarity and poverty: "Deviant or non-normative gender expressions exclude queer people from work, constrain the industries where we can find work, and make experience at work contentious and dangerous."[47] While there are certain professional and service industry niches where some trans people are able to find employment, "there are many African-American and Latina trans women who have survived through criminalized sex work."[48] The precarity of trans people in employment and monetized labor highlights the ways "all working-class people are subject in their jobs to various forms of gender discipline and regulation."[49]

Employers developed strategies for the gendered, racialized and sexualized formation of their workforce that mapped together elements of standardization and differentiation. On the one hand, these management strategies required standardization, the formation of interchangeable deskilled workers who could be rotated through jobs as needed. On the other hand, these strategies were founded on differentiation, the formal or informal designation of jobs on the basis of gender, racialization, national status, disability and/or sexuality, organized around hierarchical divisions of labor that legitimate disparate pay, security and working conditions.[50] Employers have deliberately built erotic containment, gender discipline and racial formation into their strategies to mold the working class into the labor force required to maximize profitability by enhancing productivity.

NORMATIVE REGIMES AT WORK

The dominant normative regimes of gender and sexuality tend to be organized around sustainable relations for living given dominant divisions of labor and the specific organization of work. People may resist these normative regimes, but without a wider ranging reorganization of work and access to resources that alters the calculus of sustainability, the parameters of change will tend to be limited by the need to form viable survival strategies within the existing structures. In this section, I will examine the relationship between heteronormativity and the organization of work.

Heteronormativity can seem elusive, as it does not primarily take the form of an articulated code such as a legal framework: "It consists less of norms that could be summarized as a body of doctrine than of a sense of rightness produced in contradictory manifestations – often unconscious, immanent to practice or to institutions."[51] I am arguing here that sex and gender normativities develop to the point of providing "a sense of rightness" through processes of contestation framed by the existing and historical landscape of alienated labor and social reproduction.

Members of the working class must organize their survival projects around preexisting relations of work and household, which structure the choices available to them. The price of opting for non-normative ways of life rather than participating in these preexisting relations can be very high, including lack of access to fundamental resources for living and the violence of policing, surveillance and carceral detention. Adrienne Rich argued in the 1980s that heterosexuality was, in essence, compulsory for women: "the absence of choice remains the great unacknowledged reality, and in the absence of choice, women will remain dependent upon the chance or luck of particular relationships and will have no collective power to determine the meaning and place of sexuality in their lives."[52] Rich cited Lorraine Hansberry's 1957 letter to the lesbian publication *The Ladder*, which described women as trapped if they "are not prepared to risk a life alien to what they have been taught all their lives to believe was their 'natural' destiny – AND

– their only expectation for ECONOMIC security."[53] The compulsory character of heterosexuality for women was grounded in their limited access to the means of economic and social autonomy, which meant they have often needed to be reliant on men to attain the requirements for living.

Specific configurations of work support particular ways of living gender and sexuality. The apprenticeship system used to train craft workers in European cities early in the development of capitalism required young men to move away from their families to learn specific skills under the guidance of an accomplished practitioner. Chris Chitty argues that this organization of work created the conditions for specific arrangements of sexuality associated with weakened kin relations, in which "norms of late marriage, bachelordom, and casual sex with other men were common ..."[54] Similar norms were supported by the organization of work on the seas, in ports and in the military. [55] In contrast, nearby in the countryside, the organization of work intensified kin relations: "Among tenant farmers, labor-intensive seasons of planting and harvesting required the labor of every family member who could toss seed, heave a scythe, or direct a plow."[56]

Among women, domestic service was the most common form of monetized work from the rise of capitalism up to the early twentieth century. Domestic service, like apprenticeship, often required a move away from one's family of origin. Servants, who often resided in their employers' households, faced strict regulation: "Stringent codes of class and gender marked the relation between master and servant as one of personal dominance and subordination. Female servants lived as dependents, tied to their masters' households."[57] Domestic servants were generally expected be sexually abstinent and to conform to "exaggerated codes of meekness and cleanliness."[58]

While some women worked in domestic service for their whole adult life, others left once they were in a position to marry: "'Better' servants and their suitors, usually skilled or semi-skilled workers, shared their masters' sense of respectability. They aimed to acquire some economic security as a basis for marriage."[59] While there is clear evidence of historical patterns of same-gender sexual activity among men in homosocial work situations removed from kin, the evidence of women's sexual practices in the household realm is rather sparse. For Raffaella Sarti, some servants might have continued in service rather than marrying as a result of their own same-gender preferences: "Though evidence on this is scarce, it seems likely that the dislike of marriage felt by some servants was due to their homosexuality, which in some cases may even have found some gratification within the employer's household, in the case of both female and male servants."[60] In the absence of historical records, cultural representation in literature may provide some indication of life-practices, though of course fiction is never a simple record of life as it is lived. Erotic dimensions of relations between the elite mistress of the household and female servants were explored in Victorian nineteenth-century fiction.[61]

These examples show ways that the organization of alienated labor structures embodied experience and frames possibilities for sexual expression. More broadly, the emergence of sexuality as a form of social identity was linked to the organization of work in capitalist societies. John D'Emilio developed a path-breaking analysis of the connection between the dominant organization of labor in capitalist societies and the rise of the homosexual as a type:

> Only when individuals began to make their living through wage labor, instead of as parts of an interdependent family unit, was it possible for homosexual desire to coalesce into a personal identity – an identity based on the ability to remain outside the heterosexual family and to construct a personal life based on attraction to one's own sex.[62]

Capitalist dispossession and the restructuring of everyday life around alienated work and privatized reproduction provided the historical basis for the development of sexuality as a distinct realm of existence, marked by the emergence of social identities focused around the gendered orientation of one's sexual attraction (homosexual, heterosexual, bisexual). Ross and Rapp argue, "The separation, with industrial capitalism, of family life from work, of consumption from production, of leisure from labor, of personal life from political life, has completely reorganized the context in which we experience sexuality."[63]

It was in these conditions that homosexuality came to be understood as a way of life. For Gayle Rubin, "The idea of a type of person who is homosexual is a product of the nineteenth century."[64] Sexual practices in non-capitalist societies, whether same-gender or different-gender oriented, were generally a part of existing kinship relations which were the basis of all life-making activities. In certain cultures, men engaged in same-gender activities as initiation into manhood or in connection with apprenticeship in warfare or philosophy, but this did not tend to define their identity as they would also engage in different-gender activities as prescribed by kinship relations. It was only after the homosexual, the person who specialized in same-sex desire, was named that it became necessary to develop a term that labelled the taken-for-granted dominant form of different-sex desire as "heterosexuality."[65] From the outset, the forms of heterosexuality that developed as normative were defined in part by their counterposition to homosexuality ("no homo").

Capitalist dispossession and the reorganization of productive and reproductive labor created the conditions in which people forged emergent sexualities from below, structured around the organization of work and the limited freedom afforded in the private realm. State policy-makers developed modes of sexual regulation designed to organize these emergent sexualities around the requirements for sustaining the current social order. The development of sex as a *public* issue took place as the bodies of wide layers of the laboring population were becoming *private*, the property of self-owning persons. Foucault noted that officials began to focus in new ways on the regulation of sex in the eighteenth century: "Between the state and the individual, sex became an issue, and a public issue no less; a whole web of discourses, special knowledges, analyses, and injunctions settled upon it."[66] Policy-makers made sexual activity an object of public scrutiny and intervention as the new private realm of self-reproduction was developing. Sexual normativities were developed through a process of contestation from above and below in the context of dynamic capitalist social relations that included the ongoing restructuring of work to maximize profitability.

In the later twentieth and early twenty-first centuries, feminist and queer struggles, along with processes of capitalist restructuring associated with lean production and neoliberalism, have created the possibility for the formation of viable and sustainable same-sex relationships, modelled largely on the dominant heteronormative forms.[67] Lisa Duggan described this as 'the new homonormativity': "a politics that does not contest dominant heteronormative assumptions and institutions but upholds and sustains them while promising the possibility of a demobilized gay constituency and a privatized, depoliticized gay culture anchored in domesticity and consumption."[68] Such lives of domesticity and consumption depend on participation in capitalist employment and particular forms of household labor.

In short, people make sexual lives in relation to the dominant organization of work, which renders certain ways of living relatively viable or unviable. The spaces of sexual freedom and unfreedom are not structured on moral grounds alone, but are organized around the particular institutions and practices of work, both in the form of capitalist employment and household labor.

WORK AND SURVIVAL PROJECTS

People actively make lives, negotiating the constraints of alienated labor and regimes of sexual normativity. We organize this life-making activity into survival projects, building relationships to aggregate our efforts and share out resources: "people must enter into various kinds of affiliation to secure the basic necessities of life."[69] We construct families, households or other forms of relationship, configured around the need to engage in alienated labor which is structured in particular ways.

These survival projects are contradictory as they tend to combine the compulsion and drudgery of alienated labor with some degree of self-realization. To make their survival projects viable, members of the household must engage in reproductive work and employment (or monetized equivalent). At the same time, such projects offer at least some possibility for a space of self-realization outside of the direct supervision of employers and authorities, though that is limited both by the internal power relations of the family itself and persistent policing by various state regulatory agencies.

People form families, households and communities to survive, thrive and resist as best they can in capitalist societies. These survival projects undergird their identities: "patterns of affiliation are fundamental to how individuals define the boundaries of their solidarities, how they position themselves in relation to others, how they organize a worldview, and how they develop their various definitions of self, including their gendered identities."[70] People forge survival projects that organize their experiences of work and form a crucial dimension of their sense of self, including sexuality and gender expression.

Survival projects necessarily trace out what Ferguson and McNally describe as "the inner connections of household, neighbourhood and community activities with the monetized social activities (predominantly wage-labour) necessary to market-dependent reproduction, wherein food, housing, transportation, clothing and so on must be purchased as commodities."[71] People form affiliations in order to make lives in the context of a given landscape of work and life that frames sustainable possibilities. In the words of Johanna Brenner,

Social reproduction includes caring labor but also includes how sexuality is organized – not only because of biological reproduction but because intimacy and desire are mobilized in and through institutions that organize social reproduction – in capitalism, for example, the privatized, nuclear family household.[72]

People organize their survival projects around the local and global landscape of alienated labor, including divisions of labor, possibilities for secure or precarious employment, prevailing wage levels, forms of oppression, colonialism and state regulation, access to housing, and temporal rhythms of work. These configurations of work tend to frame the realm of possibility for life-making, including sexual activity. Certainly, members of the working class can resist, influencing these conditions through mobilization to fight for better wages and/or working conditions, access to affordable housing, decent health care and education, social provision and other necessities of life; and struggles for power and rights for racialized people, queers, women, those designated disabled and others. People can also make lives in defiance of these conditions of alienated labor, though at the risk of poverty, incarceration and denial of status.

SEX AS WORK

People engage in sex work as one of a range of survival strategies in conditions of alienation that compel the dispossessed to trade on their human capacities. Sex work undermines erotic containment, transgressing the boundaries between the confinement of sexuality to private spaces and the creation of public spaces marked by continence and productivity. Indeed one component of the ongoing criminalization of sex work is the violation of the boundaries of erotic containment that demarcate between work and sex.

The notional boundary between sex and work is clearly inoperative in the various forms of sex work and is complex in the realm of reproductive labor. In the latter, the line between sexual engagement with a partner and the requisite labor of caregiving in the reproductive realm may be difficult to discern, for example, in the situation of an economically dependent household member who feels compelled to fulfill a partner's desires as part of the deal (explicit and/or implicit) that provides access to resources for living. Sex within marriage and other forms of household arrangement can be a form of labor required for access to sustenance, even if it may not be reducible to work.

Paid sex work takes a variety of forms, providing very different degrees of agency and a range of experiences for the workers themselves. The definition of sex work as "work" – a form of monetized labor – has derived in part from the self-organization of sex workers, who developed a frame built around agency that was distinguished from moral categories. Gowri Vijay-akumar notes that sex worker organizing in India changed the way words were used: "especially in the 1990s, this activism has grown both in scale and formality, and the term 'sex worker' has become more central to organizing in India and transnationally."[73] The increasing use of this term is associ-ated with the development of a new collective identity through mobilization. Despite this emergent identity, Vijayakumar observes that activists diverged on the basis of "different interpretations of sex work as 'sex' or as 'work,'" as well as "different experiences of anonymity and visibility in public spaces."[74]

In the Global North, a wave of sex worker organizing began in the early 1970s, inspired by the general insurgency of the period, including queer and feminist mobilizing. Melissa Gira Grant attributes the importance of San Francisco as a hub in the emergence of sex workers' mobilizations in the United States to its vibrant history of recent mobilizations: "Without its student liberation movement, its black liberation movement, its women's liberation movement, and its gay liberation movement I can't imagine San Francisco birthing a prostitutes' rights movement ..."[75] Chi Adanna Mgbako notes the particular importance of queer liberation, given the specific history of mobilizing against the police, and the crucial role of trans activ-ists, including sex workers, in these mobilizations: "In response to rampant police abuse against the queer community, transgender women who engaged in sex work participated in uprisings such as the 1966 Compton's Cafeteria Strike in San Francisco and the 1969 Stonewall Riots in New York City."[76] The militant workers mobilizations of the 1960s and 1970s certainly offered a model of transforming conditions of work through mass direct action.

While mass insurgency was widespread in the early 1970s, sex workers in certain North American urban centers also faced defensive struggles against new forms of policing and regulation. Sarah Beer argues that sex worker self-organization in the Canadian state in the 1970s was driven in part by the need for a defensive response to increasingly punitive policing and new measures to drive out sex work in the interest of gentrification of urban cores and the reorientation of main streets towards new forms of commerce: "By the mid-1970s, however, plans were underway for a renewal of com-mercial development, with municipal politicians anxious to make urban centres more appealing to middle-class shoppers, with police set to re-estab-lish control over prostitution areas, and with major newspapers garnering support for 'clean-up' campaigns."[77]

The relationship of sex and work in sex work is sharply debated. The elimination frame maintains the suppression of sex work is the only way to pursue justice, as these practices are founded on compulsion and violence (particularly violence against women). In this frame, the organization of sex workers simply perpetuates violence: "When prostitution is understood as violence, however, unionizing prostituted women makes as little sense as unionizing battered women."[78] Advocates of elimination argue any move to treat sex work like other forms of labor ignores its fundamental basis in forms of compulsion and violence against women: "Legal sex businesses provide locations where sexual harassment, sexual exploitation, and violence against women are perpetrated with impunity."[79] One of the key foundations of this frame is the impossibility of true consent within the power relations of compulsion and violence that characterize the sex trades: "The silence of most of those in prostitution is a result of intimidation, terror, dissociation, and shame. Their silence, like the silence of battered women, should not be misinterpreted, ever, as their consent to prostitution."[80]

In contrast, the labor frame stresses the parallels between sex work and other forms of alienated labor. For Chateauvert, women in sex work as well as "homeless boys, undocumented immigrants, transgender people of color, and other marginalized and social undesirables" do what they need to do to get by:

They hustle, using sex – the one form of labor capital they possess – to obtain food, shelter, clothing, medicine, physical protection, and other necessities. Such trades are survival strategies for a population shut out of other forms of work, in a nation that does not affirm a human right to shelter, food, or health care."[81]

Kimberly Hoang observes that sex workers she interviewed in Vietnam favorably compared their work conditions to "their personal experience of factory work, domestic work, and other forms of service work, which they saw as far more exploitative than sex work."[82] This is not to deny the specificity of sex work, but to locate it within a spectrum of control and exploitation. Truc, a sex worker, told Hoang in a conversation that the NGOs focused on uplifting sex workers "should go save factory workers who are forced to work long hours for little pay, [are] beat by their bosses, and [who] sometimes have to offer sexual [favors] to get higher pay."[83] Most importantly, the sex workers Hoang interviewed worked in bars in which "the actual practice of sex work operated according to strict moral codes oriented toward freedom and consent rather than forced labor."[84]

The criminalization of sex work has tended to undermine the agency of workers to construct codes based on freedom and consent, casting sex workers simply as victims in need of protection. Despite the impressive strides in sex worker organizing in the Canadian state, "sex workers today remain bound in webs of criminalization and regulation whereby access to legal protections is legitimated only when they are conceptualized as victims."[85] The overall legal context for sex workers in the Canadian state "is one where sex workers' safety strategies have been disrupted, antagonistic relationships with police and other regulatory officials continue to persist, and stigma and discrimination remain."[86]

Whereas the elimination frame sees consent within sex work as essentially impossible given the dominant regime of violence and the dehumanization of women and other sex workers, the labor frame sees consent as problematic across the spectrum of employment situations. Durisin argues that the understanding of consent as impossible in sex work is based on the implication "that the body is appropriated in its totality in prostitution."[87] This framing of sex work as the "commodification of the body in its entirety, as in slavery" leads to the conclusion "that there is no way for prostitution to be anything other than total victimization, precluding the possibility of sex workers' resistance."[88]

The key question in these debates is the extent to which the alienation of sexual activity as property is different from, or parallel to, the alienation of other core human capacities in the everyday sale of labor power. The elimination frame is based on an analysis of sexual activity as distinctly foundational to the self, so that its alienation can only mean the total loss of one's humanity. In contrast, the labor frame is based on the conception that all wage labor involves alienation of fundamental human capacities to think and do, and that sexual activity is not necessarily a completely distinct category of activity. As Durisin points out, violence and sexual exploitation can be present "in many forms of employment."[89] The question of consent is complex across the whole spectrum of requisite labor as self-owning members of the working class are compelled to alienate core human capacities as property as it is the only available means to meet their wants and needs. Self-ownership is the fundamental precondition for consent to alienated labor, but it is never separate from compulsion as it is necessarily paired with dispossession. Many of the key issues in the discussion of sex work as work echo those in others areas of alienated labor.

Heather Berg posits that porn workers engage in that work specifically because it allows them to complete their requisite labor more efficiently than might be possible in more conventional forms of employment: "one of porn's major draws is that one can make more money in less time, leaving space for a life not wholly focused on earning next month's rent."[90] This is not necessarily a simple equation, as porn work is generally precarious and involves a great deal of work to keep the body marketable. Berg contends that the nature of porn work "blurs the lines between working, preparing for work, and cultivating the kind of self that makes work possible."[91] Porn workers, outside of paid activity, must engage in "the constant labors of self-making and marketing ... in workspaces ranging from gyms and salons to homes and vacation spots."[92] The need for porn workers to create a self, according to the standards of images that can only be attained through intense work (gym, diet, hair removal, makeup, etc.), rather than real life certainly intensifies these labors of self-making in certain realms, though more broadly it is a feature of alienated labor under capitalism that workers must engage in various forms of self-making in their "free" time, blurring boundaries between work and leisure.

In porn work, there can be a complex and contradictory relationship between workers' own fulfillment and the apparent authenticity that managers demand for the viewing pleasure of the audience. For porn workers themselves, actual fulfillment distances porn work from the drudge labor associated with other forms of paid work: "Authentic pleasure creates that distance from straight work, which performers overwhelmingly frame as pleasureless."[93] But this authenticity is at the same time alienated: "Managers do use this dynamic to extract more work for less; they frame authentic pleasure as a substitute for good pay and compel additional emotional labor of performers, who must demonstrate their personal investment in the work."[94] This creates a complex situation where the performance of authenticity becomes work: "the performance of 'wanting to be there' is part of the job when managers want workers to come to set for the 'fun aspect'..."[95]

Berg summarizes her conversations with porn workers who discuss elements of inherent fulfillment in their work: "Sometimes, even with a bad contract, a long day on set, and the demand to open up for the camera, porn work also feels *authentically* good."[96] This is in part a contrast with other kinds of paid labor: "This says as much about straight work – and why many porn workers reject it – as it does about porn. One problem with work is indeed its 'falsity,' the way it alienates workers from their own bodies and relations with others."[97] The contrast with the repression of sexuality in "straight" work can create a sense of authenticity in the realm where sexuality is work, even if this can never be simply distinguished from elements of compulsion.

RESISTANCE AND SELF-REALIZATION

Members of the working class actively engage in survival projects, building community with others not only to negotiate the existing landscape of work and life, but also at times to change the world. In these survival projects, people deploy individual and collective agency to bend the alien worlds of monetized and reproductive labor around their own wants and needs, working to attain not only reasonable remuneration, but also livable hours of work, mental and physical health and safety, dignity and freedom from harassment. Workers mobilizing to make lives have played a crucial role in shifting the terrain of sexual normativities and challenging regimes of gender discipline.

One crucial dimension of survival projects, spanning monetized and reproductive work, has been the struggle for sexual subjectivity, the resources and bodily autonomy for erotic self-realization. This has included, for example, mobilization around the length of the working day, which aims to maximize the time outside of the direct control of employers as well as resistance to the sexual objectification and harassment that pervades many workplaces. Ryan Patrick Murphy noted the influence of the new wave of feminist and lesbian/gay liberation struggles in the 1960s and 1970s on flight attendant mobilizing, providing activists with "a new set of conceptual tools" to challenge such inequities as sexual objectification and pay differentials between women and men.[98] He provides the powerful example of a flight attendant who was reinstated due to activist mobilization after being removed from a flight for insubordination on the basis of her refusal to wear lipstick in defiance of the orders of a flight captain.[99] Murphy shows the ways flight attendants successfully mobilized against employment practices that forced out older workers on the basis that they were less attractive, and specific management practices to control the personal appearance of racialized employees.

The struggle for sexual subjectivity was not simply about combating objectification and harassment, but also access to fulfilling ways of living: "Unlike teaching, nursing, or administrative work, becoming a stewardess gave middle-class white women unprecedented access to an urban, cosmopolitan world, one usually reserved for businessmen."[100] Flight attendants gained access to a world of travel associated with particular kinds of sexual freedom and exploration often denied to women. For gay male flight attendants, work in the travel industry offered the opportunity to explore the queer scene in the major metropolitan centers, home to particular cultural expressions of sexuality on a larger scale.

The realm of social reproduction has also been a crucial site of struggles around sexual subjectivity. Angela Davis and Saidiya Hartman both argue a sexual revolution took place among African-American women in the early twentieth century, as they accrued formal self-ownership and migrated to northern cities following legal emancipation from conditions of enslavement. The end of slavery produced certain degrees of freedom in the personal realm for African-Americans, but offered little improvement in their economic situations or social and political experiences as white supremacy and racism persisted in slightly restructured forms. For Angela Davis, "Sexuality thus was one of the first domains in which emancipation was acted upon and through which its meanings were expressed."[101] Black women played a leading role in creating new models of sexual freedom for women, shifting the terrain of social reproduction in important ways. Saidiya Hartman described this process:

> After the slave ship and the plantation, the third revolution of black intimate life unfolded in the city. The hallway, bedroom, stoop, rooftop, airshaft and kitchenette provided the space of experiment. The tenement and rooming house provided the social laboratory of the black working class and the poor. The bedroom was a domain of thought in deed and a site for enacting, exceeding, undoing, and remaking relations of power.[102]

Indeed, the organization of production and social reproduction along the lines of gendered, sexualized and racialized divisions of labor can create spaces for collective self-formation by bringing people together. Allan Bérubé argues that queer work could be contradictory, both an occupational dead end to which one was shunted when other doors were closed, and also a place of community: "It was in queer jobs where many of us first discovered that we weren't alone. It's where we first learned how gay people can cover for each other and even create camaraderie in the workplace."[103] Elements of queer cultural expression could thrive in these situations: "Here we could sometimes use our own language, make up secret codes, and give each other campy nicknames."[104]

Bérubé explored the radical potential of queer work in his path-breaking study of the Marine Cooks and Stewards (MCS) Union on the west coast of North America in the 1930s and 1940s. The union, after long internal struggles which vitalized the rank and file and transformed practices, took up the fight for justice for queer and racialized crew members on passenger liners, which meant among other factors overcoming a history of racist exclusion.[105] Given predominant divisions of labor, stewards jobs tended to be associated with queer and racialized workers. In the 1930s, at a time of rising worker insurgency and a radical left with genuine social weight, the divisions of labor on these passenger liners became the basis for organizing based on new forms of solidarity and combativity.

MCS militants developed a new ethos of solidarity, described by activist Revels Cayton: "If you let them red-bait, they'll race-bait, and if you let them race-bait, they'll queen-bait. These are all connected."[106] The sense of mutual support in the face of baiting and attacks buttressed a new audacity in everyday practices at work and in union negotiations. Frank McCormick recalled his response to being summoned to a table he was waiting on by a diner calling him "boy": "If you want my service, I am not your boy, I am a steward, and I have a name. If you do not treat me with respect, I can and will refuse to serve you."[107]

The situation in the MCS was exceptional in the 1930s and 1940s. Union action around queer issues reappeared after the rise of lesbian and gay liberation in the 1960s and 1970s. Ultimately these struggles played an important role in making new forms of open queer existence viable, which created new possibilities for more integrative identities that moved out of the private realm into public life. Workers mobilized to make it possible to be out at work, overcoming the sanctions that had confined queer life to the nighttime and private life.

The militant Canadian Union of Postal Workers achieved a precedent-setting breakthrough in their 1981 strike, winning collective agreement on language prohibiting discrimination on the basis of sexual orientation, at a time when such protection was absent from all human rights codes in the Canadian state, with the exception of Quebec.[108] The same strike also won paid maternity leave, and both of those gains were taken up by many other unions in the Canadian state, particularly in the public sector. A few years later, Canadian Union of Public Employees library workers in Toronto won recognition for same-gender relationships as part of a strike settlement, providing partners and their dependents access to benefits.[109] These union victories anticipated state recognition in terms of human rights codes and social policy frames. Same-gender domestic partnerships were only recognized in legislation in the later 1990s in Canada, after these relationships were recognized in many collective agreements, particularly in the public sector, conferring the same coverage for benefits and leave as heterosexual marriage. In each of these situations, queer workers played a key role in mobilizing to engage fellow workers. The struggle to transform work, both monetized and reproductive, is a crucial dimension of the struggle for sexual subjectivity and genuine fulfillment of our self-defined wants and needs.

4
Market Model Sexualities

INTRODUCTION: SEXUAL LIBERALISM AND THE COMMODIFICATION OF INTIMACY

Over the history of capitalism, relations of alienation have entered more deeply into our everyday lives, transforming our social engagements increasingly into transactions organized along the lines of market exchange. People more and more organize their sexual lives, ranging from casual encounters to marriage, as transactions governed by contract. People have sex not simply to fulfill their own erotic desires and those of their partners, but also as the means to such ends as economic security, companionship, self-esteem, social standing or personal care. A regime of sexual liberalism has developed through a process of struggle, organizing our erotic lives along market lines.

The consolidation of the regime of sexual liberalism has made the contract the dominant form of regulation for intimate relations, including marriage, common law coupledom and consent to sexual activity in any form. Mobilization from below played a crucial role in the development of sexual liberalism, as women, queers and people who are racialized and/or colonized have fought for the right to bodily autonomy including the requirement for full consent to sexual activity. The regime of sexual liberalism is thus contradictory, on the one hand, providing crucial tools for bodily autonomy and, on the other hand, drawing on market exchange as the model for interpersonal agency. Among other key issues, the contract frame is organized around the formal equality of parties to a transaction, despite substantive inequalities based on age, gender, racialization, colonial or migration status, categorization as disabled, class and/or sexuality.

SEXUAL LIBERALISM AND THE MARKET MODEL

Sexual liberalism was an important dimension of the generalization of market relations as capitalist alienation was woven more deeply into the fabric of daily life. The liberal model of market transactions freed from fetters and regulated by contract was extended into the realm of interpersonal relations. For Pamela Haag, the development of sexual liberalism marked "a cultural transition from classic to modern liberalism, from laissez-faire in economic contract to laissez-faire – profoundly uneven, to be sure – in sexual 'contracts' under the right of privacy ..."[1] The development of sexual liberalism in the early twentieth-century United States expanded the use of consent linked to the social contract form that regulated the labor market and relations of citizenship: "the deployment of consent or violence in one type of relationship necessarily affects and is modified with reference to other social 'contracts' inherent in citizenship and labor."[2]

The development of sexual liberalism was also driven from below, as women, queers and trans people, Black and Indigenous people, migrants and those categorized as disabled created new ways of living that allowed them to realize the contradictory and limited freedom of bodily autonomy grounded in self-owning personhood. In the United States, the early twentieth-century struggles against rape conducted largely by Black women played a crucial role in the development of new ways of organizing sexuality. The activism of Black women was prominent, given the context of racist dehumanization which made Black women particularly vulnerable to sexual assault while Black men were treated as a sexual threat.

Angela Davis argues that sexual assault was a defining feature of relations of enslavement: "Sexual coercion was ... an essential dimension of the social relations between slavemaster and slave."[3] This rape culture outlasted the specific conditions of slavery: "The pattern of institutionalized sexual abuse of Black women became so powerful that it managed to survive the abolition of slavery."[4] Racialized and gendered dehumanization contributed to the persistence of sexual assault, and indeed was reinforced by it.

Black women such as Ida B. Wells played a crucial role in the politicization of sexual consent and coercion in the struggle against lynching. In the words of Bettina Aptheker, "the anti-lynching movement of Black women may also be understood as a movement against rape. The women used the only political forms and arguments available to them. They forged a movement that, for the first time in United States history, made rape a political issue."[5] The lynching of Black men drew on a mentality that "required the dehumanization of Black men (as rapists), Black women (as prostitutes) and white women (as property whose honour was to be avenged by the men who possessed them)."[6] The mobilization of Black women against lynching necessarily challenged this whole logic: "In defending the racial integrity of

Black manhood, Wells simultaneously affirmed the virtue of Black woman-hood and the independence of white womanhood."[7]

In this context, the fight for the right to engage in consensual sexual activity and refuse non-consensual activity was a crucial component of the mobilization for the full right to autonomous personhood, challenging the dehumanization on the basis of gender and racialization. This fight was a crucial dimension of Black women's remaking of intimate life that Saidiya Hartman described as a "revolution in a minor key": "This upheaval or trans-formation of black intimate life was the consequence of economic exclusion, material deprivation, racial enclosure, and social dispossession; yet it, too, was fueled by the vision of a future and what might be."[8]

This "revolution in a minor key" played a crucial role in the development of the regime of sexual liberalism that reoriented sexuality around concep-tions of bodily autonomy grounded in self-ownership and property exchange regulated by contract. Yet, full personhood grounded in self-ownership is not the same thing as substantive equality. Haag writes that the consent frame in sexuality "presupposes, implicitly – as does consent in economic transactions, or any other free contracts – that women and men already have sufficient equality and parity in heterosexual relations that they *can* make straightforward, verbal assertions that adequately reflect desires."[9] Further, the organization of erotic life around consent falls far short of relations of mutuality and reciprocity in which people take responsibility for meeting each other's needs as a condition of shared existence, as our outcomes are deeply interwoven.[10]

At its core, the regime of sexual liberalism is built on contradictory con-ditions of freedom and compulsion, so that members of the working class feel a degree of bodily autonomy grounded in self-ownership while alienat-ing their most human capacities. Breanna Bhandar argues that self-owning members of the working class experience themselves as "composed of qual-ities that are both alienable (I alienate my labour in the external world and through this act of alienation, come to own things) and inalienable (as the labour of continually constituting myself through reflection, and exercis-ing my power of appropriation over my own processes of reflection)."[11] Full personhood in sexual liberalism is rooted in real but limited freedom that is inseparable from compulsion and measured relative to the unfreedom of others who are dehumanized on the basis of gender, racialization, colonized or migrant status, social class, sexuality or categorization as disabled.

Elaine Freedgood points out that people must negotiate this contradiction on an ongoing basis, feeling fully human while treating their most characteristic human capacities as property for exchange: "Ideally, modern subjects must be capable of selling parts of themselves or capable of alienating parts of themselves economically without becoming alienated psychologically."[12] We must alienate our must human capacities without losing our sense of humanity, maintaining, "the constant aura of inalienability, an aura that any object can possess and that need only be imagined to be sustained."[13] The aura of inalienability is crucial to sustaining the limited and contradictory freedom of sexual liberalism, in which ownership of our own bodies is inseparable from the compulsions to alienate our most human capacities.

THE ROLE OF COMPANIONATE MARRIAGE

One of the central features of the regime of sexual liberalism was the generalization of companionate marriage, based on the contractual relationship between formally equal partners with a basis in sexual attraction. Tina Simmons described the specific characteristics of this emergent form of intimate relations: "Companionate marriage reflected a more individualistic society and a vision of marriage as the union of two individuals bonded through sexual love, rather than the traditional institution of childbearing, kin, and property relations."[14]

Feminist and anti-racist mobilizations in the early twentieth century created the grounds for the generalization of companionate marriage. One of the key prerequisites of contractually based sexual and intimate engagement was the formal equality between the partners who freely entered the relationship. Early twentieth-century feminists mobilized for rights that opened up a new, active conception of women's sexuality linked to a broader conception of women's full humanity: "Men's right to nurture their sexual selves was also important, but women are more central to the story. People at the time believed women's increased freedom was driving sexual and marital change."[15] D'Emilio and Freedman argue that companionate marriage "redefined marriage in more egalitarian terms" so that a "successful relationship rested on the emotional compatibility of husband and wife, rather than the fulfillment of gender-prescribed duties and roles."[16]

Yet, despite the apparent egalitarianism of companionate marriage, it was still grounded in privatized responsibility for sustaining the household and raising the next generation organized around dominant hierarchical gendered and racialized divisions of labor in capitalist employment and reproductive work. The equality between partners was primarily the formal equality of participants in market exchange and contract relations. This formal equality has been inseparable from substantive inequalities based on gender, racialization, income and national status. Heterosexual relationships have continued to be based on women's disproportionate responsibility for unpaid or poorly paid caregiving labor and gender gaps in pay, as well as other dimensions of male dominance, violence against women and gendered violence.

Sex reformers played an important mediating role in translating these trends into new codes of state regulation, which meant certain innovations from below were generalized while others were rendered invisible and/or repressed. These sex reformers in the United States engaged in the development of new modes of normativity that placed sexual attraction at the center of an emergent form of romantic marriage. Tina Simmons suggests, "The revisions of marriage proposed in the 1920s were a new phase in the development of love marriage, one in which reformers sought to stress the specifically sexual component of romantic love."[17]

The emergence of companionate marriage was driven both by the deeper commodification of all aspects of life, including human capacities, and by resistance from below in the form of freedom struggles which included sexual dimensions. Eva Illouz argues that the romantic model of companionate marriage is related to the generalization of market relations: "What we call the 'triumph' of romantic love in relations between the sexes consisted first and foremost in the disembedding of individual romantic choices from the moral and social fabric of the group, and in the emergence of a self-regulated market of encounters."[18] The generalization of alienated labor undermined broader kinship networks and created openings: "Production for the market created wage-dependency for broader swaths of the population, unseating the family as the primary economic unit of self-reproduction and opening up sexual and life options outside its restrictive form."[19] Yet, this opening up of sexual life was inseparable from the compulsion to alienate one's human capacities.

SEXUAL ALLURE AND INTIMATE RELATIONS

Feminist, queer and anti-racist struggles throughout the twentieth century expanded the purview of sexual liberalism beyond companionate marriage to frame the whole range of forms of sexual and intimate engagement. In Canada and other places in the Global North, the sexual revolution since the 1960s generalized the hegemonic forms of sexual liberalism beyond heterosexual companionate marriage to include a wider range of contractual relations including: lesbian and gay marriage, unmarried common-law couple relations (whether same or different gender), and sexual relations more generally (as governed by consent).

Sexual attraction was the cohesive element in forging and sustaining these contractually regulated relationships. Illouz contends that this understanding of sexual attraction was a specific historical departure:

> although "sexiness" has probably been somewhat implicitly present throughout history, as an aspect of attraction and love, its deployment as an explicit, pervasive and legitimate cultural category and criterion of evaluation is essentially modern in that it is underpinned by vast economic and cultural organizations codifying sexual allure and sexiness.[20]

This organization of relationships around sexual allure was central to the development of emergent market exchange forms. People began to treat their sexual allure as alienable property, to be exchanged for some combination of companionship, respect, shared leisure, caregiving, economic security, co-residence or similar factors. People invest great work in honing this allure through fitness, fashion, development of appropriate repertoires of leisure activity; primping their property to ensure demand when it reaches the market. The honing of sexual allure was associated with a shift in the understanding of the body: "Such search for sensuous satisfaction gave way to the sexualization of the body: the body could and should evoke sexuality and eroticism, arouse it in others, and express it."[21]

In these circumstances, people necessarily work hard to enhance the value of their body, both in terms of productivity and sexual allure. It is increasingly common for people to apply the methods of scientific management, designed to enhance the productivity of alienated labor, to discipline their own bodies and maximize allure. People self-monitor using mobile devices to improve their performance, for example, by counting steps. Adam Greenfield notes the power of mobile technologies such as wristbands to intensify scientific management by rigourously tracking workers' movements. The methods of scientific management, developed in the early twentieth century by Frederick Taylor and others, sought to maximize efficiency by measuring outcomes through time-motion studies. Mobile technologies dramatically enhance the tool chest for measurement and control: "the rise of wearable biometric monitoring can only be understood as a disciplinary power traversing the body and all its flows. This is a power Frederick Taylor never dreamed of ..."[22]

Employers, health care organizations and the state have attempted to blur the line between private and public in the use of these tracking device. One of the issues that triggered the 2018 strike by teachers in West Virginia was the cost of health insurance coverage and the means offered by their insurer to reduce billings. Teachers were offered the option of submitting biometric data from a device to a private contractor who would reduce premiums if their lifestyle was deemed sufficiently healthy:

> As costs rose to astronomical levels with no signs of slowing, teachers and staff were offered the "opportunity" to defray costs by submitting biometric data to the private company in charge of the Go365 "preventative health" program; for a discount on access to health care, workers were asked to upload their daily "steps" as well as individual body measurements, weight, height and updates about sensitive health tests.[23]

The idea of fitness marries conceptions of productivity and attractiveness, all to be accomplished through the application of scientific management methods to the development of the self. Kelly Moore argues that neoliberalism, with its intensified precariousness and elimination of community infrastructure, has put pressure on members of the working class to make themselves into entrepreneurial citizens, seeking "opportunities to 'invest' in the self, to improve it, and to publicly demonstrate these commitments."[24]

Indeed, these methods can be applied to transform sexual performance into metrics of time and effort. English cricketer Andrew "Freddie" Flintoff was quoted in the *Telegraph* as saying he wears his Fitbit during sex because "it makes him try harder." His wife described the experience from her point of view, "Things are happening and then your husband's wrist is flashing telling him his heartbeat and how hard he's working. It's really wrong. It's putting me off though. It's like you're seeing it as another training session rather than anything else. It's really not nice."[25]

The honing of sexual allure and expansion of dating culture becomes a labor process in itself, particularly for women. Moira Weigel points out that dating involves substantial physical and emotional work: "The fact that dating is work is not necessarily a bad thing. Labor is how we shape the world around us."[26] The problem is that the work of dating is largely about finding a mate for marriage or coupledom: "If marriage is the long-term contract that many daters still hope to land, dating itself often feels like the worst, most precarious form of contemporary labor: an unpaid internship."[27] The uncertainty of precarious labor makes it particularly demoralizing and exhausting, but the grind of the permanent job, ever more rare in contemporary neoliberal conditions, is nonetheless a commitment to a long-term regime of draining work. This work includes the honing of sexual allure and transactional practices of hooking up and dating.

Sexual allure is mystified in capitalist societies, where it is freighted with our many-sided needs for fulfillment and connection.[28] The destruction of social and ecological connection and enforced individuation leaves people without adequate support or means to make lives. Bruce Alexander maintains that psychosocial dislocation in free market society was "not the pathological state of a few, but the general condition."[29] We engage in sexual relations in the context of this psychosocial dislocation, using a narrow and specific activity as the means to filling a wide range of needs.

People form family, household or community relations, often on the basis of sexual attraction, that bear the weight of our many-sided needs. These contractually regulated relationships are thus deeply contradictory, combining the romance of sexual allure with the drudgery of requisite labor. George Bernard Shaw, writing in the early twentieth century as these new forms of companionate marriage were developing, was particularly scathing about the contradictory combination of magic and toil in these contractually regulated relationships. He described the marriage ceremony as "an honest attempt to make the best of a commercial contract of property and slavery by subjecting it to some religious restraint and elevating it by some touch of poetry."[30] He notes the limits of sexual attraction as the basis for lasting love: "But the actual result is that when two people are under the influence of the most violent, most insane, most delusive, and most transient of passions, they are required to swear that they will remain in that excited, abnormal, and exhausting condition continuously until death do them part."[31]

The assumption that sex and caring go together is a very historically specific sense of how humans should live. Edmund White describes the orientation towards sex for sex's sake among layers of the gay male community: "Well perhaps sex and sentiment *should* be separated. Isn't sex, shadowed as it always is by jealousy and rules by caprice, a rather risky basis for a sustained, important relationship?"[32] In the regime of sexual liberalism, sexual attraction is seen as the key marker of a multidimensional economic and social relationship. Alain de Boton sees contemporary marriage as a misguided attempt to make the exhilarations of sexual attraction into a permanent life bond. "We married to make such sensations permanent but failed to see that there was no solid connection between these feelings and the institution of marriage. Indeed, marriage tends decisively to move us onto another, very different and more administrative plane ..."[33]

People form relationships on the basis of sexual attraction in which sex actually plays a quite limited role. Sexual attraction seems to have a power over us, determining our partners for relationships we form to meet our needs for enjoyment, economic security, care, a sense of home, child-rearing. In conditions of alienation, we lose touch with our own purposive and creative making, at the individual and collective level, and thus misattribute our formative powers to forces that seems to operate independently of our will. Desire is reified, so that relationship formation seems to result from mystified sexual attraction rather than our own labor. Sexual attraction seems to be an immensely powerful force as it channels our multidimensional human needs for each other.

SELF-OWNERSHIP AND DIFFERENTIATED DISPOSSESSION

In conditions of alienation and dispossession, people are compelled to treat their human capacities, the only resource they control, as property for exchange. People trade on their erotic capacities, using them as the means to such ends as building sustained relationships. This market model sexual exchange is the basis of the regime of sexual liberalism, oriented around contractually regulated interchange. People are in a position to consent to these contractual relationships on the basis of their formal equality as owners of their own bodies.

Yet, capitalist dispossession does not simply level humanity, producing an undifferentiated working class upended from relations with community, land and the cosmos. Susan Ferguson contends that "while *all* workers are alienated from their humanity when they sell their labour power to a capitalist, the degradation involved in that alienation varies in degree and intensity."[34] All members of the working class are dispossessed, however, processes of gendered subordination, categorization as disabled, sexual regulation, nationalization of populations creating status and non-status conditions, racialization, settler-colonialism and enslavement integral to the development of capitalism produce differentiated forms of subordination. Ferguson describes this as a "differential dispossession" produced through "oppressive practices and institutions" that creates conditions in which "workers are more-or-less precarious, more-or-less able and willing to work at dangerous or dirty or low-paying jobs."[35]

The freedom of self-owning members of the working class is inseparable from the compulsion to alienate their most human capacities. Some people (e.g. white, male, full citizens) experience this contradictory combination of freedom and alienation as freedom in part relative to the unfreedom of other layers of the laboring population due to colonialism, disability, gender, migrant status, racialization, non-normative sexuality and/or stateless status. The unfreedom of sections of the laboring population is not simply a pre-capitalist leftover that will diminish, but is reproduced over time, taking different forms through history and in different social and geographic locations. As Rioux, LeBaron and Vervošek argue, "Contrary to the expectations of liberal and neoclassical economists, as well as many Marxist theorists, the deepening and extension of capitalism seem to have reinforced unfree labor rather than diminished it."[36]

Saidiya Hartman argues that in the United States, free white labor was specifically relative to the unfreedom of African-Americans: "the rights of the self-possessed individual and the set of property relations that defined liberty depend upon, if not require, the black as will-less actant and sublime object."[37] Even those formally granted full ownership of their bodies, not enslaved or incarcerated or indentured, may be dehumanized – in part through devaluation of those very bodies. Charles W. Mills describes this as the "relation between the individual body and the larger social body: we come to respond to the physical body in a certain way because its corporeality has become embedded in the body of law, a body that fleshes it out, incarnated it in a larger juridical anatomy."[38]

The bodily autonomy of dehumanized people is further undermined by the state regulation to limit their reproduction. For E. San Juan, "It is difficult to deny that the racial polity pivots around the sexualized-gendered division of labor."[39] The reproduction of racialized populations was cast as a problem to be solved by those in power by restraining or preventing procreation. For Dorothy Roberts, "The belief that Black procreation is the problem remains a major barrier to radical change in America."[40]

The bodies of people who engage in undervalued forms of labor, such as the caregiving performed disproportionately by women and people who are racialized, are devalued. For Rosemary Hennessey, abjection creates differentiation in the laboring population: "In devaluating some bodies, abjection helps to produce subjects who are worth less – that is, subjects who forfeit more of themselves in the labor relations that produce capital."[41] The devaluation of caring labor is central to the gendered character of differential dispossession. For women, "motherwork and housework have a negative bearing upon their relationship to paid labor."[42] Women in capitalist society tend to be more tied (to caregiving, the household) than men and therefore are somewhat less free to sell their capacity to work, which is at the same time generally devalued as it is measured against the gendered expectation of participating in unpaid work. In the words of Kay Gabriel, *"Gender for capital assumes the form of an accumulation strategy,* an ideological scaffolding that sustains an unequal division of labour, contours practices of dispossession and predation, and conditions particular forms of exploitation, including and especially in the form of un- and low-waged reproductive labour."[43]

As full personhood in capitalist societies is based on self-ownership, the racialized and colonial construction of property rights plays a crucial role in differential dispossession and sustained unfreedom. Brenna Bhandar argues, "The settler colony is a space where the self-possessive, proprietorial subject emerged in relation to property relations that were thoroughly racial."[44] The destruction of Indigenous relations to the land was a crucial feature of this construction of property rights: "The privatisation of the land base was intimately connected to colonial identity formation."[45] At the same time, the settler-colonial regime suppressed and outlawed "independent, aboriginal ways of holding land and self-governance."[46] The overall goal was the destruction of Indigenous ways of life, in part through the attempted annihilation of history: "the *Indian Act* and the imposition of private property relations it embodied were premised on the denial of First Nations' memory of their relationships to land and place."[47]

The Canadian state created a status for Indigenous people that included disqualification from full rights as possessors of property (and therefore exclusion from full self-ownership): "The Indian subject of the *Indian Act* cannot be the individual who engages freely in exchange, nor can she be a private owner of land in *fee simple.*"[48] Assigned status through the settler-colonial regime attempted to erase the self-administered constitution of membership in given First Nations. For Bonita Lawrence, the construction of status through the *Indian Act* was based on "utter indifference to traditional Indigenous ways of evaluating who was a member/citizen of the nation and who wasn't (which was precisely their purpose, in terms of reshaping Indigenous identities) …"[49] The denial of agency to Indigenous peoples was an important dimension of the construction of status by the settler-colonial state, creating "the inherent dehumanization of having one's identity regulated by (largely biological) standards of 'Indianness.'"[50]

There were specific gendered dimensions to this dehumanization through state-imposed colonial status. Bonita Lawrence posits that women's roles were fundamental in sustaining Indigenous communities' relationships to the land. Thus, the demands of the settler-colonial regime "were most strenuously resisted by the women, who saw holding on to the land base as the only way in which the social fabric of the society to nurture the next generation would survive at all."[51] The settler-colonial regime "required Indian women to be treated as property of their husband."[52] Indigenous women's status was determined by that of their husband, so that women lost status if they married someone who was not recognized as Indigenous by the state or would be assigned to membership in the First Nation of the man she married. This gendered dispossession was a key feature of state-assigned Indigenous status until a long battle succeeded in overturning this aspect of the *Indian Act* in 1985.

The freedom of the self-owning individual is associated with a conception of bodily autonomy based on specific ways of living and working that grant certain freedoms and undermine others. Sarah Ahmed suggests that the dominant models of sexual freedom in the Global North draw on a conception of freedom in terms of mobility, being untied and unencumbered: "The idealization of movement, or transformation of movement into a fetish, depends upon the exclusion of others who are already positioned as *not free in the same way*."[53] This vision of sexual freedom "may exclude others, those who have attachments that are not readable as queer, or indeed those who may lack the (cultural as well as economic) capital to support the 'risk' of maintaining anti-normativity as a permanent orientation."[54] This vision of sexual freedom in terms of autonomy and lack of attachments is deeply connected to masculinity, whiteness and wealth. Relative to men, women are more likely to be tied to others through caregiving responsibilities that require different practices in many areas of life. People who are racialized may have a different kind of community connection fulfilling very specific needs in conditions of dehumanization and oppression.

The distinctive trajectories of gay male and lesbian communities provide a valuable example of the ways sexual liberalism based on the unencumbered individual can frame sexualities. Relative to gay men, lesbians are more likely to have responsibilities for caregiving and limitations on their use of urban space due to gendered and racialized safety concerns grounded in routinized sexual assault. As a result, lesbians and gay men tend to live differently in cities and elsewhere. Lo and Healy contrasted the urban experiences of lesbians and gay men in Vancouver: "lesbians' spaces are not only different from gay men's territories, but that they are also more hidden and significantly less privileged."[55] There were specific reasons for this. Lesbians tend to have lower incomes, given overall earning differentials between men and women; are more likely to be raising children in their households, which will affect the choice of location; and face greater concerns about the risk of violence and assault in public spaces.[56]

Further, members of racialized and/or cultural minority communities often value and need community ties that reduce their ability, need and desire for unencumbered mobility. In their historical study of lesbian communities in Buffalo, New York, Lapovsky Kennedy and Davis found that African-American women tended to be "firmly established in their Black communities and, in the 1950s, their social lives were led within these communities."[57] Rather than participating in the lesbian bar scene, Black women tended to create "lively house parties reminiscent of rent parties and buffet flats of the 1920 and 1930s" grounded in "the strong Black tradition of self-activity to resist oppression."[58] Similarly, two-spirit identity among Indigenous peoples is importantly defined in relation to one's place in community. Margaret Robinson named this as a process of "coming in," described by her interview participants in terms of "the fit between two-spirit identity and their own understanding of the distinct cultures, histories and traditional knowledges of Aboriginal peoples."[59]

THE CONSENT FRAME

A crucial feature of contractually regulated sexual liberalism has been the centrality of the consent frame in struggles for bodily autonomy and erotic liberation. The consent frame is a necessary but not sufficient dimension of struggles for sexual justice. On the one hand, freedom from sexual assault and sexual self-determination are foundational requirements for erotic fulfillment grounded in mutuality. One the other hand, the consent frame reflects the contradiction that parties are formally equal as property owners (specifically self-owners), yet substantively unequal based on processes of differential dispossession creating hierarchies of class, disability, gender, sexuality, colonial or national status, and racialization. Further, sexual consent is based on an instrumental model of rational exchange which does not necessarily fit the complex emotional and interpersonal dynamics of sexual engagement.

Carole Pateman explored the contradictions of the consent frame in radical feminist terms in *The Sexual Contract*. Pateman states, "contract is the specifically modern means of creating relationships of subordination, but, because civil subordination originates in contract, it is presented as

freedom."[60] Despite formal equality, sexual contracts reproduce male dominance: "exploitation is possible precisely because, as I shall show, contracts
about property in the person place the right of command in the hands of
one party to the contract."[61] She argues that the struggle for formal equality
and autonomous personhood was not sufficient for the emancipation of
women: "the conclusion is easy to draw that the denial of civil equality to
women means that the feminist aspiration must be to win acknowledge-
ment for women as 'individuals'. Such an aspiration can never be fulfilled.
The 'individual' is a patriarchal category."[62] Further, Pateman argues that
the conception of sexual consent as we understand it is already founded on
women's relative unfreedom, casting consent as the acceptance or denial of
the advance made by a male initiator: "The 'naturally' superior, active, and
sexually aggressive male makes an initiative, or offers a contract, to which a
'naturally' subordinate, passive woman 'consents.' An egalitarian sexual relationship cannot rest on this basis; it cannot be grounded in 'consent.'"[63]

The relationship of formal inequality to substantive inequality is not a
unique characteristic of sexual contracts, but rather a defining feature of
capitalist exchange relations including the fundamental labor contract
between employer and employee. The worker and employer meet as formal
equals, both property owners, one purchasing the capacity to work that
the other is selling. Yet, the worker is ultimately compelled to sell to gain
access to the necessities of life, so that "the relation of capitalist exploitation
is mediated through the form of contract."[64] Indeed, consent to one's own
subordination is a central feature of the forms of hegemonic rule that have
developed in many capitalist societies, particularly liberal democratic states.
Antonio Gramsci argued that consent and coercion are woven together in
parliamentary capitalist states: "The 'normal' exercise of hegemony on the
now classical terrain of parliamentary regime is characterized by a combination of force and consent which balance each other so that force does not
overwhelm consent but rather appears to be backed by the consent of the
majority, expressed by the so-called organs of public opinion."[65]

Consent and coercion are woven together in sexual engagement in part
through the routinization of sexual assault. For Nicola Garvey and Charlene
Senn, "sexual violence is not a clearly bounded and aberrant phenomenon
that is separate from sexuality, but that it arises out of and sits alongside sexuality as usual."[66] This perspective of the embeddedness of sexual coercion
in dominant sexual normativities "allows us to better recognize the mundane
workings of power in the realm of sex and sexuality, particularly gendered

forms of power within heterosexual sex, and thereby to be sensitive to the nuance and complexity of questions to do with sexual choice and consent."[67]

Kimberlé Crenshaw maps out these "mundane workings of power" in the many dimensions of subordination faced by women who enter shelters following experiences of violence and sexual assault: "In most cases, the physical assault that leads women to these shelters is merely the most immediate manifestation of the subordination they experience."[68] The violence these women faced was grounded in multiple subordination due to: job market discrimination, childcare responsibilities, lack of access to affordable housing, poverty, racism, migration status and many other factors.

Women, trans people, people who are racialized, Indigenous people, those who are gender non-binary and those categorized as disabled are dehumanized through regimes of degradation that undermine personhood grounded in formal equality, including agency in contract. In the words of Lewis R. Gordon, "Rape, as a form of violation, depends upon human agency for its existence."[69] When people are dehumanized, as in systemic anti-blackness, it removes the presumption of agency and therefore the meaning of consent. "Where agency is denied, so, too, is violation."[70]

Sexual assault reinforces power relations both by marking the conquest by the dominant and the abjection of the subordinated. It is deeply connected to existing forms of power and vulnerability. In military and carceral contexts, sexual assault is an ongoing dimension of conquest and efforts to achieve domination. Angela Davis wrote of US policy in Vietnam, "It was the unwritten policy of the US Military Command [Vietnam] to systematically encourage rape, since it was an extremely effective weapon of mass terrorism."[71] The Japanese army in World War II enslaved women from occupied nations (Chinese, Korean, Taiwanese and others) as sex slaves (called "comfort women"). In the words of Yoshimi Yoshiaki, "an attitude privately acknowledging rape as a 'wartime benefit' permeated all ranks of the Japanese military."[72] Israeli prisons use sexual assault and humiliation against Palestinian women who are political prisoners: "Sexual harassment and humiliation in all forms, including attempted rape and rape, are used to deter women from participating in the struggle."[73]

Sexual assault is systemic and indeed normalized. Nicola Gavey argues that the "everyday taken-for-granted normative forms of heterosexuality work as a cultural scaffolding for rape."[74] Specifically, she argues that heterosex is based on gendered norms of "women's passive, acquiescing (a)sexuality and men's forthright, urgent pursuit of sexual 'release'."[75] Action against sexual assault must undermine this cultural scaffolding by "the 'queering' of sex and sexuality in the broadest of ways."[76] This queering is to be accomplished through a combination of education, cultural critique and social activism. One of the crucial dimensions of this queering is the development of "opportunities for girls and women to experience and develop physical strengths, pleasures and acumen necessary for an embodied agency."[77]

The political mobilization around consent has been crucial in highlighting the pervasiveness and taken-for-grantedness of sexual assault in contemporary contexts. College and university campuses in Canada and the United States have become crucial sites for the development of new policies and practices concerning sexual assault and harassment. Grigoriadis classifies this new frame as "one of the greatest cultural shifts to happen on American campuses in decades: a reframing of sexual dynamics."[78] This reframing is a remarkable goal, and it is having an important effect. A male undergraduate interviewed by Grigoriadis said, "It got me reflecting on my life experiences, asking, 'Do I know what consent looks like? Do I ask for consent?'"[79]

Effectively designed programs to build consent practices on campuses can make a real difference. Charlene Senn et al. designed and implemented a program for women to reduce sexual assault focusing on the enhancement of sexual agency and self-valuation while also teaching self-defense and actualizing the right to say "no." The clinical trial of this program demonstrated that it "was successful in substantially reducing the occurrence of sexual assaults among first-year female university students, including those at higher risk because of previous rape victimization."[80]

The consent frame is an important tool chest for transforming sexual culture, yet it has limits. Katherine Angel maintains that "consent has a limited purview, and it is being asked to bear too great a burden, to address problems it is not equipped to resolve."[81] The consent model is based on rational negotiation between formally equal partners, despite the substantive inequalities that mark real sexual activity, and the affective complexity of desire in interpersonal relations. Women may consent to unwanted sex, "because they agree to it under duress, or out of a need to feed and clothe themselves and their family, or a need to remain safe."[82] Further, desire is complex and dynamic, "our desires emerge in interaction; we don't always know what we want; we sometimes discover things we didn't know we wanted; sometimes we discover what we want only in the doing."[83]

Octavia Butler explored the complexity of consent through fiction in the novel *Fledgling*. A female vampire discovers that her saliva relaxed the man she was engaging and made him happy. As he became addicted to this sensation, she recognized the importance of attaining his consent. She offered to let him go: "Because I think … I think it would be wrong for me to keep you against your will."[84] He stays, but the reader is left with questions about his willing consent, given that her saliva is addictively pleasuring.

In practice, erotic engagement is often an emergent dance of bodies in which people discover desires they did not expect, or realize that they do not want to pursue something they thought they wanted. Commonly, little is spoken in this encounter between partners who often hold different amounts of power. Jacqueline Rose posits that it is possible both to support campaigns around deliberate consent and raise questions about the complexity of "the murky world of sexuality, where all bets are off, where desire can flare up and be followed by a change of heart in the space of a single breath."[85] This does not mean giving up on consent education, but rather recognizing the limits of sexual justice within the constraints of a market model of contractually regulated sexuality based on rational negotiation between formally equal partners.

THE MONEY SHOT

People seek much more than erotic fulfillment when they engage in sexual activity in the context of the regime of sexual liberalism. Sexual engagement is freighted with our many-sided wants and needs for human connection and embodied satiation, given our dispossession from land, community and direct control over the resources we require to make lives. People come to understand "'good sex' as the glue that forms and sustains relationships."[86]

The orgasm has become the metric by which the quality of this sex is evaluated, creating an "orgasmic imperative" in which erotic fulfillment through intimate engagement is focused primarily on a very specific kind of climax.[87] The orgasmic imperative directs erotic engagement towards specific genital-centered coital activity in which the orgasm marks the key moment in the exchange transaction. Nicola Gavey contends that the conception of heterosexual sex in terms of a "coital imperative" is a key foundation of the cultural scaffolding of rape, constructing "the main point of heterosex as the penetration of the vagina by the penis …"[88] This narrow definition of sex abstracts one moment in the complex relations of bodies and lives that shape actual sexual engagement and makes it the pinnacle of heterosex. This tends to have an impact on women's erotic experiences: "Women find it difficult to take their own desires and pleasures seriously, since the heteroerotic norm is, simply, that women are not supposed to care about sexual pleasure."[89] Women are to subordinate their own embodied pleasure to the need to steer the engagement towards the required climax.

The orgasmic imperative is reflected in the centrality of the "money shot" in pornography. In hard core porn, the "money shot" is the moment of ejaculation from a penis shown on the screen, and it was so named as performers were paid extra for those scenes.[90] The money shot is the moment where the exchange value of the sexual encounter is realized. This is supposedly the climax of the sexual encounter, "cue the drum roll, he has come."[91]

The money shot is clearly oriented around male sexual satisfaction. It has a male masturbatory element: "the male pornographic film performer must withdraw from any tactile connection with the genitals or mouth of the woman so that the 'spending' of his ejaculate is visible."[92] Sexual encounters organized around the money shot are not, then, about mutual fulfillment: "The money shot utterly fails to represent the satisfaction of desire as involving a desire for, or of, the other ..."[93] Rather than mutuality, the money shot represents "the more solitary (and literally disconnected) visual pleasure of the male performer and the male viewer."[94]

The emphasis on the money shot in porn is one dimension of the organization of sexual engagement around the orgasmic imperative, putting pressure on the participants to perform a moment of climax, a "money shot." The absence of orgasm is thus seen as problematic.[95] This has a highly gendered impact given the dominant frame in which male orgasm is more or less taken for granted while female orgasm is seen as contingent. The understanding of the female orgasm has changed over the past century: "the *absence* of female orgasm has shifted from being depicted as expected and 'natural' to being unnatural and dysfunctional."[96] Feminist, queer and anti-racist struggles have recast desire so it is no longer understood simply as an attribute of men's bodies.

This changing understanding of the female orgasm demonstrates the ways apparently biological facts of life can be shaped by societal change. Indeed, Elisabeth Lloyd argues that the female orgasm has no straightforward evolutionary purpose and is not in any direct way connected to reproduction.[97] The understanding of the female orgasm and its place in sexual practices varies a great deal across time and place. Hannah Frith posits that through the twentieth century, "the fate of the female orgasm has fluctuated amid shifting articulations of gender relations."[98] Lynn Comella traced out the role of feminist activism and the commercialization of sexuality in the development of a new understanding of female orgasm that changed women's expectations and desires. She suggests that feminist sex activists "challenged the patriarchal status quo that had taught women to see sex as an obligation rather than something they were entitled to pursue for the sake of their own pleasure."[99] Even with this increasing emphasis on women's sexual fulfillment, including orgasm, the orgasmic imperative encodes a deeply male-centric understanding of erotic engagement.

Disability activists and scholars have developed an important critique of the orgasmic imperative, which produces forms of sexual exclusion for those who do not practice eroticism in this way. Tobin Siebers notes that sexuality framed through the lens of disability "reveals unacknowledged assumptions about the ability to have sex and how the ideology of ability determines the value of some sexual practices and ideas of others."[100] People living with disabilities may be disqualified as sexual agents if they do not meet the requirements of the orgasmic imperative: "On the one hand, the stigma of disability may interfere with having sex. On the other hand, the sexual activities of disabled people do not necessarily follow normative assumptions about what a sex life is. Neither fact means that people with disabilities do not exist as sexual beings."[101] Indeed, Anne Mollow points out that people living with disabilities are caught in a double bind, and may be cast as both too sexual, insufficiently regulated and not sexual enough: "if sexuality can easily be interpreted as both sexual lack and sexual excess (sometimes simultaneously), then it seems nearly impossible for any expression of disabled sexuality to escape stigma."[102]

People who do not conform to the norms of the orgasmic imperative are disqualified as fully sexual and dehumanized. In an ethnographic interview about the sexual experiences of people with spinal cord injuries, participant Sergi described the sense of disqualification: "There is a part of sexuality that is not for me and that is not something that just a few people tell you. The whole world is telling you that: ads, TV, cinema … they say – this is not for you."[103] Sergi's response has been to develop a more fulsome erotic sensibility:

> Sexualizing the whole body is an attitude and it has to do with how you feel your body, how you relate to your body, and being in this arrangement means that you love your body and that every part of your body at any given time can be lived in a way and be in a way.[104]

The orgasmic imperative directs this potential whole body eroticism towards specific genital-centered activity oriented towards a particular form of climax. The rise of sexual liberalism, in which sexual relations take the commodified form of property exchange governed by contact, provides the context in which the orgasmic imperative becomes a form of fetishism. Marx identified commodification as foundational in the mystification of everyday life in capitalist societies, as products of our labor in circulation on the market seem to take on a subjectivity, setting the terms for our relationship with them. The human capacity for purposive making is misattributed to the products of our labor in circulation as commodities.

We come to understand our own sexual allure in relation to the magnetic attraction of commodities in circulation. Walter Benjamin examined the penetration of commodity exchange more deeply into everyday life in his study of the Paris Arcades, the nineteenth-century precursor to the shopping mall. He noted the allure of goods in circulation at the mall: "The arcade is a street of lascivious commerce only; it is wholly adapted to arousing desires."[105] He observed the role of the flâneur at the mall, the forerunner of the window shopper who is there to see and to be seen: "he is no buyer. He is merchandise."[106] Benjamin argues that desire in these circumstances crosses over between living others and non-living objects: "In fetishism, sex does away with the boundaries separating the organic world from the inorganic. Clothing and jewelry are its allies."[107]

Allure has generally been organized around the male gaze, given the organization of contemporary sexualities around male dominance. Esther Leslie maintains that women, in Benjamin's analysis of commodification, are "Always on view, like wares, they view themselves on view, like buyers snared in a circuit of self-consumption."[108] Women are not only objectified, but objectify themselves. Queer, feminist and anti-racist struggles have created a great equity in objectification, so that men are now more likely to "view themselves on view." The male-centric foundations of the orgasmic imperative and contemporary sexual exchange remain, but in a form that accommodates some conception of women's sexual agency.

As commodity exchange is universalized in capitalist relations, the social engagement between people increasingly takes the form of market exchange between things: "a relation between people takes on the character of a thing and thus acquires a 'phantom objectivity', an autonomy that seems so strictly rational and all-embracing as to conceal every trace of its fundamental nature: the relation between people."[109] The orgasmic imperative endows the orgasm with such a "phantom objectivity," capturing the powers of erotic fulfillment and human connection in fetishized form. The orgasmic imperative endows the orgasm with important powers as the gatekeeper to human connection, and people do their very best to meet its standards. The money shot becomes the moment of currency exchange that seals the deal.

People form and sustain various forms of connective relationships through hard work within the frame of normativities that are socially constructed, historically made by people through contestation around societal relations. The active formation of the most intimate of these connections is misattributed to mystified sexual attraction, concretized by the metric of the orgasm. In conditions of alienation and sexual liberalism, people form relationships in the context of interpersonal liaison organized as market exchange processes, in conditions where our personhood is not based on our humanity, but on ownership of property (even if only our own body). Sexual allure is the source of market value for these bodies in circulation, and the money shot is the moment that value is realized. People still find ways to realize their humanity through sex and many other forms of interpersonal connection, but often framed by a taken-for-granted understanding of their own subjectivity framed by sexual liberalism.

5

The State and Sexual Hegemony

The state plays a central role in the development of normative sexualities through social policy regimes designed to shape the population around the formation of a workforce that is willing and able to engage in alienated labor. The goal of social policy is to reproduce a working class that will participate in transforming themselves into human resources. Programs ranging from public health to unemployment insurance, from compulsory education to old age pensions, aim to shape the practices and frame the expectations of the population, so they will maintain themselves and each other at a certain work-ready standard. Social policy regimes develop historically as state policy-makers forge and reshape programs in the face of working-class resistance and capitalist crises. As part of a strategy of containing working-class mobilization within the limits of capitalist relations, the most forward-looking policy-makers seek to incorporate elements of the innovations in life-making generated by communities from below, though doing so in ways that are compatible with profitability and the existing social order.

The formation of sexualities is a crucial, if underexplored, dimension of social policies. The role of the state in the development of sexual normativity may seem limited at first, given the centrality of informal regulation in sustaining these codes. Certainly, laws and carceral mechanisms do play an overt role in enforcing sexual normativities, ranging from the war on queers waged by state security apparatuses through to the regulation of family forms permissible for immigrant sponsorship. Yet, people tend to learn about these normativities, and face consequences for transgression, from informal social networks of peers, family and community, backed up by cultural representations in the media and advertising.

Even these informal elements of sexual normalization are profoundly influenced by social policy. Sexual formation is an explicit element of social policy, for example, in laws proscribing homosexuality, limiting access to abortion and contraception, or regulating family form through such programs as social assistance. At the same time, sexual formation is an implicit dimension across the whole range of social policies, as the regulation of eros plays a key role in disciplining people's relationships with their bodies, each other, their labor and the nation. Children in schools, for example, learn to accept instruction and assessment, rather than producing knowledge actively by sensory engagement with the world. The self-regulation required to arrive on time, sit still, and attend on command is an important dimension in the development of particular modes of time-discipline and self-regulation, oriented around extrinsic rewards (such as grades) rather than inherent fulfillment. Children learn to synchronize their bodies and minds with a disciplinary regime, timing their bathroom visits, hunger, thirst and attention span to the schedule of the institution. Formal education builds the foundation for erotic containment, even if that is not formally listed as a learning outcome in the lesson plans.[1]

Social policy in capitalist societies weaves together elements of productivism, based largely on deferring gratification to conserve life-energy for draining alienated labor, with aspects of pleasure, based on the potential to escape from the horizons of deadening work through moments of leisure achieved largely through the consumption of commodities. The most effective social policy regimes have balanced productivism with pleasure, so that the toil of alienated labor is matched to certain kinds of potential reward or moments of escape. The complex balance between sexual repression and the unleashing of desire is dynamic rather than fixed, aligned with the broad development of social policy to contain working-class resistance and motivate participation in alienated labor.

The role of the state may not appear central in the development of normative sexualities, as social policy-makers must negotiate the complex balance between actively intervening to forge a national population with particular capacities and characteristics; and downloading the responsibility for social reproduction fully onto the shoulders of working-class households. The most effective forms of moral regulation are often self-effacing, appearing not as commandments from above in the form of coercion, but as resources to negotiate the world, producing hegemony that resonates from below, generating elements of consent.

One of the important contributions of queer marxism to our understanding of sexualities is a specific focus on the role of the state in sexual formation. Sexual normativities do not necessarily take the form of formal legal codes, but often operate at the level of everyday experience rendering the dominant organization of gender and sexuality obvious to the point of being taken for granted. The practice of "coming out" as queer, for example, arose in the context of a heteronormativity so pervasive that it need not be spoken, so that announcing one's sexuality was a disruptive practice of breaking silence. Dominant modes of sex and gender normativity are present everywhere, apparently emanating out of the pores of family relations, religious institutions, education systems, the design of housing stock, employment structures, leisure activities and social services. Students learn sexual normativity in the schoolyard as well as in the classroom; it is reproduced through informal social engagement as well as formal institutional governance.

It can be difficult to socially locate processes of sexual formation, given the combination of formal and informal dimensions in the development of normativities. Berlant and Warner maintain that heteronormativity "is produced in almost every aspect of the forms and arrangements of social life: nationality, the state, and the law; commerce; medicine; and education; as well as in the conventions and affects of narrativity, romance, and other protected spaces of culture."[2] The currently dominant regime of heteronormativity has become so pervasive that it is commonly taken for granted and naturalized as the expression of eternal hard-wired urges and evolutionarily determined desires. Yet, this particular hegemonic organization of heterosexuality is very recent, dating back to the early 1900s (in certain places, among specific social strata). A very specific form of heterosexuality has been institutionalized and cast as the pinnacle of sexuality, "from which everything else remains a falling away."[3] As discussed above, by the early 2000s, this heteronormativity was in many social locations expanded to include an emergent homonormativity which framed certain forms of same-gender relationships as equivalent to the heterosexual norm, eligible for parenthood, access to partner benefits, and state recognition in the form of marriage.

People experience heteronormativity (and now homonormativity) organically, as something learned through everyday life rather than a formal code or imposed set of rules. Yet, an active process of state formation underlies this organic informal way of life. Chris Chitty rejects the conception of normativity as "some free-floating, regulative idea, perhaps taking shape in particular institutions, according to which human activities are monitored and judged."[4] Chitty instead argues for the understanding of "the normal as a status, one which – given certain concrete socioeconomic conditions – accrues material advantages to those who achieve it or happen to be born into it."[5] The normal in Chitty's sense is accomplished through the establishment of sexual hegemony in which "sexual norms benefitting a dominant group shape the sexual conduct and self-understandings of other groups, whether or not they also stand to benefit from such norms and whether or not they can achieve them."[6]

The state plays a central role in establishing sexual hegemony, organizing moral regulation through social policy to shape sexual norms, in part by containing, coopting and directing specific elements of new ways of life emerging from below. Chitty argues that the proscription of homosexuality, one of the key foundations of heteronormativity, was directly connected to state formation: "Homosexual repression, as such, was largely a product of an expanded state bureaucracy, increased police power and capital's twentieth-century concern for the welfare and health of working populations."[7]

Sexual hegemony is a fundamental dimension in the capitalist state's broader hegemonic project of forging subjectivities that naturalize and eternalize conditions of capitalist alienation. This process of developing social policies to forge subjectivities is never simple, as people are not blank slates upon which the state and employers write a script, but living, thinking and potentially powerful individual and collective agents making lives oriented around their wants and needs. The state formation of subjectivities, including sexual normativities, is contested through resistance ranging from political mobilization to everyday non-conformity. Further, this process of formation must marry together elements of differentiation (along such lines as class, gender, racialization, colonial status, sexuality, designation as disabled, employment status), with sufficient standardization to reproduce the formal equality required for a contract, as discussed in the previous chapter.

The Italian Marxist Antonio Gramsci used the term "hegemony" to describe a mode of regulation in which the rulers do not rely on coercion alone, but also on the consent of those who are governed. He wrote, "the fact of hegemony presupposes that account be taken of the interests and tendencies of the groups over which hegemony is to be exercised, and that a certain compromise equilibrium is formed."[8] A core condition of such a "compromise equilibrium," or settlement, was that it did not threaten the ongoing reproduction of capitalist social relations. According to Gramsci, these compromises "cannot touch the essential."[9] State hegemonic regulation emerges to contain working-class resistance from below, ranging from the individual act of work avoidance to collective mobilization up to and including mass insurgency. Sexual hegemony is one dimension of this broader hegemonic project, in which state policy-makers seek to manage normativities through repression but also through cooping and directing elements of life-making survival projects from below.

THE STATE AND SOCIAL POLICY

The social policy of capitalist states is framed by working-class self-ownership and the privatization of responsibility for social reproduction. This privatization creates certain contested spaces of freedom, inseparable from the burdens of privatized life-making with inadequate resources. Capitalists need sources of labor for production, but they do not take direct responsibility for its reproduction, which is downloaded onto members of the working class themselves. Marx wrote, "The maintenance and reproduction of the working class remains a necessary condition for the reproduction of capital. But the capitalist may safely leave this to the workers' drives for self-preservation and propagation."[10]

In fact, the capitalist state has been far more involved in regulating privatized working-class reproduction than Marx envisioned in this quote. States developed new forms of social policy to regulate private self-reproduction, in response to both employer concerns about the quality, quantity and discipline of the existing labor force, and struggles of members of the working class for the resources, time and social rights to reproduce themselves. Policy-makers developed a range of interventions to regulate social reproduction in the private sphere, ranging from cultural policy to welfare payments, and from national health care to public housing. Sexual regulation features as a fundamental dimension of social policy, both explicitly in direct controls over sexual practices such as laws proscribing gay relationships, censorship of sexual content and laws against prostitution; and implicitly as a dimension of programs ranging from compulsory education to immigration controls, and from public health to social welfare.

The development of social policy was driven by the need to establish a hegemonic frame in the face of resistance from below. The state regulation of social reproduction far exceeded Marx's expectations in large part due to the trajectory of class struggle after his death. State policy-makers developed new forms of social policy to attempt to solve the problem of sustaining capitalist profitability in the face of working-class resistance that culminated in moments of mass insurgency. Social policy therefore had an improvisatory character, as policy-makers attempted real-time problem-solving in situations of economic and social upheaval. In the words of Michael Kidron, "the state's growth has been in a series of disjointed steps that bear every sign of not representing a coherent attitude working itself out in institutional forms, but rather a series of ad hoc responses to short-term problems which could not be dealt with in any other way."[11]

Yet, despite the improvisatory, problem-solving character of state policy, there is a consistency based on the need to sustain capitalist relations as the basis for reproducing society. State policy-makers did not simply develop innovative social programs to grant rights and resources to members of the working class in response to mobilization. Rather, they worked to address the problem of working-class militancy in ways that accorded with the needs of employers and the capitalist system more broadly. Christian Topalov contends that there was "a process of transformation, reformulation and displacement" between the demands from below and the instruments of social policy that emerged to address issues of working-class sustainability, from state education to health care, from social housing to social assistance.[12] Struggle from below won the franchise, social programs, national health care and certain forms of human rights protection, but always structured through policies that disciplined and incorporated sections of the working class into the nation and the economic system.[13]

Simon Clarke points out that the state developed historically to solve problems in sustaining capitalist reproduction in the face of working-class resistance:

> The necessity of the state is, therefore, not formal or abstract, it is the historical necessity, emerging from the development of the class struggle, for a collective instrument of class domination: the state has not developed logically out of the requirements of capital, it has developed historically out of the class struggle.[14]

State policy-makers are confined to orienting their projects around capitalist profitability as there is no other option for sustaining social life within the limits of capital. The state identifies the national interest with the perpetuation of capitalist relations.

Social policy is oriented around the formation of a working class with particular capacities and expectations, as well as sufficient wellbeing to engage in required labor. Sexual regulation is fundamental to this project of shaping the national population through social policy, even where it was not an explicit focus of particular programs. As discussed above, sexual regulation is a fundamental feature of compulsory schooling. At the most explicit level, programs such as sex education classes teach a perspective on sexualities. More broadly, schooling has been founded on practices of gender and sexual normativity, ranging from historically segregated schoolyards and gendered curricula through to dress codes and school social rituals such as dances. At the most general level, the overall form of schooling involves the deliberate suppression of the erotic and sensual dimensions of learning, so that education becomes primarily a process of students attempting to absorb the teaching of experts while holding their own bodies constant in the class-room. Freire describes the dominant pedagogical frame in schooling as the banking model where education "becomes an act of depositing, in which the students are the depositories and the teacher is the depositor."[15] The banking model habituates students to understanding their own body and mind not as active elements in their own world-making, but rather as a storage vessel for the accumulation of second-hand knowledge from certified experts.

Sexual discipline builds on this process of disembodied education in which students learn self-regulation and erotic restraint through sitting quietly and attending to the front of the room. People learn everywhere and all the time, but in formal educational settings the intrinsic satisfaction of learning for its own sake is generally replaced by extrinsic rewards for learning that the teachers deem important. Freire argues that students in the banking model of schooling "become collectors or cataloguers of the things they store" and therefore, "it is the people themselves who are filed away through the lack of creativity, transformation, and knowledge," deprived of full embodied sub-jectivity as "apart from inquiry, apart from the praxis, individuals cannot be truly human."[16] The banking model contributes to the development of a self oriented around extrinsic rewards and a productivist ethos in which defer-ring one's own thoughts, feelings and physical states is central to acceptable performance. The very form of compulsory education, then, contributes to the development of subjectivity associated with particular modes of embod-iment that are foundational to sexual regulation.

STATE FORMATION, SUBJECTIVITY AND SEXUAL REGULATION

The state is pedagogical, shaping the lives of the population through forms of social policy ranging from border controls to arts funding, from education to labor law, and from human rights enforcement to policing and imprison-ment. Philip Corrigan and Derek Sayer maintain that an adequate account of state formation must attend to the "meaning of state activities, forms and rituals – for the constitution and regulation of social identities, ultimately of our subjectivities."[17] Through a wide range of social policy activities, cap-italist states "define, in great detail, acceptable forms and images of social activity and individual and collective identity; they regulate, in empirically specific ways, much – very much by the twentieth century – of social life."[18]

Corrigan and Sayer describe the social policy of the state as a project of moral regulation, "a project of rendering natural, taken for granted, in a word 'obvious', what are in fact the ontological and epistemological premises of a particular and historical form of social order."[19] Sexual formation is a foundational dimension of this moral regulation, rendering obvious and naturalizing particular practices of gender and sexuality crucial to the development of a laboring population with particular characteristics and expectations. The sexual pedagogy of the state is a taken-for-granted grounding for the whole range of social policy instruments playing out in a variety of ways in social welfare, health care, approaches to homelessness, compulsory education, immigration controls, colonial administration and indeed even tax policy (e.g. who qualifies as partners or dependents).

Social policy has tended to involve a complex and shifting balance between productivism, constraining desire to direct life-energy to requisite labor, and hedonism, unleashing and managing desire so that satiation is associated with complying with the conditions of alienated labor. The fulfillment of desire is deferred to serve as a reward for productive work, whether in paid or reproductive labor. Desire also fuels fantasy, making drudgery sustainable by fueling dreams of ease and leisure, for example, through the sale of lottery tickets. Capitalist hegemony does not depend on the dull compulsion to labor alone, but also on the aspiration for fulfillment of desires despite alienation and dispossession. Both the mobilization and repression of desire are crucial to sustaining capitalist relations.

The moral regulation of the working class in capitalist societies involves a complex and shifting balance between constraining and unleashing desire. The constraint of desire takes the form of state regulation aimed at fostering values of temperance, saving and productivity, for example, in the governance of alcohol, drug consumption and gambling, the management of public comportment including the suppression of non-normative sexual expression, and the punishment of those cast as unproductive or dependent. At the same time, state regulation also stokes and directs desire through the promotion of normative cultural and leisure activities (spectator sports, local and national festivals, subsidies to and governance of the culture industries), controlled access to legalized alcohol and drugs for at least certain sectors of the population, lotteries, and the removal of elements of censorship of normative eroticism associated with sexualized social formation. The state plays a fundamental role in the development and generalization of reified forms of desire through social and cultural policies that open up certain forms of fulfillment and foreclose others. The over-constraint of desire inhibits profit-making, limiting both the pursuit of economic self-interest by corporate bosses and the hedonism that fuels consumerism among members of the working class.

Miguel de Beistegui drew on Foucault's work to explore the conception of desire in the emerging science of political economy, noting the ways theorists such as Adam Smith argued for unleashing rather than curtailing desire: "All of this is to say that the 'good' method of government now consists in knowing how to say yes to individual desires, to self-love and self-esteem."[20] The issue was not to constrain desire, but to unleash it in ways that drove specific economic forms of self-interest. Desire was to be assessed in terms of economic efficacy rather than moral character: "The problem no longer has to do with the moral quality of the object that one desires, but with the manner in which we make choices in order to maximize individual and collective satisfaction."[21] The goal of political economy was to analyze the ways market forces can enhance the efficacy of desire in maximizing satisfaction: "And that's precisely what the new 'science' of economics, and the newly defined space of the market, is meant to help us achieve."[22]

Desire acquired a twofold meaning through processes of capitalist regulation, on the one hand, in terms of sexual longing and, on the other, in terms of economic interest: "in addition to the rewriting of desire as interest, the bourgeois order found it necessary to reframe the old thematic of desire in terms of a natural and specifically *sexual* instinct."[23] Capitalism requires an opening up of desire and self-interest to sustain the system, yet this desire must be channeled in the direction of maximizing "individual and collective satisfaction" through rational calculation. In the words of Foucault, "In the eighteenth century, sex became a 'police' matter – in the full and strict sense given the term at the time: not the repression of disorder, but an ordered maximization of collective and individual forces …"[24]

One key feature of the rationalization of desire was the distinction between normative and perverse longing. The treatment of perversion emphasized the regulation of desires more than acts: "Not only was sexual activity displaced from the sexual acts themselves to the desires that produced them, or failed to produce them … sexual desires were clinically framed, that is, integrated into a strict distinction between a normal and deviant sexuality."[25] The goal of the regulation of sexuality was not simply to proscribe specific activities, but to organize, direct and rationalize desire to align with economic interests. Sexual perversion was seen as the key basis for unrationalizable interest: "the 'discovery' of the sexual instinct is the discovery of not just one instinct among many, but, potentially at least, the key to understanding all the other instincts, and psychical life as a whole."[26] The regulation of sexuality was thus cast as a fundamental aspect of the channeling of desire towards capitalist rationality understood as economic self-interest, controlling the perversion that manifests in multiple forms of unrationalizable desire.

The problem of working-class hedonism had a special place in the disciplinary regulation of desire, as members of the working class needed to be taught temperance in order to preserve the regime of alienated labor in a society of unleashed self-interest. John Clarke described an "unending struggle about control in the area of working class leisure," marked by "activities to control, discipline and 'improve' the working class."[27] These regulatory activities ranged from "the attempt to suppress popular football" to programs aimed at "giving working class youth 'something constructive to do.'"[28] The rationalization of desire through social policy has included both proscriptive dimensions, to eliminate "perverse" behaviour (e.g. laws governing homosexuality, prostitution and public comportment) and prescriptive dimensions, to shape normative practices (school dances, sports, public health access for contraceptives, family policies, festivals and holidays). The character of this disciplinary regime has varied over time. Neoliberalism over the past 50 years has been associated with the relaxation of this regime of temperance and continence, opening up a more market-based hedonism that has restructured but not eliminated the distinction between normative and perverse.[29]

SOCIAL POLICY AND NATIONAL FORMATION

Capitalist states have organized moral regulation on a national basis, bounding off a particular population, establishing status systems (e.g. citizen, migrant, colonial) and shaping their social reproduction through social policy. This process of national formation has become so pervasive that it is now largely taken for granted. Nigel Harris compared this process to the enclosure of land as capitalism developed in Britain, "the appropriation of common lands by private owners to the point where all territory within Britain was officially parcelled up among a category of 'owners.'"[30] The net result of the national formation of populations was that states claimed people just as owners claimed land: "The process both within the territory of any given State and internationally eliminated all 'free lands' and all free men and women: all who do not officially belong to one or other local ruling class (and can, in principle, acquire a valid passport to prove that they actually exist)."[31]

The enclosure of national populations was part of a global process of capitalist state formation organized around imperialism. Colin Barker notes that the capitalist state cannot be understood in the singular (e.g. *the* Canadian state, *the* British state), but must be understood within "a world system of states."[32] The nation-state serves a dual purpose within capitalism, "both as an apparatus of class domination and as an apparatus of competition between segments of the bourgeoisie."[33] The development of the capitalist state is driven by a process of problem-solving to sustain capitalist profitability within a specific territory, in the face of working-class resistance, capitalist crises and global competition. Further, capitalism developed as an imperialist system in which specific modes of colonial administration were developed to appropriate land and resources and to dispossess the colonized population. The process of national formation involved important elements of differentiation, for example, between full citizens, migrants, colonized peoples, and those denied full citizenship on the basis of disability, age, gender, racialization, sexuality or social class.

The regulation of sexuality emerged as a dimension of social policy in the nineteenth century, as states attempted to solve problems associated with the ungovernability of the working classes and the colonized. The hedonism, unruliness, ill-health, work evasion, and overt resistance of the working class, colonized people and other subordinate classes created massive challenges to national and imperial sustainability. Visionary policy-makers innovated in response to these challenges, developing new modes of regulation. The working class and subordinate classes made themselves a problem for employers and state policy-makers. They did not show up for work on time, attempted to sustain their relationship to the land, developed their own cultures and ways of living, and resisted up to the point of mass insurgency. State social policy developed as a mode of regulation to teach the working class and other subordinate classes how to calibrate their desires to the prevailing conditions of alienation and dispossession in order to maximize their wellbeing within the context of a system of exploitation and domination. This was driven in large part by mobilization from below, as people organized to fight for the right to socially reproduce themselves in a system that was killing them through disease, hunger and overwork.

One of the key dimensions of the social policy regime that emerged to control unruly populations was the partial nationalization of social reproduction. Through this partial nationalization, the state assumes limited responsibility for the development and maintenance of the population through such programs as education, health and social welfare, seeking to create sufficient levels of compliance and productivity to meet the needs of employers and sustain social order.[34] This nationalization of social reproduction is necessarily partial, as the state must assert control without undermining self-ownership and the responsibility to sustain one's own existence.

Sexual regulation is a crucial dimension of this partial nationalization, built into practices of family formation, the normalization of productivity, the design of public housing, and expectations around public comportment and the uses of public space. This was emphatically a partial nationalization, as social policy was organized around the privatization of responsibility for social reproduction, the centrality of wage labor, and the gendered division of labor that cast women as caregivers primarily performing unpaid reproductive labor in the household. Women's access to welfare state benefits and services was limited by the devaluation of reproductive labor, and came disproportionately through their relationships with men.[35]

This partial nationalization of social reproduction is necessarily contradictory as it must not undermine the privatized responsibility for self-reproduction. One of the ways state policy-makers negotiated the contradiction between partial nationalization and privatized responsibility was to enshrine in various forms the principle of less-eligibility, which dated back to the British New Poor Law of 1834. Jones described less-eligibility as the stipulation "that the condition of the 'able-bodied pauper' on relief be less 'eligible' – that is, less desirable, less favourable – than the condition of the very poorest independent labourer."[36] The principle of less-eligibility included both a lower standard of living and a stigmatization of social provision: "Thus the labourer would be discouraged from lapsing into a state of 'dependency' on poor relief and the pauper would be 'encouraged' to work."[37] The application of less-eligibility has extended far beyond determinations of the level of social assistance for those who are not employed, up to and including constraints that undermine the bodily autonomy of those who receive services or benefits. For example, the personal relationships of people receiving social assistance benefits are policed in ways that severely limit their autonomy in the areas of sexual and gender expression.

The principle of less-eligibility is necessary but not sufficient to ensure that workers actually show up to the site of employment willing and able to work. Economic need alone does not ensure that workers show up punctually to the site of paid employment prepared to alienate their human capacities and produce to the point of exhaustion or beyond. Social policy benefits and programs work to align the expectations of the laboring population with the dominant conditions of requisite monetized and reproductive labor. Aumeeruddy, Lautier and Tortajada argue:

> the wage-worker must be a social subject who is partially autonomous: at the moment of exchange he or she must be free; the capitalists as a whole must ensure that this autonomy is limited in such a way that, despite him or herself, the wage-worker will duly come and re-engage under conditions that they fix …[38]

The goal of capitalist social policy is to create a laboring population who exercise sufficient autonomy to consent to alienated labor, intervening through a range of programs and benefits to regulate the process of social reproduction. The formation of children is a crucial dimension of social policy, as the exercise of constrained autonomy framed by the expectation of subordination must be practiced from a young age to produce workers willing and able to participate in alienated labor. Harry Braverman suggests:

> the habituation of workers to the capitalist mode of production must be renewed with each generation, all the more so as the generations which grow up under capitalism, are not formed within the matrix of work life, but are plunged into work from the outside, so to speak, after a prolonged period of adolescence during which they are held in reserve.[39]

Schooling and child services weave together elements of productivist discipline, to habituate the young to subordination, with elements of pleasure associated with rationalized play. Children learn to identify their own fulfillment with subordination through active participation in a school curriculum that marries time-discipline, responsible citizenship and erotic containment with elements of playful self-realization. Schooling folds together elements of productivism and pleasure to try to develop workers who participate willingly in hegemonic relations, consenting to their own alienation as they define it as the only path to their own fulfillment.

Children traverse a trajectory over their educational career from a greater emphasis on pleasure and play in pre-school and early elementary school through to a more disciplinary orientation in secondary school. The locus of discipline also shifts over the educational career, so that post-secondary education is oriented around a greater degree of self-regulation and relative absence of direct supervision. The university classroom tends to combine low degrees of pleasure with high expectations of personal responsibility.

The balance between productivism and pleasure in social policy varies not only through the life cycle, but also according to social location. Social policy regimes create degrees of standardization, forming the population as responsible citizens, though always combined with differentiation along such lines as gender, sexuality, social class, racialization, colonial status, age or disability designation. The balance between productivism and pleasure in social programs is not the same for all members of the working class. Social policy forms a population organized around a hierarchy of statuses, marked in part by a differentiated balance between productivism and pleasure. Higher status groups (e.g. well-off white men with full citizenship) are accorded greater bodily autonomy and sexual subjectivity, while lower status groups are expected to accept more intense subordination in all aspects of life.

The historical process of criminalization of recreational drug use in North America, for example, aimed to repress the pleasure of particular racialized groups by targeting the consumption of substances associated with sex and disinhibition.[40] In the 1990s, Black women in the United States were targeted for arrest if they used drugs during a pregnancy, purportedly in the name of preventing harm to the fetus. Enid Logan argues,

> The primary utility of stigmatizing and punishing poor drug-addicted black women lies not in the prevention of fetal harm, but in the defense of normative standards of gender and motherhood, the resuscitation of public innocence concerning the plight of the black poor, and the legitimization of a status quo characterized by continuing oppression and inequality.[41]

Sexual formation is intimately linked to racial formation. In the words of E. San Juan, "How the idea of the nation is sexualized and how sex is nationalized are topics that may yield clues as to how racial conflicts are circumscribed within the force field of national self-identification."[42] Black women's sexuality has been subjected to particular forms of sexual regulation, including limits on access to contraception and abortion as well as forced sterilization. Dorothy Roberts maintains: "The systematic, institutionalized denial of reproductive freedom has uniquely marked Black women's history in America."[43]

Social policy is organized around dominant forms of heteronormativity that are structured around racialized, gendered and colonial hierarchies of personhood. African-American families tended to look different in response to specific conditions of life and work, and did conform with heteronormative standards established through the lens of whiteness. Roderick Ferguson notes, "As racial differences in how people make a living affected domestic life, producing increasingly diverse forms of family, family became an index of those differences."[44] Sex and gender non-normativity, or queerness, took different forms in African-American communities, organized in relation to non-heteronormative family forms: "Though African American homosexuality, unlike its heterosexual counterpart, symbolized a rejection of heterosexuality, neither could claim heteronormativity."[45]

Global divisions of labor mean that many people who migrate do not live in heteronormative families, as they often find themselves scattered across households in different geographic locations, sustained in part by the transfer of resources and transnational caregiving. Sue Ferguson and David McNally remind us of "the complex patterns by which labour migration has become central to the reproduction of hundreds of millions of working-class households, whose well-being relies on wage remittances."[46] Conely de Leon examines the ways Filipino kin networks organize on a transnational basis, often combining employment as paid caregivers with unpaid labor in many forms organized among geographically dispersed participants. In this situation, people sustain themselves and each other through "broader communities of carers such as siblings, nieces, nephews, neighbours, partners, grandparents, and grandchildren – those who are not often considered active care givers in the dominant gender, migration, and care literature, but who are clearly 'doing' the work of care."[47] Rather than facilitating these complex transnational configurations of care, social policy has generally constructed obstacles ranging from the constraints of border regimes to the geographic limits of social, health and educational programs.

The development of domestic social policy was tied to colonial administration, where the rule over populations required more than raising a flag or coloring in a particular territory on a map upon agreement between colonial powers. Colonialism required ongoing regimes that combined (in different proportions under changing circumstances): brutal authoritarianism, racialized dehumanization and measures of limited inclusion to promote hegemony. Kenneth Ballhatchet traced out the origins of the colonial social policy regime developed by the British in India. This regime was founded on assumptions of differential sexualization: "The British often suspected that Indians were by nature more lascivious that they were themselves."[48] This view was often reciprocated: "Yet Indians, on the other hand, were often shocked by European manners, not only in eating, drinking and personal hygiene but in the indecorous behaviours of ladies baring their shoulders and even dancing on social occasions."[49]

The British regime sought to preserve and regulate certain forms of prostitution seen as essential to sustaining military occupation, while generally preventing sexual activity between colonial administrators and Indian women. According to the understanding of colonial authorities, rank and file military personnel needed sources of heterosex while in India to preserve their masculinity:

> Indian prostitutes were therefore seen in a positive role as necessary to the satisfaction of the soldiers' physical needs. If those needs were denied satisfaction, dire consequences were envisaged. The soldiers' masculinity would be at risk: the prospects of homosexuality was revealed in guarded terms by the authorities whenever there was talk of excluding prostitutes from the cantonments.[50]

The concern was solely the masculinity and wellbeing of soldiers, with no attention to the lives of the Indian women who were at the center of this policy. This form of prostitution was cast as a specific exception to a broader policy of racialized separation:

> There is an obvious contradiction between the care with which the military authorities provided facilities for sexual relations between British soldiers and native women, and the care with which other authorities tried to discourage sexual relations between British officials and native women. In both cases the fundamental concern was to preserve the structure of power. In the one case the soldiers' virile energies had to be maintained. In the other case the social distance between the official elite and the people had to be preserved.[51]

Imperialism up to the nineteenth century was largely marked by the claim of sexual continence amongst the colonizers who cast themselves as civilized, in contrast with the diverse and unruly sexualities of those who were colonized and racialized. Mousab Younis noted the way twenty-first-century maps of homophobic threat zones bear remarkable similarity to those that demarcated almost exactly the same regions as sexually unruly places where homosexuality was widespread in the nineteenth century:

Sexual liberation is now seen as a pillar of Western freedom: Africa, the Arab and Muslim world, Asia and the Caribbean constitute an anti-gay empire, marked in forbidding red on maps that chart homophobic legislation around the world – a perfect inversion of the 19th-century Arabist Richard Burton's "Sotadic Zone", a vast geographical space, named for the scurrilous Greek poet Sotades, in which the "vice" of homosexuality was allegedly rife.[52]

The social policy tools being developed by colonial administrations in India and elsewhere aimed at subordination through dehumanization were taken up by social policy-makers in the Global North, who began to construct a perspective presuming that layers of the working class were amoral, feckless, hedonistic, ignorant and impressionable, vulnerable to charismatic leaders, diseases, drink and sex. Through the nineteenth and early twentieth centuries, the British government developed forms of moral regulation to shape the social reproduction of the working class in new ways, including public health measures, compulsory education, limits on working hours, occupancy and building standards for housing, bans on homosexuality and prostitution, regulations on alcohol consumption and immigration controls.

The partial nationalization of social reproduction through social policy was developed in the global context of imperialism and migration. The nation-state did not simply claim the population of particular territories, but designed regimes to reproduce differentiation on a local, national and global level. The social rights of self-owning individuals were not organized universally, but on a national level oriented around hierarchies of status, gender and racialization. Differential sexual formation was a crucial dimension of social policy, oriented around a complex balance of productivism and pleasure to reproduce a population willing and able to work and live in conditions of capitalist alienation.

HISTORIC PHASES OF SOCIAL POLICY AND SEXUAL FORMATION

Social policy has developed historically through a series of phases that vary with the rhythms of class struggle and colonial dynamics in different states within the global system. In Canada, the broad welfare state lasting roughly from 1945 to 1980 was the pinnacle of prescriptive social policy, marked by the extensive though still partial nationalization of social reproduction through a range of social, cultural and health programs. After that, social policy in Canada and globally was restructured towards the neoliberal lean state, which combined deep cuts in services and benefits with a heavier reliance on policing and carceral detention and elements of moral deregulation in such areas as sexuality, gambling and alcohol or drug use.

Each of these social policy regimes was associated with particular modes of sexual regulation. Peter Drucker developed a framework that connected historical shifts in social policy with changes in same-sex formation, which he defined as "a specific hierarchy of different same-sex patterns (like transgender, intergenerational and lesbian/gay patterns) in which one pattern is culturally dominant (if not necessarily more prevalent)."[53] The restructuring of capitalism in the Global North has created the conditions for the development of three different same-sex formations, each associated with a particular social policy regime: the invert-dominant before the broad welfare state (roughly 1870–1940), the gay-dominant generally corresponding to the broad welfare state (roughly 1940–90) and the homonormative-dominant associated with the neoliberal lean state (roughly 1990–present).

The invert-dominant mode of same-sex formation developed in a social policy regime before the broad welfare state that was primarily proscriptive, oriented around "suppressing alternatives to wage labour and prohibiting or constraining a wide variety of working-class activities."[54] Social policy in this period focused largely on the carceral (e.g. the workhouse, the asylum, the orphanage, the prison), at times paired with stigmatized and limited outdoor relief for the destitute. Proscriptive social policy prominently featured the use of legal measures to attempt to eliminate or at least punish and stigmatize aspects of working-class life ranging from trade union organization to prostitution and from vagrancy to homosexuality. Over time, policy-makers developed limited forms of prescriptive social policy, which focused more on actively shaping working-class social reproduction, including public health regulation around housing standards and access to clean water, factory acts setting conditions on employment (including who could be employed and the structure of the working day), and limited compulsory education. The early years of the twentieth century saw some expansion of prescriptive social policy, including more years of compulsory education, widening public health measures and a new immigration regime, driven by the intensification of imperialist competition and a new level of working class militancy that culminated in the post-World War I revolutionary upsurge.

The proscriptive social policy mode before the welfare state was associated with measures to outlaw homosexuality and prostitution as well as strict censorship of cultural representations of erotic life. It was in this context that the invert-dominant mode of same-sex formation emerged, characterized by a tendency towards homosexual relationships organized around polarized identities, whether that be on the basis of gender (e.g. butch/femme), class (e.g. working class and bourgeois) or racialized/colonized status (e.g. colonizer and "native"). It was only transgendered people (i.e. feminine men and masculine women) who tended to identify as members of a distinct community in these relations, while other (cis-gendered) people tended not to develop specific identities around their same-gender sexual practices, and indeed often fit in to the dominant (normative) order, including heterosexual marriage, despite participation in homosexual activity.[55]

The broad welfare state developed in response to the massive upsurge of working-class mobilization in the 1930s and 1940s. State policy-makers developed measures to try to contain working-class insurgency through a tremendous expansion of prescriptive social policy through which the state took "responsibility for some of the costs of reproduction in order to forge a population with a specific national identity as well as certain standards of health, education and discipline."[56] The state attempted to diffuse working-class resistance and build a base for sustained capitalist profitability by creating a range of social programs which "established social minima (using programmes and benefits to provide at least a specified minimum level of income, housing, health and education) and enforced norms."[57] The broad welfare state was based on a form of "social citizenship" that mapped together political and social rights, though in practice those rights were not universal but highly differentiated on the basis of gender, sexuality, racialization, employment history, migration status and Indigeneity. Esping-Andersen argues that social citizenship combined a limited decommodification of the means of sustenance, providing non-market access to some necessities of life (education at certain levels, health care, public housing) with the stratification of social rights so that access to benefits and services was differentiated and accorded varying levels of stigma.[58]

The broad welfare state was associated with a heteronormative mode of sexual regulation, oriented around the family wage in which a single (presumably male) wage worker earned enough to support a household, based on the situation of limited strata of the working class employed in particular industrial or office settings who had won significant improvements in wages and benefits through union struggles. The social policies of the broad welfare state contributed to the capitalist profitability of the long post-war boom linked to increased productivity. As outlined by Chris Chitty, "The investment of capital into a highly-disciplined and rationalized laboring body normalized the reproduction of labor power within family units, allowing for the adoption of technologies that made the production process far more efficient."[59]

In the context of the broad welfare state, queer communities began to mobilize in new ways (alongside women, racialized populations and others) to demand full personhood and inclusion in social citizenship. The result of these mobilizations was the emergence of what Drucker labeled the gay-dominant mode of same-sex formation, characterized by a shift to less polarized forms of lesbian and gay relationship, often consisting of partners with roughly similar gender identities.[60] It also saw gay and lesbian identities grounded in sexual orientation begin to separate off from trans identities based on gender expression.[61]

The shift from the broad welfare state to the neoliberal lean state began in the mid-1970s, driven both by a profitability squeeze and a decline in working-class militancy. The development of the lean state included a partial de-nationalization of social reproduction, narrowing the scope of social programs and forcing members of the working class to meet more of their needs through the market. At the same time, states engaged in a certain degree of moral deregulation in such areas as gambling, substance use and sexuality, associated with an emphasis on consumerism disciplined through the marketplace rather than direct state regulation. Women faced the intensification of unpaid labor and the devaluation of paid caregiving often associated with privatization of services or contracting out of employment.

From the perspective of employers and state policy-makers confronting the economic downturn of the mid-1970s, the social policy of the broad welfare state was seen as a fetter on profitability, producing "labour market rigidities in the form of high wages, limited wage differentials, entitlements through social programmes and labour market regulations."[62] Capitalists began an intensive process of restructuring associated with the generalization of lean production methods which aimed to squeeze out "waste," eliminating the buffers associated with previous mass production systems by introducing "just-in-time" delivery of parts and a more flexible workforce willing to accept movement between jobs and to tolerate a variety of working conditions. The ideal flexible worker incorporated a lean ethos which combines comfort with risk and lack of security with the drive "to maintain herself or himself at peak levels of fitness" and the organization of life "around lean principles, avoiding waste and dependence."[63]

The homonormative-dominant mode of same-sex formation developed in connection with the emergence of the neoliberal lean state. The recognition of lesbian and gay partnership and/or marriage rights folded certain queer relationships into the dominant family form, creating an important distinction between socially acceptable forms of lesbian, gay and (to a lesser degree) trans identities and other forms of same-sex or gender non-conforming practice that remained highly stigmatized and punished.[64] The development of the homonormative mode of sexual hegemony was connected to particular characteristics of the social policies of the lean state.

The shift to the lean state deliberately undermined social programs that policy-makers identified as offering alternatives to participation in wage labor or monetized equivalent to purchase goods or services on the market. This included limited moral deregulation, in which the state reduced the use of "a few of the tools it used to attempt to shape the morality of the population" that had focused on promoting "values of temperance and prudence among working-class people."[65] This limited moral deregulation included a shift in sexual hegemony: "A much wider-ranging collapse of the hegemony of the normal enabled a dramatic cultural redefinition of marriage and sexuality in the space of a few decades, despite substantial moral backlash."[66]

This partial moral deregulation was accompanied by a sharp coercive turn in social policy, including a dramatic increase in imprisonment, particularly of racialized and Indigenous people, harsher policing tactics, increased regulation of people accessing social services and more restrictive immigration controls. Ruth Wilson Gilmore examined this coercive turn in California, the political jurisdiction that modeled many dimensions of the neoliberal transformation to the lean state that were subsequently taken up elsewhere. In California, the prisoner population increased by almost 500 percent as neoliberalism took hold between 1982 and 2000, despite a general downward trend in the crime rate.[67] During this period, the orientation of prison policy shifted away from the rehabilitation emphasis that has been dominant for the previous 60 years.[68] At the same time, there was a shift in the character of crimes for which people were imprisoned, "from a preponderance of violent offences in 1980 to nonviolent crimes in 1995."[69] This increase in imprisonment was associated with a "remarkable racial and ethnic shift in the prison population" in which "[w]orking-class African American and Latinos – especially Chicanos – experienced the most intensive criminalization, trailed by urban and rural Anglos of modest means."[70] Before 1977, Anglos had been the predominant segment of the California prison population.[71]

The social policy of the lean state freighted working-class households with responsibility for their own sustenance and wellbeing by slashing social programs, and created heavy consequences for those who could not do so.

Some queers gained new rights with the rise of the lean state, particularly those who were better off, white and whose recognized couple relations or marriages fit the new regime of sexual hegemony. Others faced "an extension and intensification of certain forms of sexual policing and censorship" affecting "a number of our sex-related practices, from men who have sex in washrooms and parks to gay hustlers, to young lesbians, gay men and bisexuals who need access to information about queer sexual practices, to community AIDS workers, to lesbians, gay men and bisexuals who read, view, write and produce erotic materials."[72] While certain layers of queer communities gained social rights associated with relationship recognition and increased cultural representation, others who could not afford to participate in commodified queer life, or who did not conform with the standards of homonormativity, faced increased policing and coercion.

Sexual formation is a foundational element of social policy, even where it is not an explicit goal of particular benefits, programs or services. Through social policy measures, capitalists states attempt to shape their populations by regulating social reproduction to construct certain life practices as normative. State policy-makers craft programs and benefits to foster productivity and rationalize pleasure. Erotic containment and normativity in sexual and gender expression are core requirements of the national population shaped through social policy to be prepared to engage in paid or reproductive labor at least somewhat accommodated to their place in the hierarchy of social statuses organized around national status, gender, sexuality, racialization, colonial dispossession and disability designation.

6

Sexuality and Ecology

While our erotic sensibility may feel profoundly personal and physiological, it is at the same time social and ecological. The dominant social relations not only shape the conditions of our labor, but also frame our engagement with nature, both internally with our own bodies and externally with our environment. The rise of capitalism as a global system has created a qualitative shift in ecological relations. As discussed previously, dispossession destroys relations of mutuality and reciprocity with other humans, other species and the world around us, transforming human capacities, other living species and the land into commodities for exchange. Capitalism undermines human responsibility for the sustainability of our interchange with nature, creating the multidimensional ecological crisis of our times, which crucially includes, but is not limited to, climate change.

Jason W. Moore maintains we must understand human experience as "unavoidably, irreducibly socio-ecological."[1] We make sense of the world through our active transformative work; learning, tasting, crafting, naming. This embodied experience of knowledge production is socially and environmentally located. Yet, human life is not simply environmentally determined by external forces. People are at once products and producers of their social and natural environment. The importance of labor in Marx's social analysis derives from the centrality of life-making activity in framing human experience. "Labour … is an eternal natural necessity which mediates the metabolism between man and nature, and therefore human life itself."[2]

People do not work on nature from the outside, but as part of it. Marx argued that the laboring person "sets in motion the natural forces which belong to his own body, his arms, legs, head and hands, in order to appropriate the materials of nature in a form adapted to his own needs."[3] As people transform nature to meet their needs, they also change themselves: "Through this movement, he acts upon external nature and changes it, and in this way he simultaneously changes his own nature."[4] Thus, planning, imagination and deliberate decision play particularly important roles in human life-making activity: "He develops the potentialities within nature, and subjects the play of its forces to his own sovereign power."[5]

Capitalist alienation undermines purposive life-making and shatters existing relations of mutuality and reciprocity with other humans, other species and our environment. This is not to romanticize or flatten pre-capitalist social relations, which included a wide range of societal forms ranging from the relatively egalitarian to those characterized by long histories of enslavement, war and class domination. It is to argue that capitalist dispossession and alienation represented a qualitative break with previous practices, remaking ecological and social relations on a global scale in ways that affected everybody, though not in the same way given relations of class, colonialism, gender, racialization and sexuality.

Leanne Simpson characterized her Indigenous nation's ways of living as an "ecology of intimacy" that is based on an expansive sense of connectivity and responsibility: "It is a web of connections to each other, to the plant nations, the animal nations, the rivers and lakes, the cosmos, and our neighbouring Indigenous nations."[6] This web of social and ecological relationships is not based on domination or subordination, whether of other humans, other species or the land. "It is an ecology of relationships in the absence of coercion, hierarchy, or authoritarian power."[7]

In conditions of alienation, the dominant class levers its ownership and/ or control over the means of production to orient all aspects of the metabolic interchange between people and nature around profit-making. People in capitalist societies begin to treat nature as a supply of resources to plunder for profit. This focus on extraction as opposed to mutuality had a huge impact on conceptions of sexuality, gender and embodiment. The human interchange with nature under capitalism is part of an integrated system of domination and exploitation mapping together social relations (of class, gender, racialization, sexuality and colonialism) and ecological relations between humans and the rest of nature. The dominant regime of sexualities is framed by ecological relations with our own bodies (internal nature) and our environment (external nature).

Marx explored the disruption of the metabolism between humans and nature under capitalist relations primarily through the lens of soil depletion, noting the way:

> large landed property reduces the agricultural population to an ever decreasing minimum and confronts it with an ever growing industrial population crammed together in large towns; in this way it produces con-

ditions that provoke an irreparable rift in the interdependent process of social metabolism, a metabolism prescribed by the natural laws of life itself.[8]

Marx contrasts this metabolic rift under capitalism with a post-revolutionary "[f]reedom" in which "socialized man, the associated producers, govern the human metabolism with nature in a rational way, bringing it under their collective control instead of being dominated by it as a blind power ..."[9]

John Bellamy Foster generalizes Marx's conception of "the metabolism between man and nature" to understand the ways that human life-making is an ongoing ecological interchange: "An essential aspect of the concept of metabolism is the notion that it constitutes the basis on which life is sustained and growth and reproduction become possible."[10] Bellamy Foster builds on Marx's conception of a specifically capitalist disruption in the human interchange with nature: "Marx employed the concept of metabolic rift to capture the material estrangement of human beings in capitalist society from the natural conditions of their existence."[11] Capitalist social relations frame a view of nature that focuses on extraction not reproduction, ultimately creating massive threats to sustainability. The unsustainability of the capitalist social-ecological system represents a metabolic rift, a disruption of ongoing interchanges between people and their environment.

This metabolic rift frames our understanding of our own bodies, each other, and the world around us. People in capitalist society are deprived of the capacity to take responsibility for sustainability in our interchange with nature by alienation through dispossession and the profit-making imperative that shapes all capitalist decision making. Sexual engagement organized along the lines of market transaction undermines the responsibility for care and sustainability in our interpersonal relationships. The responsibility for mutuality is not simply a lovely ideal, but is grounded in the reality of human sociability in ongoing metabolism with nature that inextricably links our future outcomes. Within the frame of capitalist dispossession, responsibility is privatized, care is individualized, and nature is transformed into resources for extraction. People form relationships as part of their survival projects, as discussed above, but in capitalist conditions these projects are necessarily organized around participation in alienated labor rooted in an extractive economy.

People in contemporary capitalist societies negotiate sexual life in the context of metabolic rift. At a simple level, sex has to compete for life-energy with the exhausting demands of overwork through alienated labor in a situation of dispossession and atomization created by the destruction of networks of mutuality and reciprocity. People face a new kind of loneliness and the challenges of finding the time, space and life-energy for intimacy. Our relations with our own bodies are shaped by the metabolic rift, to the extent that there is a tendency to prize bodies that look like products and shame those that look "natural" in the sense that they are not shaped by training, diet and fashion in the dominant beauty hierarchies of the Global North. The question of sustainability is at the forefront of these times.

SECOND NATURE

The interchange with nature in contemporary capitalism is characterized by the development of what Neil Smith described as "second nature." Smith drew on Hegel and Marx to distinguish between "first nature" untouched by human transformative activity and "second nature" produced through the metabolic interchange between humans and nature. Second nature is no less "natural" (the laws of physics, for example, are not suspended), but it is not the same as first nature as it bears the fingerprints of human activity. George Monbiot, for example, has argued that it was problematic to designate the Lake District, the birthplace of Britain's modern conservation movement, as a UNESCO World Heritage Site:

> Stand back from the fells and valleys, and try to judge this vista as you would a landscape in any other part of the world. What you will see is the great damage farming has inflicted: wet deserts grazed down to turf and rock; erosion gullies from which piles of stones spill; woods in which no new trees have grown for 80 years, as every seedling has been nibbled out by sheep; dredged and canalised rivers, empty of wildlife and dangerous to the people living downstream; tracts of bare mountainside on which every spring is a silent one. Anyone with ecological knowledge should recoil from this scene.[12]

The beauty of the Lake District is a clear example of second nature; and UNESCO designation would mean enshrining a certain phase of human development of the area (sheep-intensive farming) as the ecological standard. This organization of life in the Lake District is a result of historical human activity now defended by specific humans with particular interests in relation to future transformations. The natural and the social in second nature are deeply integrated.

Second nature has existed through human history, as it is the character of human life-making activity to transform nature. Capitalism has intensified second nature and extended it to the bounds of the planet, so that first nature in its pristine sense no longer exists. The impact of human action, whether through development of infrastructure or the dumping of contaminants, is present everywhere. The second nature produced under capitalism is a contradictory mixture of alienation and the innovation driven by competitive profit-making, so that human transformative capacities are massively increased while control over the outcome of human activity is located in the hands of capitalists who are necessarily oriented around the extraction of surplus. This has created the ecological crisis of our time. Andreas Malm points out that global warming is only one dimension of the widespread human impact on nature:

> Besides carbon, several cycles of elements essential to life – notably nitrogen, phosphorous and sulphur – are now out of joint due to human over-extraction and over-emission; the water cycle has been upset by the damming of rivers and the clearing of land; the sixth major event of species extinction is underway; oceans are acidifying; ozone is depleted; and the list goes on. Signs of planet wide human ascendancy seem to criss-cross all spheres of life.[13]

The development of capitalism has qualitatively shifted the human interchange with nature. Smith posits, "The development of capitalism, however, involves not just a quantitative but a qualitative development in the relation with nature."[14] Capitalism did not merely expand the realm of second nature, but reproduced it at a world scale. In these circumstances, "first nature is deprived of its firstness, its originality."[15]

Second nature is driven to the edges of the earth – and indeed beyond the bounds of the planet – by capitalist exploitation that combines ever-increasing productivity and endless plunder. As Jason W. Moore outlines, the "basic logic of capital owes its success as much to the extension of appropriation as it does to the capitalization of production – this, the dialectic of productivity and plunder."[16] Second nature is produced by the combination of the capitalist drive to enhance productivity for competitive advantage in the accumulation of profits and the naked plunder that fuels the system.

Andreas Malm maintains the crucial moment of qualitative shift in the human interchange with nature was the rise of the fossil economy, "an economy of self-sustaining growth predicated on the growing consumption of fossil fuels, and therefore generating a sustained growth in emissions of carbon dioxide."[17] The rise of the fossil economy through the process of Industrial Revolution has been driven by power in the dual sense of sources of energy and a relationship of domination and subordination between humans. The specific turning point Malm points to is the introduction of steam power in the British cotton industry in response to the capitalist crisis of 1825–48. Ryan Cecil Jobson argues that Malm's account of this qualitative shift in the human interchange with nature needs to further examine the specific role of the enslavement of African peoples in the cotton industry: "the private ownership of energy necessitates extractive violence, whether the source of that energy is fossil fuels, the harnessed energy of solar, wind, or water, or human labor power."[18]

The rise of the fossil economy and the extension of second nature was integrally tied to the capitalist drive to enhance profitability by undermining the power of workers and exploiting the labor of enslaved people in cotton production. Capitalist strategies for profitability drew together the use of steam power, the employment of women as cheaper laborers, and the unfree labor of enslaved people whose work provided cotton at low rates, which together allowed for substantial accumulation and the investment in new technologies. The struggle for control over the workplace, the drive for profit through exploitation, the transformation of nature into resources for plunder, the cheapening of women's labor and the brutal exploitation of enslaved people were hard-wired into the character of the fossil economy.

The production of second nature was driven by the integrated development of imperialism as a foundational feature of capitalism. Edward Said contends that imperialism, focused on the domination of peoples through the conquest of land, was the crucial process through which second nature was driven to a world scale. The transformation of the land was fundamental to the process of dispossessing Indigenous peoples. The land has thus remained a central reference point in anti-imperialist and decolonizing struggles: "To the anti-imperialist imagination, our space at home in the peripheries has been usurped and put to use by outsiders for their purpose."[19] Imperialists transformed the ecosystem as they dispossessed the Indigenous peoples of the lands. The colonizers brought with them new diseases, new plants, new animals and new relationships with the land and bodies. The development of second nature was intimately linked with genocide, cultural destruction and dispossession on a massive scale. The deliberate cultural genocide of Indigenous ways of knowing and living through residential schools in Canada was part of the dispossession of Indigenous peoples in relation to the land and their own bodies.

Jason W. Moore pointed out that this ecological regime depletes both nature and the working classes through interconnected processes. The current ecological crisis is not only creating climate change and the extinction of huge numbers of species, but is also pushing large sectors of the human population beyond sustainable limits, one more chapter in a long history of working-class deprivation. Even the relatively well-off workforce in the United States is "maxed out": "it can no longer deliver a rising stream of work/energy into – or in support of – the circuit of capital."[20] Kim Moody demonstrates the specific ways the US working class is being driven to exhaustion by employers who have restructured work since the 1980s by reducing breaks, lengthening shifts, driving up the pace of work, increasing surveillance of the workforce and undermining union organization.[21] This has increased productivity by driving workers to the point of exhaustion or beyond.

Capitalist speed-up is not limited to paid labor alone, but crosses the whole terrain of life. Parents, for example, face very real time pressures in their child-rearing relations, and thus play time might be curtailed as parents rush to leave for work in the morning. Yet, there are limits to how much work can be squeezed out of members of the working class. A sick child needs care, just as no adult can work endlessly day after day without ultimately collapsing. "The *real* working day – of paid and unpaid work – cannot be extended without limit."[22]

Clearly, the exhaustion of members of the working class has a huge influence on their personal lives in every sense: "Time for education, for intellectual development, for the fulfillment of social functions, for social intercourse, for the free play of vital forces of [their] body and [their] mind, even the rest time of Sunday (and that in a country of Sabbatarians) – what foolishness!"[23] The capitalist drive to exhaust the working class is part of a productivity ethos in which human worth is associated with engaging in activities that generate profit for capital. Sexual practice is, in this context, an unproductive waste of energy, to be confined to the margins of the daily lives of members of the working class except in those limited cases where it is directly connected to reproduction.

The toll of exhaustion is greatest and the sustainability of life most threatened among those who are at the lower end of hierarchies of labor and who must work for low wages or for free. Women and people who are racialized have most often made up a disproportionate share of those performing cheap or unpaid labor, given the global organization produced by colonialism, racism and gendered divisions of labor and particularly the compulsion to perform unpaid labor.

RESISTING SECOND NATURE

People mobilizing against capitalism and imperialism, challenging the dispossession that is central to second nature, often invoke a return to first nature. William Blake's 1804 poem *Jerusalem* (made into a hymn of the English labor movement but also English nationalism) contrasts "England's green and pleasant land" with "these dark satanic mills." This is just one example of nineteenth-century romanticism that contrasted visions of first nature before capitalism with those of capitalist devastation of human life and the environment. Similarly, Palestinian culture is rich with images of the magnetic draw and resilience of the land from which the bulk of the population was displaced by the Nakba. The Palestinian poet Mahmoud Darwish wrote, "Like orphans I ran to you/asking about the wisdom of the ancestors:/'Why is the green orchard dragged/ to a prison to exile to a harbour/&despite its journey/&despite the odors of salt and of longing/why does it remain green forever?"[24]

The return to first nature is not simply a romantic dream, but a practical strategy as people use wilderness as a place of freedom or refuge. This includes important histories of forbidden sex in the urban wilderness of parks. The Ramble in New York City's Central Park is an area of "dense vegetation, serpentine paths, giant boulders and meandering streams created by the park's designer, Frederick Law Olmsted."[25] It feels like a nature reserve in the midst of New York's hyper-urban environment, though it is a very deliberate creation seen as a model of landscape architecture and park craft. The Ramble is "a magnet for bird-watchers, who know it as one of the best spots around to see migrating warblers and other songbirds on the Atlantic flyway."[26] It might be a deliberate product of human design, but it is a very attractive spot for a wide variety of birds: "From the sky, the birds spy the verdant rectangle of the park amid the grey cityscape and gravitate toward the Ramble, with its ample sources of food and water."[27]

The Ramble is not only attractive to birds, but also has a long history as a cruising area, a place for gay men to have sex. The Central Park website soberly describes this history:

One notable fact about the Ramble is its status as a gay icon, which has developed since the early 1900s. A well-known site for private homosexual encounters throughout the 20th century, the woodland is now an important part of LGBT history.[28]

The same ecological conditions that make wooded parkland an attraction to bird life also make it hospitable to sexual activity. Frederick Law Olmstead described his goal that the design of the Ramble would "create a degree of obscurity not absolutely impenetrable, but sufficient to affect the imagination with a sense of mystery."[29] Parks designed to create a sense of natural respite from the intense demands of the city open up spaces for certain kinds of freedom. The woods in urban parks create a degree of obscurity in the midst of the city streetscape designed for transparency and surveillance. There is a long history of the use of urban parks as a cruising ground for gay men and others needing some sort of cover for marginalized or outlawed sexual activity.

Forbidden or marginalized sex is just one example of the dissident or resistance activities that have developed in the spaces of wilderness since the rise of capitalism. Andreas Malm points to the important examples of the use of forests as shelter for maroons fleeing and resisting slavery on Dominica and other Caribbean Islands; and for Jewish partisans fighting fascism and escaping deportation or murder in Eastern Europe. Malm suggests that relative wilderness has an important place in histories of dissent and resistance. The Rambles in Central Park is a clear example of "relative wilderness," where the direct ongoing control exercised by the forces of authority is relatively limited. He distinguishes this from absolute wilderness, areas completely untouched by the impact of human activity associated with first nature which simply no longer exist on this planet. Relative wilderness is a space within second nature where direct human control is more limited than in many of the places of daily life:

> water springs forth in a stream without anyone having pushed a button, wolves and lemmings and foxes feed and reproduce of their own accord, plants grow and leaves fall with no investors pulling the strings: natural processes play out without direct human control.[30]

The dominant powers in capitalist societies have tended to invest remarkable resources to bringing the wilderness under control through felling forests, diverting rivers into canals, draining wetlands, laying track, building roads, planting fields, digging pipelines and constructing structures. The conquest of wilderness is a settler-colonial project integrally connected to the dispossession of Indigenous peoples. Glen Coulthard discusses the centrality of land in Indigenous anti-colonial struggles, which is "deeply *informed* by what the land *as system of reciprocal relations and obligations* can teach us about living our lives in relation to one another and the natural world in non-dominating and non-exploitive terms ..."[31] The land is the crucial point of connection to other ways of living and knowing.

The destruction of the wilderness is practical, it provides the immediate means and the longer-term infrastructure for corporate profitability which is at the core of the system. But the domestication of wild spaces is also a political and moral project to enhance hegemony by creating an environment that naturalizes the dominant power relations. Malm noted that on Caribbean Islands:

> while the plantations were confines for the tyranny of the masters, beyond them now lay a relative wilderness. The masters detested that space as not-yet-cleared, untamed, savage – and in exactly the same proportion, slaves cherished it as a land of freedom.[32]

Wilderness provided both elements of material protection for those fleeing or resisting domination and the inspiring and nurturing image of unconquered spaces of freedom. The wild can provide a practical and symbolic space beyond the immediate control of authorities. John Rechy's 1977 novel *The Sexual Outlaw* highlighted the lives of the "sexual underground," particular layers of emerging gay communities that he cast as an insurgent band resisting the authorities, and particularly the police and courts. He described Griffith Park in Los Angeles as "the capital of the sexual underground ... Miles of sexhunting along declining paths, hills to the sides of the road ... hundreds of outlaws hunt ..."[33] The sexual underground thrives in wild spaces. One character on his way to the hunt for sex breathes in the forest air: "The sweet musty odor of moist wood and greenery – he smells its definite presence. It mixes with the sounds of grass, leaves, moisture, twigs, branches, shadows, stillness."[34] The sensory experience of wilderness and untamed sexuality co-mingle. However, after less than an hour of hunting, the stillness is broken. "The unmistakable roar of the hated helicopter! The cops! Men move for cover."[35]

The sexual underground Rechy sketches is engaged in dissident sexual behavior and active, at times militant, resistance to the cops. He begins his picture of the gay parade down Hollywood Boulevard with images of struggle: "Where else but on the turf they've tried deviously with ordinances, openly with violence, to wrest from us year after year. Site of how many gay battles fought cruising and hustling, being chased away by the envious cops, and returning to cruise, and hustle on the same corner, your favourite?"[36] Rechy traces the sexual underground through the city, and notes its headquarters is in the relative wilderness.

Men have used wild spaces (such as ravines in Toronto or the Rambles in Central Park in New York) to have sex with each other in the face of repressive regulations, but also restrictions on access to private space. The prohibitive cost of housing means that some people live in crowded units which afford no private space, while others are unhoused. Marcus McCann observes, "The parks provide an alternative to all of this."[37] Parks are among the locations that have historically been turned into "erotic oases" which operate as cruising grounds that are at once bounded (limiting through traffic and surveillance) and open (public spaces with free access).[38] Parks as erotic oases offer an element of liberation from the everyday. A participant in Richard Tewksbury's research on men who had sex with men in erotic oases stated,

> I see it as the perfect escape plan. Well, not perfect, but as near to perfect as you can be. I mean, you don't have to cook breakfast for them in the morning, you don't have to try to get them out of bed because you have to go to work in the morning. You don't have to sleep with them at all. All you have to do is go fuck them or be fucked by them.[39]

The wilderness of the park can enhance the sense of escape from highly regulated social life through wild sex in an untamed and unmonitored setting. The legalization of same-sex relations has often been accompanied by a crackdown on sex in the wilderness and the cruising areas used historically by men to have sex with men. This has a highly differentiated impact, so that men who have the inclination and means to live open gay lives that fit certain patterns are legalized and domesticated through marriage, while those who for various reasons (often including racialization and class) cannot or do not form such relationships face new forms of arrest and surveillance. Gary Kinsman argues that legalization tended to intensify a distinction between "responsible" LGBTQ who settled down into relations officially classified as family and those who cruised for sex: "for those who are not constructed as 'familial' or 'spousal,' there is continued policing and oppressive regulation in areas regarding sexuality and social life outside spousal/familial contexts."[40]

At a more general level, sex outside of certain constraints (e.g. couple formation) has been constructed as a connection to wildness outside of society, with its rhythms of daily life, productivity ethos and commodified leisure regime. Sex is contradictory, at once cultural and biological; raging and controllable. At some level, sex might remind us of a part of ourselves that cannot be conquered or completely alienated. However, before we all start going wild there is another side to this discussion of the wilderness and ecology. The connection to wilderness might at times be insurgent, but it can also be very much part of the dominant power relations. White masculinity in a settler-colonial context is often expressed as a heroic relation to wilderness:

> The prototypical wilderness subject is a white male bourgeois individual. By making wild nature his realm, he symbolically re-enacts his conquest of the world. He leaves effeminate civilisation behind, demonstrates his survival skills and penetrates virgin nature: this is how he becomes a real man.[41]

A particular kind of white masculinity is affirmed by surviving the engagement with wilderness. The ordeal of wilderness is a litmus test, proving that he is an individual who can survive without the nurturing maternal embrace of society. Of course, this individuality is a myth for an inherently social species, but it serves the purpose of validating men's work and degrading nurturing and caregiving disproportionately done by women. Further, this is very specifically a white settler-colonial survival ritual that depends on the prior dispossession of Indigenous peoples.

> His masculinity is bound up with an unmistakable racial identity – most obviously, the national parks in which he roams can be perceived as wild only because the indigenous populations have been expelled. He is the white settler who takes hold of the land again.[42]

At the same time, it is not simply true that society represses sexuality that is naturally free. Indeed, society creates sexual possibilities and expands erotic horizons. Over the history of capitalism there has been ongoing contention between creative remaking of sexual life from below and efforts to repress, limit or harness it from above. Gay men might have had sex in the

urban wilderness of parks along with other locations (such as lanes and lav-
atories), but in contradictory ways this "wild" impulse was seen as a very
specifically urban form of behavior. Steven Maynard believed that Judge
Morgan, who delivered a verdict on a gross indecency case that he intended
to be his last, saw the act as a product of urban life: "Like many of his con-
temporaries, Morgan also believed that ... the historical development of
indecency was intimately linked to the growth of the city."[43]

Sexuality, in short, is lived in a web of social and ecological relations that
have a great impact on our relations with our own bodies and each other.
The ecological crisis of our time is one of sustainability, the development of
a relationship with nature that reproduces conditions in which humans and
other species can thrive. Capitalist social relations frame nature as a field
for extraction rather than a partner in reproduction. The extraction from
nature and exploitation of the labor of working classes are integrally connected in the same process of reproducing capitalism. The social experience
of gender and sexuality is framed by this extraction orientation. It is not surprising that our relations with external nature and with our own bodies, the
piece of nature that is us, are connected. The call for a shift to a more sustainable interchange with nature around us is connected to creating conditions
in which humans can thrive. Social and ecological reproduction are part of
the same cycles.

There is no full return to pristine first nature possible as a route out of
global capitalism and second nature. Rather, the path to liberation must
build on the potential for transformation in a world already characterized
by the globalization of second nature. Second nature is contradictory, it
combines the destruction of metabolic rift with the development of human
transformative capacities in ways that open up new ways of living, including
emerging conceptions that gender and sexuality crafted from below, even if
these are indelibly marked by alienation and dispossession in the context of
capitalism. There is no return to first nature, despite its apparent attractions
in the face of dispossession, commodification and violence. Said maintains
that the goal of anti-imperialism cannot be to return to first nature, however
strong the longing, for that no longer exists as such. "It is therefore necessary
to seek out, to map, to invent, or to discover, a *third* nature, not pristine and
pre-historical ... but deriving from the deprivations of the present."[44] Even if
it cannot return to before, the relationship with the land is crucial to decolonizing. Said writes of anti-imperialist struggles, "One of the first tasks of
cultures of resistance was to reclaim, rename and reinhabit the land."[45] John
Bellamy Foster wrote of Said's conception of third nature: "All of this gave a

more radical meaning to ecological aspirations, in which the recovery of the human connection to the earth, and therefore to labor, and to human community – as well as to past traditions – played an indispensable role in the urge to resist and create a new cultural reality."[46]

Ecological and sexual liberation are interconnected in the development of third nature through a transformative struggle against capitalism and imperialism. Sexuality develops in the context of a political, social and natural ecosystem. Our vision of sexual freedom is intimately associated with second nature, a nature that has been transformed by human agency in the context of particular social relations. It is still nature – after all, there is nothing outside of nature – but a nature touched in many ways by human production under conditions of capitalism. When humans look in the mirror of second nature, they catch a glimpse of their own productive capacities but always framed by climate change, the devastation of soil, land and water. Colonialism, racism and sexual violence are all part of second nature.

Second nature offers certain glimpses of freedom, as human transformative capacities are expanded, for example, through the development of health-sustaining treatments. But second nature is rooted in plunder, enslavement, colonialization, dehumanization, and the development of productive forces specifically to enhance exploitation. Processes of dispossession and devastation were the conditions of the development of second nature and remain central to its dynamics. The alienation of second nature is not due to the power of natural laws, but the domination by a small layer of humans and a system of social relations oriented around profit. Real sexual liberation requires that we follow Said's move to third nature through revolutionary processes of reclamation, democratization, reparation and transformation.

This provides some sense of third nature as a goal for radical political transformation, which requires the development of movements of radical resurgence. Indigenous resurgence is a fundamental dimension in this process, and to get there Simpson posits that it is necessary to create the spaces for collective analysis and strategic thinking: "about how to organize and build resurgent movements, about how we move beyond everyday acts of resurgence to collective actions in the short and long term, and about how to create community that embodies and practices our nation-based processes in the present."[47]

The move forward to third nature is only possible if it includes a process of return, restitution, reparation and/or reconciliation as redress for the ongoing multigenerational harm and trauma of differential dispossession associated with colonial, genocidal violence. This must include the right of return to the land/of the land that was taken through dispossession, depriving peoples of their livelihood, their networks of reciprocity, and their place in the world. The move forward to third nature necessarily includes elements of a return to/of first nature, even in a form altered by second nature. The struggle to move forward to third nature requires the resurgence of Indigenous and colonized peoples in league with the mobilization of workers and others who are dispossessed. This transformative project must include ecological and social projects of redress, reparation and reconciliation, addressing the legacies of colonization, dispossession, exploitation and destruction. We will come back to what this means at the level of sexuality below.

SEXUALITY AND EMBODIMENT IN SECOND NATURE

The dominant ideas of sexuality in contemporary capitalist society flow from the relations of second nature, even though the ideological claim that sexuality is an evolutionary product of first nature "hard-wired" into our bodies is prominent in these conceptions. In important ways, second nature has contributed to an opening up of imagination and practices of gender and sexuality. The development of new forms of contraception, medical innovations including trans surgery and global communications offer certain possibilities for new ways of living. Yet, at the same time, the frame of exploitation, plunder and market transaction, including violence towards subordinated humans and destruction of external nature, frames experiences of social life and embodiment in global second nature. People engaging around sex and gender politics often end up navigating the contradictory terrain of second nature embodiment and sexualities, in which transformative potential for self-making is mapped together with alienation, violence and reification.

People make sexualities through a historical process of formation in particular social-ecological conditions. Human nature is thus dynamic, the product of the interaction between people and their environments. Our action is neither socially nor biologically determined, but produced by the interaction between the two. Richard Levins and Richard Lewontin put this at the core of their conception of *dialectical biology*, "organism and environment as interpenetrating so that both are at the same time subjects and objects of the historical process."[48] The wide range of human experiences is a reminder that human nature, combining culture, biology and environment, is somewhat open-ended and not fixed in narrow terms by evolutionary processes: "The evident fact about human life is the incredible diversity in individual life histories and in social organization across space and time."[49]

This is not to deny the importance of bodily experiences and biological causation. At the most basic level, one must be alive to engage erotically and therefore must have access to resources to meet one's wants and needs. But the simple sorting of natural/biological from cultural/mental and the attribution of causality to one or the other does not match the complexity of human embodiment. As Anne Fausto-Sterling notes, "Bodily experiences are brought into being by our development in particular cultures and historical periods. As we grow and develop, we literally, not just 'discursively' (that is, through language and cultural practices), construct our bodies, incorporating experience into our very flesh."[50]

Indeed, Nigerian anthropologist Oyeronke Oyewumi describes the narrow focus on biological causation as part of a Eurocentric world view. There is a bio-logic connected to the specific racialized and gendered hierarchies of capitalism: "certain kinds of bodies are superior to others by virtue of having certain favored body parts; men are superior to women and whites to blacks."[51] In Yoruba culture, age-based seniority is far more important than gender attributed to bodies: "the Yoruba language does not 'do' gender; instead it does seniority defined by relative age."[52] Europeans have tended to project gender constructions based on their own onto societies they colonize, without attending to the specific modes of social organization that actually apply in a cultural context.

People produce themselves through work on nature. Moore argues we should not simply see nature as passive and humans as active in this process through which humans meet their wants and needs and make lives. Rather, "[w]ork is a co-production between the human and the rest of nature; it is indeed a metabolism, as Marx suggests."[53] This metabolic conception unfixes our understanding of nature and social construction. Social construction is not a cultural process apart from nature, nor is nature an external force shaping our experience outside of our life-making.

Humans know external nature through our work on our environment, producing things and meanings through the transformation of the world around us. We produce, among other things, our conception of nature and our relationship with the world around us in the context of specific social relations. As Moore argues, "nature is a *historical* relation." At the same time, we need to be clear that nature is not reducible to history. Kate Soper defines nature as "those material structures and processes that are independent of human activity (in the sense that they are not a humanly created product), and whose forces and causal powers are the necessary conditions of every human practice, and determine the possible forms it can take."[54] Nature exists independently of and prior to human life, but nature is only available to people through transformative life-making activity, which historicizes nature for humans. Humans, on the other hand, do not exist independently of nature.

This dynamic interchange with nature plays out at the level of our relationship with our own bodies. We experience sexuality through our own embodiment, which in contemporary capitalist societies is framed by the metabolic rift in the interchange with nature. We view our own bodies (internal nature) through the frame of our engagement with external nature. In conditions of metabolic rift, when external nature is reduced to property and resources for plunder, we see our body as alienable property and a resource we are obligated to cultivate. The bodies that tend to be held up as desirable in these circumstances are those that are obviously processed so they appear to be a product, constructed through human design and labor rather than a natural phenomenon. In contrast, bodies that seem unworked and untamed, that do not bear the signs of deliberate effort, are cast as unattractive and immoral, as indicators of waste and laziness.

Roxane Gay described her own body as "wildly undisciplined." In this society, self-discipline deeply connected to norms of productivity is held up as the ideal and those whose bodies are seen as too fat or unworked in other ways are cast as a threat, a human form of wilderness. Gay wrote of weight loss television show *The Biggest Loser*:

The Biggest Loser is a show about fat as an enemy that must be destroyed, a contagion that must be eradicated. This is a show about unruly bodies that must be disciplined by any means necessary, and through that discipline, the obese might become more acceptable members of society.[55]

Gay describes herself as practicing brutal self-denial in order to avoid claiming space and attracting notice.

My body is wildly undisciplined and I deny myself nearly everything I desire. I deny myself the right to space when I am public, trying to fold in on myself, to make my body invisible even though it is, in fact, grandly visible. I deny myself the right to a shared armrest because how dare I impose? I deny myself entry into certain spaces I have deemed inappropriate for a body like mine – most spaces inhabited by other people.[56]

This regime of self-denial includes starving herself of human intimacy. "I deny myself gentler kinds of affection – to touch or be kindly touched – as if that is a pleasure a body like mine does not deserve."[57] It also includes a denial of gender expression as her body falls outside the dominant expectations for legitimate femininity: "I deny myself certain trappings of femininity as if I do not have the right to such expression when my body does not follow society's dictates for what a woman's body should look like."[58]

The body that has not been deliberately built (too fat, too thin) is a thing of contempt. Bodies are to be a product of design and craft. Indeed, body-making has proceeded so far that the dominant images of hotness in popular culture in North America in the early twenty-first century are based on bodies that are literally unsustainable, captured at the transient moment of aesthetic peak. Models, influencers and actors spend tremendous effort training, dieting, shaving, being altered surgically, supplementing and dehydrating to pose for images after being deliberately made up in conditions of careful lighting in idealized locations cloaked in the finest fashions that are then refined through photographic techniques.

Victoria's Secret model Adriana Lima discussed the ways she prepares for a show. It begins months in advance with an intense physical training regime. But it also includes a brutal diet and fluid restrictions, organized by a nutritionist "who has measured her body's muscle mass, fat ratio and levels of water retention."[59] The regime includes protein shakes, vitamins, supplement and a gallon of water a day.

> For nine days before the show, she will drink only protein shakes – "no solids" ... Two days before the show, she will abstain from the daily gallon of water, and "just drink normally". Then, 12 hours before the show, she will stop drinking entirely. "No liquids at all so you dry out, sometimes you can lose up to eight pounds just from that," she says.[60]

The body the model creates for the photo shoot literally disappears quickly when they resume normal eating and drinking. This kind of cycling regime, combined with supplementation, tends to be very unhealthy, and water deprivation can be very dangerous. This image of the unsustainable body is further based on photographic aesthetics during and after shoots with many touch-ups. The dominance of images of unsustainable bodies is rooted in an ecological regime that is oriented around productivity, property and plunder, rather than reciprocity and the sustenance of life.

These images haunt us, from social media posts to gigantic posters in malls, from movies to magazines. Our own bodies are a disappointment compared to the unsustainable standards in circulation in the world of commodity exchange. Hotness and health become mixed up in our relationship with our bodies, so people do incredibly unhealthy things to their bodies to reach images they associate with health and attractiveness. This is integrally related to the process that David McNally describes as "forgetting" the body, the flight from the body we come to understand as a despised instrument of labor in capitalist societies.[61] It is not uncommon for workers to describe themselves as dehumanized through their labors, turned into an animal or a machine.

This dehumanized relationship with the body gets incorporated into training regimes that aim to transform the body from a piece of nature to a human product. Indeed, many gym training practices build body mass drawing on mass production methods developed to maximize the productivity of subordinated labor in factories. The training makes the body the raw material to be processed through an assembly line of standardized repetitive movements. The overall work of training is broken down into a series of distinct tasks, and work is quantified and monitored in regimes that echo time-motion studies at the Taylorist factory. The result is a body produced as an image, focusing on appearance and not functions. Mark Greif described this industrialized leisure:

> Nothing can make you believe we harbor nostalgia for factory work but a modern gym … .with the gym we import vestiges of the leftover equipment of industry to our leisure. We leave the office, and put the conveyor belt under our feet, and run as if chased by devils.[62]

The industrialization of athletic training started in the early twentieth century, and was pushed much deeper into society with the neoliberal lean state which married the downloading of responsibility for self-maintenance and preparation for productivity with elements of moral deregulation that opened up certain forms of rationalized desire. Note that Greif refers to "nostalgia for factory work," indicating that the peak period of industrialized body-making came after, and looked back upon, the apex of mass production in the Global North, from the early twentieth century roughly through to the 1980s.

The development of industrialized gym techniques for athletic training and bodybuilding dates back to the early years of the assembly line. Here I will focus on bodybuilding, a set of training and performance practices developed through the application of industrial methods to accomplish aesthetic goals in the construction of physiques. The bodybuilder represented the masculinity of the "self-made man," based on male self-creation and effacing women's role in reproduction. The built body was associated with a form of masculinity which the "ideal male body owes its being to no one else … it gives birth to itself through the thought products of its own mind."[63]

The dominant forms of masculinity in the twentieth century have been oriented in part around a negative sense of gender, assessing masculinity as the absence of femininity.[64] Men built their bodies through a harsh gym regime which proved one's masculinity through endurance of pain. Those who failed the test of pain were marked as feminine or queer. Alan Klein notes, "Once established, the definition-by-negation principle encourages a young male striving to be a man to aggressively negate any female attributes in himself and others."[65] Male bodybuilders took on this ethos of masculine self-making, squeezing out any element of femininity from a constructed physique that embodied masculine strength and the absence of vulnerability. At first, bodybuilding was a very marginal activity that over time came to influence ideas of the desirable body.

Bodybuilding generalized scientific management methods from industry to physical training, and developed new techniques that over time were used more widely in the world of sports. Early bodybuilders developed a scientific approach to weightlifting, applying the methods of the assembly line to forge the body through a training regime broken down into a series of small repetitive tasks. Rather than practicing the sport to get better at it, scientific weightlifting took the athlete into the gym to work through an assembly line of lifting exercises each aimed at developing a specific area of muscle.[66] Just as mass production in the factory broke the process of making into a series of separate repetitive steps each requiring no knowledge of the way the end product came together, the production of muscle mass broke training down into small repetitive tasks with careful measurement of inputs and outputs. Weightlifters developed a scientific management approach to training around the same time as modern sports were being codified and the modern Olympic Games created. Institutionalized sport mapped together training techniques grounded in the methods of mass production with the cult of battle in the period surrounding World War I, as nation-states pushed more deeply into the lives of the population to produce a fit working class for production and military engagement in an age of intensifying imperialism and inter-imperialist rivalry.[67]

Employers introduced new mass production techniques to increase their control over the production process by removing the autonomy in labor processes that accorded workers discretion to make judgements based on their own skills accumulated through intimate knowledge of the work. David Noble described the two dimensions to this restructuring of the production process, the separation of conception from execution and the introduction of new technologies. Firstly, management established tighter control over the conception of production by introducing new approaches designed "to monopolize the 'mental' activities, which were assigned to specialists and engineers, to employ relatively unskilled and cheap 'hands', and to specify carefully the routinized 'manual' work they performed."[68] Secondly, management deployed new technologies to mechanize and automate production, "which built into the machinery the muscle, the manual skills, and, ultimately, the self-adjusting and correcting 'intelligence' of production itself."[69] Workers were forced to habituate to conditions in which machines seemed to control the processes and rhythms of work: "Men behaving like machines paved the way for machines without men."[70]

Alan Klein argues that bodybuilding emerged as the rise of mass production techniques meant that many members of the working class labored in conditions where their own bodily prowess and skills were devalued by the experience of working on assembly lines built around interchangeable workers repeatedly performing the same limited tasks. Whereas previously, "muscularity suggested some elevated level of functioning," in the age of mass production bodybuilders began to bulk up their bodies for appearance rather than performance.[71] Bodybuilders modeled a culture of crafting physiques as a leisure activity that spread, especially in the late twentieth and early twenty-first centuries, so that "the body (muscled and fit) has become almost the exclusive province of the commodity-fitness world of leisure."[72]

The marginality of male bodybuilding as it first emerged had to do with its rather complex relationship with dominant forms of masculinity. On the one hand, bodybuilders developed bulked up physiques that represented strength, determination, productivity and endurance of pain, which tended to be cast as a key feature of masculinity. On the other hand, bodybuilders undermined masculinity by becoming sculptors of the self, working around standards that were deliberately aesthetic and objectified. The bodybuilder's physique was crafted to be looked at in a feminizing way, making men the object rather than subject of the gaze. For a long time, bodybuilding survived as an extremely marginal activity with very little cultural impact. It was regarded with suspicion and seen as pseudo-pornographic, tainted with homoeroticism and associated with "cheating" through performance enhancement.[73]

In the context of the 1970s economic downturn, employers and state policy-makers developed new strategies and practices to solve problems of profitability and working-class militancy, reorganizing labor processes and social policy to intensify production and undermine workers' capacities for collectivity and resistance. Management restructured through the introduction of lean and agile production methods, discussed in Chapter 5, which were developed to reduce waste and enhance flexibility in work practices. State policy-makers echoed core lean themes in the creation of a new social policy regime oriented around undermining alternatives to the market for meeting subsistence needs, including dramatic reductions in social assistance and programs.

Beginning in the 1970s, bodybuilding began to move more into the main-stream, as the bodybuilding "look" became extremely influential among male actors, models and in advertising imagery. This move into prominence was associated with a new emphasis on personal fitness and the download-ing of responsibility for self-maintenance through neoliberalism, as well as the remapping of desire driven by queer, feminist and anti-racist mobiliza-tions in the 1960s that, among other things, opened up new forms of male objectification. By the early twenty-first century, lean muscularity set the tone for body aesthetics: "The toned and buff look has colonized advertising, where it is ubiquitous."[74] The built physique began to set the standards for the "healthy" male body in the fitness industry and for the sexually desirable body. Yet, the equation between fitness and lean muscularity through harsh gym routines is not based on health outcomes. Bodybuilding is extremely unhealthy, and the bodybuilding "look" (extremely lean muscularity – as in the "six pack" – marked by muscle striation and visible veins) is essen-tially unsustainable – to be accomplished only through a cycle of bulking and extreme dieting, dehydration, extreme exercise and supplementation often including performance-enhancing drugs.

One dimension of this shift in the hegemonic conception of beauty is the change in the desirable male body type for actors and models. If you compare pictures of a 1950s male movie star like Rock Hudson or Marlon Brando to shots of contemporary actors there is a notable difference in their conditioning. Many male actors now have highly defined muscles including six-pack abs and are very lean so that their veins are visible. The standards for these bodies are influenced by bodybuilding, which has gone from being a marginal and stigmatized activity to a mainstream influence on the standards for the appearance of an athletic male body.[75] The built body has become an ideal, produced through a deliberate process of transformation, which includes: gym training, diet, supplements, shaving and tanning as well as specific photographic techniques. The rise of the "designed body" is associated with the increasing influence of the consumption of commodities on our everyday lives and the triumph of marketing of "every element of bodily need and desire including the medical, the cosmetic, the athletic, the sexual, the erotic – everything and anything to which can be attached a price in the flow of exchange."[76]

The cult of the lean muscular male body is also a result of changing gender relations. The past 50 years have seen the rise of a consumerist masculinity engaged with fashion and grooming, displacing previous standards of masculinity which had identified objectification and concern about personal appearance with femininity.[77] Women's bodies have been measured against established aesthetic standards for much longer. This consumerist masculinity is deeply racialized, as the images of idealized built bodies are often associated specifically with whiteness, to the extent that companies like Abercrombie and Fitch have actually engaged in employment practices that discriminate against people of color, for example, prohibiting hairstyles associated with Black men.[78]

The cult of lean muscularity is associated with conquering the wilderness of the unprocessed body to craft a product worthy of desire. The character of social relations in second nature has led to a flight from our bodies, cast as nature, except as crafted products or images. Bodybuilders construct their own body as an object, the product of their labor: "For bodybuilders the view of the body as distinct from the self, and the view of the body as partible (separated into distinct parts) works to enable the bodybuilder to establish a sense of self-mastery."[79] The body is mapped in close detail as a series of muscle groups each requiring specific attention. Klein argues that bodybuilders "take alienation to new heights" in which "[t]he self is distinguished from the body, and the body is beaten into submission."[80] Rather than an expression of their bodies, bodybuilding is in many ways a war against it (no pain, no gain). Bodybuilders mobilize their resources for a battle against their body through which they "shape themselves to approximate an external ideal form."[81]

This war against the body has important ecological dimensions, it is an expression of a broader set of relationships in which reciprocity with other species and the environment (as well as other people) has been upended through dispossession and commodification; in which the dominant class controls the key productive resources and our surroundings; in which our human capacities are turned into property for exchange. In these conditions, people alienate their bodies as objects for the consumption of others, beating nature out of their physique and replacing it with idealized images that are inherently unsustainable.

Of course, body modification is a practice across a range of cultures over time. The specificity of these practices under capitalism is that individual and collective self-expression is replaced by alienated striving after idealized images. Bodybuilding is only one example of the ongoing quest to self-objectify by triumphing over the natural within and without, reflecting experiences of alienation in unsustainable capitalist relations. These practices are gendered and racialized, and have imposed the greatest toll on women.

Some people relentlessly avoid physical activity, for example, circling endlessly for a parking spot to reduce walking time at the mall. Others work out compulsively, injuring themselves and harming their health in the interest of looking great. The "couch potato" is not a natural product of human laziness, but the result of discouragement through participation in life-making in which the kinetic nature of human experience is crushed. The project of elementary school, for example, is largely the hidden curriculum of training kids to sit still at a desk and to discipline their bodily functions around clock-time.

Laziness and the flight from physical activity is based on the exhausting and unfulfilling character of much labor (whether in employment or household caregiving) in capitalist societies. The problem is not that the work is tiring, but that it is unrewarding and dehumanizing, performed under conditions of compulsion dictated by those in power. Physical activity that is done voluntarily is removed from everyday life in the specialized setting of the gym, where people seek to create their bodies as images by imposing the discipline of the factory on their own body. Human motive power is displaced even in the gym, where electricity is used to power cardio machines on which people can expend energy while perfectly quantifying the activity for calculation.

Our experience of embodiment is shaped by ecological practices based on conquest and plunder of nature rather than reciprocity and sustainability. In these conditions, people begin to reject the "natural" body in favor of the body that has been conquered, crafted around standards of desirability cultivated in unsustainable images. The answer to the fetishization of the unsustainable body in the context of metabolic rift is not the simple romanticization of the "natural" body. Humans engage in life-making which is an ongoing transformative process through which we construct ourselves and the world around us. People do not make themselves any less "natural" through this transformative process, and a romanticization of pristine first nature within or without can undermine this creative and open-ended process, naturalizing particular ways of being by denying human history-making. The issue is not that humans have lost touch with nature through the mediation of technology, but that alienation and dispossession, which rupture relations of reciprocity and mutuality, create conditions of metabolic rift that makes sustainable self-realization impossible within the limits of capitalism.

The sexualities people have constructed in conditions of alienation, dispossession and metabolic rift are organized around a flight from our actual existing bodies, as people attempt to enter into a world of sexualized images. The circulation of sexualized images is a central feature of market model sexualities, in which commodities (ranging from fashion to food, from vacation packages to vehicles) seem to have agency and humans are cast as passive consumers. Commodity fetishism is associated with the sexualization of commodities in circulation and the desexualization of actual existing bodies, as our own sexual feelings often feel so private and perverse that we might have trouble talking about them even with intimate partners.

Sexualities in conditions of metabolic rift are rich with contradictions. People get glimpses of the possibilities for different kinds of erotic making and self-creation in the context of self-ownership and the intensification of human transformative powers associated with second nature, yet always framed by alienation and dispossession. As desire is reified, abstracted from our own activity of making and our actual bodies into circulating commodities and associated images, it is also naturalized and treated as an inescapable destiny wired into our biological being by evolution.

Given the association of second nature with the scramble to enter a world of images, it is easy to see the allure of authenticity, a rejection of technology and a return to the unmodified body that might be cast as "natural" in response to the contradictions of sexual life in second nature. Of course, this hunger to renaturalize sexuality and embodiment can easily slide into yet another dimension of performance. Richard Seymour notes that in the social media world, "The performance of authenticity is also becoming a necessity for marketing."[82] Indeed, the performance of authenticity can be woven in with the effacement of genuine human self-creation, casting human transformative capacities and technologies in opposition to nature, rather than understanding transformative making as a fundamental feature of human nature.

Donna Haraway in "A Cyborg Manifesto" warns against the invocation of "an imagined organic body to integrate our resistance."[83] Indeed, the pristine natural bodies we might return to exist only in our minds: "Later twentieth-century machines have made thoroughly ambiguous the difference between natural and artificial, mind and body, self-developing and externally designed, and many other distinctions that used to apply to organisms and machines."[84] Rather than a return to the "natural," Haraway argues for "*pleasure* in the confusion of boundaries and for *responsibility* in their construction."[85]

In conditions of metabolic rift, the question of sustainable embodiment frames our erotic experiences. In these conditions, people tend to develop tastes for the unsustainable, supported by circulating images and the flight from bodies exhausted and depleted by labor. The move towards sustainable embodiment is neither through the return to nature nor the embrace of technology, but through a restoration of collective and democratic control over the key productive resources of society and active redress for the legacies of dispossession, genocide, silencing and violence that have been differentiated along lines of racialization, gender and colonialism. People are by nature engaged in creative transformative projects that open up the horizons of embodiment and eroticism. The project of liberation is not to shut down these horizons by invoking a construction of the natural, but to open them up by orienting our metabolic interchange around purposive making, mutuality and reciprocity.

Jordy Rosenberg maintains that the perspectives of trans people offer a crucial framing of embodiment in relation to metabolic rift. Rosenberg draws on Jules Gill-Peterson's history of the ways "children with 'ambiguous' sex were medicalized and experimented upon by doctors who sought in their unfinished, developing bodies a material foothold for altering and, eventually, changing human sex as it grew."[86] The practitioners, beginning in the early twentieth century, used these children and their bodies to develop a new medical frame that unfixed ideas of biological sex: "Sex, in other words, is not an autonomous property of the body; rather, it – and the body – exist in a tangled metabolic flux."[87] This frame unfixed sex but fixed gender as a clear binary. The goal of treatment was to produce a medical transition that would "align the plasticity of sex with the intractability of gender."[88]

This project was deeply racialized, as the plasticity of sex was associated specifically with whiteness. This racialized frame "allowed gate-keeping clinicians to reject black and trans of color children as *not plastic enough* for the category of transsexuality, dismissing their self-knowledge of gender as delusion or homosexuality."[89] These practitioners developed practices and theories that treated gender as a rigid binary, while recasting biological sex as at least somewhat mutable, depending on the bodies involved. Even at its best, this frame offered certain white children "access to a rigid medical model based on binary normalization."[90]

Normalization is at the core of health practice in capitalist societies, including both medical treatment and public health measures aimed at prevention. Gill-Peterson emphasizes the history-making role of trans people in pushing the development of health practices oriented around their own needs. The agency of trans children was generally suppressed rather than engaged by medical professionals: "experimental medicine practiced on intersex children, typically without either their consent or even their knowledge, directly founded the modern medical protocol for assigning a sex and then reassigning a child's body to fit that sex, first surgically and later hormonally."[91] Gill-Peterson emphasizes trans self-making, founded on community support and collective expertise: "By seeing trans people as active participants in the construction and contestation of medical discourse in this way, rather than as passive objects of knowledge, I emphasize that as many key moments trans people's embodied fluency in medical science far outpaced institutional medical knowledge."[92]

Jordy Rosenberg explored this relationship between medical practice and trans self-formation in the compelling novel *Confessions of the Fox*. Jack, living in the eighteenth century, has top surgery performed by a comrade, Bess, after the doctor (or perhaps imposter) who was to perform the experimental surgery collapses part way through the operation. Jack expresses lack of confidence in the doctor (Evans), characterizing the practitioner as "about as qualified to slice him open as any untrained person was – which was to say, *not at all.*"[93] Jack's comrade Bess takes that as an invitation to step in and perform the operation: "She bent over Evans' form, and this time she slipped the scalpel from his hand. She picked the book up from the stool where it had been placed."[94] In the end, Jack inadvertently kills the doctor, "Dead at your hand. Well, maybe your chest. You – well – smothered him to death with your bleeding chest."[95] But the surgery was successful, "For Bess had freed him of a chest-burden so great he hadn't even known, until it was removed, what weight he had carried."[96]

This is not a story of practitioner-centered medical innovation, but of trans community self-making. The knowledge of the practitioner is useful, as Bess's surgical intervention follows Evans's plan, but the doctor is also disposable. The key is trans community knowledge and self-formation. A character in the novel later suggests that self-making is not an individual action, but is grounded in history and society. The seafaring Okuh challenges Jack's idea of the self-made individual, "There are in the world, *no such men as self-made men!* We have *all* either begged, borrow'd or stolen. We have reaped where others have Sown, and that which others have strown, we have gathered."[97]

The conception of the medical practitioner as a useful support in the process of transformative self-directed life-making challenges the dominant model in contemporary health care, whether in treatment or prevention. The dominant model focuses on regulation, instruction and/or treatment by experts, paired with compliance from patients, who must be sufficiently autonomous to consent. Health is defined largely in terms of one's ability to function in their particular assigned location within dominant gendered and racialized divisions of labor. Productivity in alienated labor is taken for granted as a foundational condition for the healthy existence for members of the working class, whether in monetized labor, as members of the military, or in unpaid or poorly paid reproductive labor. The medical system, both in the spheres of treatment and prevention, "confronts an existing set of workplace relations, a family system in the home, a particular distribution of resources on a national and international scale, all outside of the purview of health interventions. It is a question of maximizing health within the limits of these preexisting sets of relations."[98]

In contrast, trans community self-formation involves a more active role for the "patient," who is part of a collective process of knowledge production grounded in practices of self-realization. This understanding of trans community self-formation demonstrates that technology, including medical treatment, is embedded in social relations, and the crucial question is not the level of innovation but who controls the development and use of transformative knowledge and practices. The metabolic rift is not simply the result of technological development but of the deployment of innovation in the conditions of alienation and dispossession to profit those who control the key productive resources.

Jordy Rosenberg argues that experiences of trans self-formation and embodiment, in conditions of racialized and gendered divisions of labor, provide crucial tools for understanding metabolic rift. Trans people have been the agents of crucial changes in the understanding and experience of embodiment that made possible the contemporary analysis of ecological relations in metabolic terms. The analysis of metabolic rift is "tied intimately to a metabolic theory of the body in general – and of *embodied sex* in particular."[99] Changes in the experience of embodiment and gender expression have provided the grounds for more dynamic understandings of the interchange with nature: "The material conditions of trans life furnish the terrain in which the seeds of abstract concepts come to fruition."[100]

The experiences of trans community self-formation highlight both the transformative potential in the metabolic interchange with nature, and the ways that interchange is shaped by capitalist social relations. Metabolic rift is a product of the development of human transformative capacities and technology in conditions of alienation and dispossession. Within this context, technology is developed to increase the control of the ruling classes over labor processes and products through subordination of the laboring population and the organization of nature as resources, rather than to meet human needs or to sustain the interchange with nature.

Sexual revolution must address ways the metabolic rift has affected our relations with our bodies – each other's and our own. This is not a call for a simple return to first nature, but rather the development of third nature as part of the revolutionary mobilization through which people take democratic and collective control over the means of production and end alienation. This development of third nature must re-establish relations of reciprocity with other humans, other species and the environment, which requires specific measures including return of/to the land, reparations, reconciliation and other deliberate acts of redress for the violent subordination of Indigenous peoples, and those who have been racialized, gendered, sexualized, categorized as disabled and/or proletarianized. The move to sexual third nature is not about the imagined return to a more natural embodiment or the rejection of technology, but about organizing society in such a way that human transformative capacities are oriented around meeting wants and needs at an individual and collective level while specifically addressing the systemic impact of differentiated dispossession.

Indeed, one of the potential strengths of queer marxism as a tool chest for examining sexualities and as a guide to sexual revolutionary activism is the ability to account for both human creative transformative activity and the natural grounding of human life-making. People make lives through a metabolic interchange with nature, engaging in creative and transformative labor to produce what they want and need. The ecological crisis of capitalism is created by conditions of alienation and dispossession that rupture relations of mutuality and reciprocity in metabolic interchange, replacing them with commodification and extraction for profit. The resulting metabolic rift plays out in relations with external and internal nature, producing among other things a flight from embodiment into a world of circulating images.

7

Utopia and Sexual Revolutions

At the core of queer marxism is the goal of sexual revolution to attain genuine erotic liberation and freedom in gender expression. Sexual revolution cannot be confined to the realm of sexuality alone, as unfreedom in the realm of gender and erotic expression is grounded in broader relations of alienation and dispossession. Rather, sexual revolution must be part of a process of anti-capitalist transformation to overcome alienation and dispossession, driven by mass insurgency from below.

Revolution through mass insurgency from below unleashes human creative capacities as people mobilize to make history. Marx argued that insurgent mobilization was necessary not only because it is required to overthrow those in power but also because the revolutionary process transforms those doing the overthrowing:

> the revolution is necessary, therefore not only because the *ruling* class cannot be overthrown in any other way, but also because the class *overthrowing* it can only in a revolution succeed in ridding itself of all the muck of ages and become fitted to found society anew.[1]

Revolution is necessary to overturn a system built on violent domination. But more than that, it is only through the process of mass insurgency that people create the democratic forms of collectivity and new ways of living that can serve as the foundation for a socialist society. It is only through revolution that people can cast aside the "muck of ages," including the naturalization of certain regimes of gender and sexuality. In the revolutionary process, people engage and develop their collective transformative power in new ways, making it possible to envision and build other possible worlds by moving beyond the taken-for-granted frame shaped by life under capitalism that makes the existing order of things seem normal.

In the realm of gender and sexuality, the "muck of ages" limiting the horizons of change includes the assumption that sexual attraction and gendered practices are based on natural and eternal impulses hard-wired into our bodies by evolution. As I have argued earlier, patterns of gender and sexuality are not simply the enactment of eternal and unchanging physiological urges rooted in biological realities. Humans forge our own relations of gender and sexuality, as we make lives in the context of particular social and ecological arrangements bequeathed by history and sustained through structures of domination developed to counter persistent resistance. As people forge relationships to remake the world from below, they begin to develop new forms of community that point beyond the constraints of the dominant social and ecological arrangements.

Mobilization from below, whether worker organizing in paid employment or activist organizing in communities, requires the development of the infrastructure of dissent, "through which people develop the collective capacities for memory, analysis, vision and solidarity required to sustain currents of resistance."[2] The infrastructure of dissent includes formal organizations, such as unions and radical political groups, as well as informal networks within workplaces and communities. People forge collective capacities through the infrastructure of dissent to remember the stories that have been hidden or forgotten about how things got to be this way, to make sense of events at an immediate and broader societal level, to envision qualitatively different futures, and to act together by creating solidarity attuned to the divergent needs of the group as a whole.

There are important affective and indeed erotic elements to the activity of forging collectivity. Rosemary Hennessy points out that despite our hesitancy to discuss love in the context of mobilizing, "we know that affective capacities are a part of the dynamic process by which political identities are formed and they bind people to one another and, sometimes, to a common cause."[3] Affective capacities are crucial as we forge collectivity to change the world, unleashing passions to fire our commitments to each other and the cause. Hennessy maintains that we have to recognize the importance of love in mobilizing, "a sense that positive social bonds that love conjured may be necessary to survival, tied to a fundamental condition of dependency on relations of care that sustain life and to the passions that motivate action on behalf of others and for a better world."[4]

For bell hooks, the absence of a deliberate love ethos in radical organizing undermines effective transformative analysis and action: "As long as we refuse to address fully the place of love in struggles for liberation we will not be able to create a culture of conversion where there is a mass turning away from an ethic of domination."[5] Love is crucial to developing struggles for liberation that move beyond narrow self-interest to broader transformation based on solidarity: "The ability to acknowledge blind spots can emerge only as we expand our concern about politics of domination and our capacity to care about the oppression and exploitation of others."[6] This invocation of love is not based on denying pain, grief and anger but rather on forging communal ways of dealing with these feelings:

> If black folks are to move forward in our struggle for liberation, we must confront the legacy of this unreconciled grief, for it has been the breeding ground for profound nihilistic despair. We must collectively return to a radical political vision of social change rooted in a love ethic and seek once again to convert masses of people, black and nonblack.[7]

The recovery of love as an ethos in mobilization means building community that can offer visions of affective connection liberated from the baggage of property exchange models, as discussed in Chapter 4. People can forge insurgent communities that offer alternatives to market model affect: "Though many folks recognize and critique the commercialization of love, they see no alternative."[8]

The building of life-sustaining political communities has material, mental and spiritual aspects, as people collectively develop and share resources to make lives and remake worlds. M.E. O'Brien refers to this as "insurgent social reproduction" based on "shared practices of mutual care."[9] Strikes present an important example of insurgent social reproduction as working-class communities must find ways to sustain themselves in the absence of wages for the duration through formal and informal means ranging from food sharing to childcare to support for arrested activists.

Kate Hardy and Katie Cruz provide an important example of affective organizing in the unionization of sex workers in Argentina. Collective organization developed "identities as workers, and feelings of belonging and dignity, achieved through socializing, debate and discussion, or gossiping and games and touch."[10] Together the workers forged what Cruz and Hardy describe as an "'intimate union' through recorridas and 'affective organizing.'"[11] Recorridas were at the heart of the union's organizing strategies, regular walks around the areas where sex workers labored:

> They circled around working areas on foot until they encountered women who were working. They would chat for 5 or 10 minutes, asking after their children and their partners and sharing gossip. Eventually, the activists offered condoms, lubricant, and the latest leaflet or information

about legal issues and campaigns. Activists invited women to workshops, parties, and other events; offered them health services ..."[12]

The encounter could end in a local pizzeria: "If there were workers whom they knew may not have eaten, they treated them to a piece of pizza and a cup of strong black coffee, often paid for with their own money."[13] The union built mobilizing capacities through forging community with many dimensions, ranging from sharing practical resources to emotional connection based on mutual interest and concern. In Chapter 2, I discussed other examples of community formation based on mutuality to sustain world-making that challenged the dominant relations.

The affective dimensions of collective organizing necessarily include erotic aspects. Hennessey described this as "collective action's capacious and unspeakable passionate attachments."[14] Mobilization is passionate, and this passion is inescapably erotic. John Rechy in his 1977 novel *The Sexual Outlaw* is most explicit in casting erotic practice as a central dimension of insurgency: "Promiscuous homosexuals ... are the shock troops of the sexual revolution."[15] He places sexual engagement at the heart of the sexual outlaw community, offering up an image of sexual revolution in the form of a global orgy: "throughout the country, throughout the world, at an appointed sun-bright time – let it be high noon – mass orgies!"[16] Rechy portrays these orgies as a challenge to the dominant authorities, and specifically the police: "Thousands of bodies stripped naked joined in a massive *loving* orgy ... and let it happen before the cops, right in front of them that we would fuck, with *joy*. Would the cops break ranks? Flee? Join?"[17]

One need not endorse this rather limited vision of the sexual revolution as an orgy to recognize that there are important erotic dimensions to mass insurgency. The formation of a vibrant world-making collective is not simply a rational process of political calculus, but is also a passionate process connecting minds, bodies and spirits in a joyful and terrifying journey. The erotic dimensions of the infrastructure of dissent need to be further explored, both in the positive sense of understanding how desire is woven into mobilization, and in the negative sense of ensuring that the passionate character of these spaces is not abused for gendered and/or racialized violence including rape and sexual assault.

SEXUAL REVOLUTION

Mobilization, then, prepares the ground for sexual revolution as people develop new ways of making lives to sustain community for remaking the world. Sexual revolution in this sense is a crucial dimension of social and political revolution to overturn capitalism, based on mass insurgency that turns the world upside down. It is a profound break with the current order that opens up a panorama of human possibility. There is a foretaste of this kind of revolution whenever mass insurgency reaches the level where participants can see other possible worlds, even if on a distant horizon.

This goes well beyond the everyday usage of sexual revolution to describe the significant changes within the realm of sexuality itself, commonly used to describe changes in patterns of sexual engagement and relationship formation since the 1960s. These changes have included the more open portrayal of sexuality in popular culture and marketing, increased recognition of women's sexual agency, increased access to contraception and abortion, important gains in lesbian, gay and trans rights, wider acceptance of sexual activity outside of marriage, recognition of single parenting and status for common law coupledom. These changes were driving important mobilizations around feminism, Black power, student activism, worker mobilizations, anti-imperialism, Indigenous resurgence, and lesbian, gay and trans liberation. Recent developments in the United States, with dramatic attacks on abortion rights and trans existence, serve as a reminder that these changes are not irreversible but rather continue to be highly contended.

The roots of the sexual revolution of the 1960s need to be traced back historically. Stephen Seidman argues that the post-war sexual revolution was the fruition of a longer-term process dating back to the early years of the twentieth century. This process of sexual revolution had three fundamental dimensions: (1) a transformation of the gendered understanding of sexualities based on wider recognition of women's sexual agency and embodied autonomy; (2) the rise and significant acceptance of queer sexualities, lives and cultures; and (3) the sexualization of the public realm, including popular culture and public or commercial spaces.[18]

In the end, the sexual revolution fell far short of the radical freedom dreams that inspired activists in the 1960s–1970s. At the most basic level, actual sexual practice is still deeply silenced, to the extent that intimate partners often have difficulties communicating preferences for sexual activities to each other, or even clarifying whether or not they want to have sex. Women still face pervasive rape, violence and treatment as mere objects for the pleasure of men. Young people still learn to either glorify or fear sexuality due to their lack of information, restricted access to contraception and the necessities for safer sex, deep needs for relationships, and the lack of the space to have sex freely. The campaign to systematically deny the rights of younger trans people to self-determination and/or medical treatment is gaining traction across North America and globally. Governments use claims about sexual freedom to build up a racist sense of civilizational superiority that is used to justify the exclusion of immigrants, discrimination against people of color and support for imperialist actions globally. Trans people, and particularly trans women of color face discrimination and violence, up to and including murder. Women still earn less than men, and are loaded with caregiving responsibilities for kids, partners, parents and others. Women also face harassment and violence in public spaces like the streets and private spaces like the home, from men they know and from strangers.

The sexual revolution of the twentieth century produced a series of substantial yet limited and indeed contradictory reforms that were ultimately confined to the generalization of sexual liberalism grounded in relations of alienation. The movements of the 1960s and 1970s around gender and sexuality were born out of broad freedom struggles that aspired to challenge war, racism, inequality and domination. Those movements faded, both as the result of victories that led to depoliticization when activists met at least some of their goals, and of defeats that crushed agency and created a sense of resignation. Over time, the idea of sexual revolution itself became separated from the goal of a wider political transformation, so that personal erotic freedom was often seen as an end in itself distinct from broader social justice goals.[19] As James Baldwin put it, "I am not certain, therefore, that the present sexual revolution is either sexual or a revolution."[20]

CAPITALISM AND SEXUAL REVOLUTIONS

One result of the sexual revolution of the twentieth century was the association of capitalism with sexual freedom rather than subordination, repression and compulsion. Queer theorist Michael Warner, for example, contends that queer marxism is irrelevant as queer culture has thrived within capitalism: "Gay culture in this most visible mode is anything but external to advanced capitalism and precisely those features of advanced capitalism that many on the left are most eager to disavow."[21] The association of queer freedom, women's rights and anti-racism with neoliberal capitalism is reflected in the widespread narrative of sexual progress (summarized by the slogan "it gets better") that constructs oppression as hold-over "traditional" life-ways that will fade over time. As I write, the rising tide of anti-abortion and anti-trans laws in the United States and elsewhere is a reminder that sex and gender progress is not a one-way street and that what gets better can also get worse.

It is true, as I have argued above, that capitalism does open up certain spaces of self-making, but always grounded in alienation and dispossession. The sexual revolutions of capitalist society have been driven by the dissolution of bonds of community and relations to the land, and by the creation of counter-normative communities and mobilization from below that open up the creative dimensions of life-making and self-realization. Kevin Floyd points out that the reification of desire creates conditions for potential change: "Like processes of industrialization, urbanization, and social migration, the reifying of sexual desire needs to be understood as a condition of possibility for a complex, variable history of sexually nonnormative discourses, practices, sites, subjectivities, imaginaries, collective formations and collective aspirations."[22]

People making lives from below have changed the ways gender and sexuality are lived, even if these emergent practices have generally been captured within forms compatible with capitalist relations. Gary Kinsman notes the ways "lesbians and gays participated in making themselves."[23] This collective self-making from below has marked the history of sexual revolutions under capitalism. Kevin Floyd posits that "capitalist development did not itself produce, but certainly participated in the production of, a space of opportunity for a certain kind of liberatory sexual and political practice."[24] Yet sexual revolution with this "space of opportunity" will necessarily be confined in scope without broader emancipatory struggles to overcome alienation and dispossession to produce genuine democracy from below.

The term "sexual revolution" developed in the anti-capitalist context of the political and social mobilizations of the early twentieth century. The period roughly from 1910 to 1930 was characterized by revolutionary uprisings in Russia, Germany, Mexico and China along with moments of mass insurgency on a global scale. Wilhelm Reich captured the sexual dimensions of this period of social and political uprising in his book *The Sexual Revolution* originally published in 1936. Reich understood the sexual revolution as a crucial dimension of the economic and political revolutions of that period; even if this dimension was sadly neglected by many within socialist movements, including the leadership that consolidated around Stalin after the early years of the revolution in the Soviet Union.

The early years of the Russian Revolution saw notable changes in the realm of sexuality, including the secularization of marriage, the liberalization of divorce, the legalization of abortion, the decriminalization of homosexuality and the launch of experiments in collective living.[25] Reich describes these changes in the realm of sexuality as part of a broader cultural shift associated with the development of new revolutionary ways of living: "This sexual revolution was the objective expression of the revolutionary restructuring of culture."[26] There were important indications in the early years of the revolution that people were beginning to remake sexuality as part of the deepening of the revolutionary process: "The disintegration of compulsory morality was only a symptom indicating that the social revolution would also result in a sexual revolution ..."[27]

The consolidation of the Stalinist leadership represented the development of new forms of authoritarian rule from above. One of the dimensions of this counter-revolution was the reversal of many of the changes in the realm of sexuality, through the reintroduction of sodomy laws, the recriminalization of abortion, and the reimposition of elements of compulsion in family formation.[28] Reich maintains that the reversal of the emergent sexual revolution in the Soviet Union was an indicator of the shift towards authoritarianism: "In the Soviet Union, regression in the sexual realm is connected with general questions of revolutionary cultural development. We know that the trend toward self-regulation of social life has yielded to authoritarian regulation of society."[29]

Reich contends that sexual revolution must be a deliberate feature of socialist revolution, as it was a crucial element in the development of workers' democracy and self-regulation as opposed to governance from above: "the affirmation of life, in its subjective form as affirmation of sexual pleasure and in its objective social form as work democracy, has to be brought to subjective consciousness and objective development."[30] While Reich made an important contribution arguing that sexual revolution was an essential dimension of socialist insurgency, his own view of sexual revolution was profoundly limited, particularly given his pathologization of homosexuality. It is important to understand writers in the context of their times, and at the time Reich was writing, there was a definite current in German socialism in support of gay rights. The pathologization of homosexuality "was not the only available perspective: many German socialists and social democrats argued publicly in support of gay rights without invoking it as a medical pathology."[31]

Sexual revolution is a vital dimension in overcoming alienation through the development of democratic control from below. Braverman described the process through which workers: "become the masters of industry in the true sense, which is to say when the antagonism in the labor process between controllers and workers, conception and execution, mental and manual labor are overcome, and when the labor process is united in the collective body which conducts it."[32] The collective body which conducts this united labor process is charged with eroticism and engaged in life-making labor that extends far beyond the capitalist workplace.

Dennis Altman developed an elaborated sense of sexual liberation in the context of the sexual revolution of the 1960s and 1970s: "Liberation would involve a resurrection of our original impulse to take enjoyment from the total body, and indeed to accept the seeking of sensual enjoyment as an end in itself, free from procreation or status enhancement."[33] This conception of sensual enjoyment is not simply describing sex for its own sake as we now know it, but also the transformation of erotic practice. Liberation is connected to overcoming alienation so that people pursue life-making activities of all sorts to attain multidimensional inherent fulfillment. Altman describes this as "the possibility of breaking down the rigid lines our society draws between art and life, or in other words the possibility of eroticizing everyday living."[34]

Liberation in this sense expands our understanding of erotic fulfillment beyond personal pleasure to encompass mutuality with others. In the words of Altman:

> Sex would be seen as a means of expanding contact and creating community with other persons, and would demand some reciprocity other than the purely physical. Sex as much as everyday life would be eroticized and would become a means of human communication rather than purely physical gratification or consummation of a sacred union.[35]

Altman makes the point that the sex-centeredness of emergent gay male communities in the 1970s did not offer a simple model for liberated sexualities. However, as a dissident community forged around access to same-sex sexual practice as well as intimacy, it was a site for the development of a sex-positivity that was distinctive from that in heterosexual communities. He wrote that the sex-centric character of gay life "represents an acceptance of sexuality in a way perhaps fewer heterosexuals have experienced."[36] A process of genuine sexual liberation must build upon these life-experiments and struggles from below.

UTOPIA REALIZED

Sexual revolution opens the possibility of liberation in the sense of realizing utopia. For Muñoz, "Queerness is utopian, and there is something queer about the utopian."[37] The utopian points beyond the frame of the present, challenging the assumption that future changes will be quantitative (more or less of the same) rather than qualitative (frame-shifting social transformation). Queerness, in the sense that Muñoz uses it, is not simply a synonym for LGBTQ (lesbian, gay, bisexual, transgender, queer or two-spirit) but a vision of liberation, a way into seeing a better world we have not yet attained. Queerness is therefore utopian, and utopianism is queer in that it defamiliarizes the world we think we know and allows us to think against ourselves to imagine living otherwise.[38]

Muñoz draws specifically on the conception of concrete utopia developed by Ernst Bloch, which emerges as shared visions of a better world generated largely by struggles that open up the horizons of possibility. This is not about untethered dreaming, but audacious envisioning of other possible futures grounded in the serious analysis of history and mapping of present conditions that allows us to find paths to realizable transformation. Bloch refers to this as the "anticipatory" that includes both structured imagining and serious attention to the actual: "But the anticipatory of course must blossom, especially when this takes place in sobriety instead of in effusiveness and clouds."[39]

Freedom struggles become self-limiting when they are bounded by the present and resigned to the limits of the dominant relations. Concrete utopian practices open up the vision of better ways of life that is sobered by a serious analysis of the present that provides tools to map possible futures. This book follows Muñoz in arguing that queer liberation is premised on the possibility that the future of sexualities could look very different than the present. Our imagination of sexual futures tends to be bound by our lived experience of our own bodies and those of others in a particular social context. This limits our vision of sexual liberation to what is obtainable by winning reforms within the present state of social organization.

I have argued in this book that queer marxism offers valuable tools for queer utopian thinking, denaturalizing the current state of relations of gender and sexuality by showing how these relations are a historical product, reducible neither to a natural order nor a set of social constructions. The critique of utopianism in the Marxist tradition has been to challenge the political project of imagining ideal societies without mapping the connections to the present that create a potential transformative path from here to there. Utopia in this sense becomes an unrealizable dream, at best an entertaining fiction.

However, a marxism that is totally divested of utopian thinking may prove rather too limited in its ability to boldly and expansively envision the better world we struggle to make. Indeed, marxism tended to lag behind utopian socialism in the development of a politics of sexual liberation through the nineteenth and early twentieth centuries. Sheila Rowbotham described Edward Carpenter's resilient "broad utopianism," reflected in works like *My Days and Dreams* in which "a vision of transformed sexual relations is integrally connected to a fundamentally different social order."[40] While marxism has been historically opposed to dreaming of new worlds that is disconnected from practical transformative mobilization in present circumstances, it can certainly draw on utopian understandings of gender and sexuality to help fuel the struggle for a better world. I want to argue here that queer marxism provides valuable tools for envisioning and strategically mobilizing realizable utopias to fuel struggles for gender and sexual liberation.

One of the great challenges we face when envisioning sex and gender liberation is that our imagination is limited by our life experiences to date and the ideas circulating in society. We learn to read the sexualized and gendered relations we inhabit as eternal and natural, the expression of connections hard-wired into our bodies. It becomes hard to envision a future that is not simply more or less of the same. Ok, maybe men do a bit more housework, gays get to marry, movies get sexier and women get equal pay; but these remain variations on a theme, built around forms of sexual normativity we take for granted, for example, the idea that lasting couple relations are the standard for intimacy and sexuality.

Our experience of normativity acts like a kind of gravity in our lives, pulling our idea of possibility down to the ground. Science fiction provides a bracing vision of other ways of doing things, breaking free of that gravity. Frederick Jameson wrote about the power of science fiction as a form of utopian writing that defamiliarizes social relations that tend to be taken for granted by those living through them.[41] W.G. Pearson argued specifically about the power of science fiction in enabling readers to re-envision gender and sexuality. Pearson observes that science fiction contributes to "a radical rewriting of the assumption within the show of naturalness, endurance and fixity, of our current understandings of sexuality and its relationship both to the sex/gender dyad and to sociocultural institutions."[42] Science fiction allows us to really envision fluidity in sex and gender connected to real freedom in personal relations.

The sex radicals of the nineteenth and early twentieth centuries developed audacious visions of sex and gender liberation, sometimes tied into utopian projections of future societies. The sexual visionary and utopian socialist Edward Carpenter developed a radical conception of a society of freedom:

I conceive a millennium on earth, a millennium not of riches, nor of mechanical facilities, nor of intellectual facilities, nor absolutely of immunity from disease, nor absolutely of immunity from pain; but a time when men and women all over the earth shall ascend and enter into relation with their bodies and shall attain freedom and joy.[43]

These visions still have a power. This kind of utopian radical project is an ongoing theme in science fiction, allowing us to know humanity more expansively by shifting the social and ecological context in ways that open up the question of what to expect. Here, I explore the visionary power of science fiction, drawing on four works suggested by the critical writing of W.G. Pearson.

Three of the books I draw on have utopian elements, allowing us to imagine a more fluid set of relations around gender and sexuality. Samuel Delany's *Trouble with Triton*, Ursula Le Guin's *The Dispossessed* and Marge Piercy's *Woman on the Edge of Time* all conjure up societies that are very different from the way we live now. These books share certain common themes, exploring situations in places that are distant in time or space where people have mobilized in revolutionary processes and developed new ways of working and living that support very different practices in the areas of gender and sexuality. These books offer rich conceptualizations of human relations in which there is a great deal more at play in the areas of gender and sexuality than we are used to at the present time, grounded in different ways of organizing work, households, child-rearing and politics.

In contrast, Octavia Butler's *Parable of the Sower* has a more dystopic edge, showing an image of social breakdown grounded very much in the neoliberal and austerity-focused social policies that have dominated state activities since the 1980s. This society has no place for the poor and unemployed who have become unrooted as the need for their labor was undermined. Relations of gender and sexuality are reorganized around the imperatives of mobility and survival as well as the threat of violence.

One of the most striking characteristics in each of the three books with more utopian elements is the fluidity in both gender and sexuality that is expressed. I have personally found these books very helpful in mapping other possible futures. In *Woman on the Edge of Time*, Connie is a mental patient led by her guide Luciente from a brutal institution to a place of freedom in a future liberated society. She has trouble making out the gender of Luciente and others in this new society, who do not refer to each other in terms of a gender binary, but rather use the non-binary "per" or "person."

When Connie needs appropriate attire (a flimsy) for a festival, Luciente remembers there is one available. "You put on Red Star's flimsy. Red Star ordered it, but that person had an accident picking cherries and is healing at Cranberry. We'll get per flimsy from the presser for you."[44]

Indeed, readers share Connie's experience of decoding gender fluidity through the lens of expectations generated in a society where gender binaries are expressed at the foundational level of everyday language. It becomes a habit in this society to try to sort people you meet into gender categories. As we meet people, we tend to assign them a gender that will be used to code our speech (he or she) and organize our memory. It is startling and challenging to read a book in which we do not know the gender of many of the characters. That disorientation is part of the power of Piercy's work.

In *Trouble on Triton*, people still refer to each other as "he" or "she," but the basis for attributing gender is much more ambiguous. Neither the physical characteristics of a person nor their name have much to do with gender attribution, "male and female names out here, of course, didn't mean too much. Anyone might have just about any name …"[45] At one point, Bron assumes the "muscular creature with the fur-bound thigh and arm, matted hair and ulcerated eye" must be male even though someone referred to them as "she."[46] But then, "Bron saw, across the hirsute pectoral, scars from which must have been an incredibly clumsy mastectomy."[47] This is a society where body transformation is wide-ranging and highly accessible. At the same time, people sometimes use cruder methods that leave scars.

The Dispossessed tracks the experience of Shevrek, visiting a more conservative earth from a rebel moon. They are surprised to hear about the rigid division of labor between women and men on earth. "That seems a very mechanical basis for the division of labour, doesn't it? A person chooses work according to what interest, talent, strength – what has the sex to do with that?"[48] In all three of these novels, the expression of gender fluidity is intimately connected to the development of societies where work is not assigned on the basis of gender.

The characters in these future societies also express great fluidity in terms of sexuality. The sexual preferences of people on Triton are mapped in detailed statistical form: "Studies have shown that 80% of the population could function sexually with either sex." Indeed, there are "forty or fifty basic sexes, falling loosely into nine categories, four homophilic … The other five are heterophilic."[49] These terms are not just about sexual lives, but also emotional preferences. "Homophilic means no matter who or what you like to screw, you prefer to live and have friends primarily from your own sex."[50]

Luciente, Connie's guide to a future society in *Woman on the Edge of Time*, nonchalantly discusses their own sexual history with women and men. Indeed Luciente is at first confused when Connie asks them about liking women. "*All* women?" ... Oh, for coupling? In truth, the most intense mating of my life was a woman ... Mostly I've liked males."[51]

In these societies, the basis for sex is relatively casual. Luciente describes the sexual morays of the society. "Fasure we couple. Not for money, not for a living. For love, for pleasure, for relief, out of habit, out of curiosity and lust."[52] People in the future society distinguish between hand friends and pillow friends, those you have sex with and those you do not. While some people rank relationships in terms of levels of intimacy, even that is contentious. "Some of us use the term 'core' for those we're closest to. Others think that distinction is bad. We debate."[53] On Triton, there is a special word for "sexualizationships" which are separate from other relationships such as co-parenting, emotional intimacy or co-residence.

Marriage is illegal on Triton.[54] People live in co-ops, organized as single or mixed gender, and specified or non-specified sexual orientation. In most of the co-ops, "sex was overt and encouraged and insistently integrated with all aspects of co-operative life."[55] But there was a range, to suit everyone's preferences, including those just not that into sex. "Most people who live in single-sex, non-specific co-ops aren't into men *or* women that much ..."[56]

The fluidity in gender and sexuality in these societies is connected to a disconnection between child-rearing and sexual coupling. Birth control is the general default on Triton, thanks to a contraceptive injection in adolescence, around the time people adopt their adult name. People can choose not to have the injection, but most proceed with it. After the injection, people who wish to conceive must take a pill to overcome the impact of the contraceptive shot: "Somewhere around nameday, you decide if you want to have children by accident or by design; if by design – which well over ninety-nine percent do – you get your injection. Then, later, you have to decide that you *do* want them; and two of you go off and get the pill."[57]

In Piercy's future society, there is no human pregnancy as fetuses are nurtured outside the body in the brooder. "Here embryos are growing almost ready to birth."[58] Connie, the visitor from our present, asks, "Were you all born from this crazy machine?"[59] Luciente, the guide, rejects Connie's assumption that this machine gestation is problematic: "You think because we do not bear live, we cannot love our children ... But we do, with whole hearts."[60]

Children are raised by configurations of loving adults who choose to parent. In Piercy's future society, children are raised by three co-mothers, a category that includes both women and men. "Co-mothers are seldom sweet friends if we can manage. So the child will not get caught in love misunderstandings."[61] People who have a special gift for parenting engage with the children of the whole community. "I'm what they call a kidbinder, meaning I mother everyone's kids."[62] On Triton, children are raised by larger communes who organize around child-rearing. Spike describes her family of origin, "My parents – all nine of them – are Ganymede ice-farmers."[63]

Men as well as women breastfeed on Triton and in Piercy's future society. Connie is at first sickened by the sight of a man breastfeeding. "He had breasts. Not large ones. Small breasts, like a flat-chested woman temporarily swollen with milk ... The baby stopped wailing and began to suck greedily."[64] Connie is worried that women have given away their power in a society where men breastfeed: "These women thought they had won, but they had abandoned to men the last refuge of women ... the last remnants of ancient power, those sealed in blood and in milk."[65] On Triton, men who are going to nurse need a course of medication. "Phillip's left nipple was very large ... Periodically when a new child was expected at Phillip's commune ... the breast would enlarge (three pills each lunchtime ...) and Phillip would take off two or three days a week wet-leave."[66] Wet-leave is certainly a sign of a society built more directly around the real needs of parents and children.

Childhood is shorter in these societies than in Canada today. In Piercy's future society, adults name children as they reach adolescence and send them into the woods to survive on their own for three months. This is a risk, but as Bee explains to Connie, "We take the chance. We have found no way to break dependencies without risk."[67] Luciente explains, "We set our children free."[68] Similarly naming occurred around the time of adolescence on Triton as on other moons. "Naming age was twelve on the moons of Saturn, fourteen on the moons of Jupiter; he wasn't sure what it was here on Triton, but he suspected it was younger than either."[69] Children have huge autonomy and even authority on Triton. Bron eats in a restaurant that "turned out to cater almost entirely to well-heeled (and rather somber) nine- to thirteen-year-olds." Indeed, the entire enterprise where Bron worked was run by twelve-year-old twins.[70]

Children were also sexually active. When Connie sees two children engaging in sexually explicit play, she asks, "Aren't you going to stop them?" Magdalena who is watching the children explains that this is how they learn: "Mostly they learn sex from each other." While adults intervene if bullying occurs or assault seems likely, they generally leave it up to the children to take care of each other, "If a child is rough, the other children deal with that."[71]

The fluidity of gender and sexuality in these portrayals goes along with a plasticity of the body. This is particularly marked on Triton, where voluntary regeneration treatments allow people to make substantial changes to their physical being. As Spike explains to Bron, "while you are at it, if you find your own body distasteful, you can have it regenerated, dyed green or heliotrope, padded out here, slimmed down there ..." People are able to choose remarkable body changes. Indeed, people on Triton are mystified by Lawrence, a 74-year-old member of Bron's co-op who does not seek regeneration. "Bron was thinking that seventy-four year olds should either get bodily regeneration treatments or not sit around the co-op common rooms stark naked ..."[72]

This body transformation can be paired with refixation to alter sexual orientation. Spike notes that Lawrence hits on Bron and others when he gets drunk, even though they have clearly expressed their lack of interest. It seems both futile and irksome to be hitting on others who have made their lack of interest clear. "I mean not only do we live in an age of regeneration treatments; there are refixation treatments too. He can have his sexuality refixed on someone, or thing, that can get it up for him."[73]

This plasticity is not bound by a narrow beauty myth. On Triton, some people cultivate the opposite of beauty: "Just as those outsized muscles were conscientiously clinic-grown, so the filth, the scars, the sores, the boils that speckled the grimed arms and hips were from conscientious neglect."[74] On Piercy's future earth, the beauty myth based on a narrow set of parameters is gone "Jackrabbit is thin beautiful. Bee is big beautiful. Dawn is small beautiful."[75]

This goes along with a compact set of sexual ethics. In *Woman on the Edge of Time*, sexual ethics are expressed in a simple formulation: "We don't find coupling bad unless it involves pain or is not invited."[76] On Triton, one can find the pleasure one is seeking without judgement: "Somewhere, in your sector or mine, in this unit or in that one, there it is: pleasure, community, respect – all you have to do is know the kind, and how much of it, and to what extent you want it."[77] The challenge for the character Bron is that he does not know what he wants: "But what happens to those of us who don't know?"[78] In most of the residential co-ops, "sex was overt and encouraged and insistently integrated with all aspects of co-operative life ..."[79]

These three books offer a vision of future societies organized around fluidity in gender and sexuality combined with plasticity of the body. Each of the books links this fluidity and plasticity to dramatically transformed social relations in which work in not assigned on the basis of gender, childhood is less distinguished from adulthood and is briefer than in contemporary Canada, and the form of households is flexible offering the individual substantial choice.

This is a remarkable contrast to the neoliberal dystopian eco-hell of Octavia Butler's *Parable of the Sower*. This book, set in the United States in the near future, shows the impact of neoliberal marginalization and ecological disaster on the impoverished and precarious working class, while the rich are living large behind high walls. A huge unhoused population roves the area scavenging for whatever sustenance they can attain, while working-class people are able to put up their own walls for self-protection. Fire and police services operate on a fee for service basis. People cling to their family units for defense and form intimate relationships on the basis of economic necessity and safety. And rape is endemic. It first shows up in the novel with a "woman, young, naked and filthy" who maybe had been "raped so much she was crazy."[80] Rape is not only a threat from the large violent scavenging population, but also within the compound and the family. Tracy had been raped for years when she became pregnant at the age of 12 by her uncle.[81]

These visions of utopian and dystopian sexualities are linked not only to changes in the sexual realm, or to new technological possibilities. They are the result of political projects to transform society. In *Woman on the Edge of Time*, Luciente who is the guide to the future society attributes changes in birth and family formation to "women's long revolution. When we were breaking up the old hierarchies."[82] Ultimately, the breaking up of hierarchies required a shift in the organization of gestation, birth and child-rearing: "Cause as long as we were biologically enchained, we'd never be equal. And males never would be humanized to be loving and tender. So we all became mothers."[83]

Delany is less specific in discussing the political transformative process, but it is clearly there. One of the accomplishments of "Brian Sanders, the old firebrand and roaring-girl" was that "she had single-handedly driven the term 'man-made' from most languages of Earth ... and Mars."[84] One of the key accomplishments of the political transformation was that women were at last treated as fully human. Indeed, the difference between women and men in Triton comes down primarily to that history:

The difference is simply that women have only really been treated, by that bizarre, Durkheimian abstraction "society" as human beings for the last – oh, say sixty-five years; and then, really, only on the moons; whereas men have had the luxury of such treatment for the last four thousand. The result of this historical anomaly is simply that, on a statistical basis, women are just a little less willing to put up with certain kinds of shit than men – simply because the concept of a certain kind of shit-free Universe is, in that equally bizarre Jungian abstraction, the female "collective unconscious," too new and too precious.[85]

Science fiction nurtures visions of ways of living sex and gender that look very different than what we can currently imagine. These visions remind us that a real sexual revolution will actually transform our erotic lives rather than incrementally expanding the realm of normative expressions of gender and sexuality. This kind of revolution will lead us beyond the bounds of what we can realistically envision right now, because our imagination is generally based on our experiences of a specific set of social relations. Utopian visions give us a foretaste of future ways of living gender and sexuality in which human potential is realized in new ways, once alienation and dispossession have been overcome as workers establish genuine collective and democratic control over processes of life-making in the broadest sense.

PERMANENT SEXUAL REVOLUTION

Sexual revolution is a fundamental dimension of socialist revolution to realize utopia by overturning capitalist alienation, including the erotic containment that channels the complex and diverse embodied fulfillment of social life-making into the narrow realm of sexuality organized around the gendered orientation of desire. Utopia cannot be realized through the development of a detailed road map of the better world to be erected on the basis of prescriptive planning in advance of a revolutionary process. It is only through the insurgent seizure of power from below that people develop the capacities and forms of organization to figure out how to make lives in a world of new possibilities. The revolution is about creating the circumstances in which people can make new ways of life from below through collective and democratic processes grounded in conversation, debate and experimentation.

The revolutionary process will necessarily be extended over a long period of time as the people who have collectively and democratically seized power set about transforming the world they have inherited, ranging from built housing stock to existing health care institution, and from transportation infrastructure to technologies built for profit and surveillance. This process must ultimately be global, spreading beyond the local, regional and national insurgencies that kick off the process. People rise up in response to immediate circumstances in their social location, and through their insurgency tend to map out the connections between their own mobilization and other struggles against a broader global power structure that is the basis for new forms of solidarity.

The relationship between the local and the global in processes of sexual revolution is complex, given the long histories of dispossession and dehumanization. Too often, the history of capitalism and sexuality has been reduced to a single story of progress, weaving together capitalist economic development, liberal democracy and the advance of sexual freedom. Chris Chitty and Peter Drucker, in different ways, applied the theory of global combined and uneven development to understand the ways differentiated and divergent patterns of capitalist development and sexual formation formed a complex and contradictory whole. The theory of combined and uneven development was originally devised by Leon Trotsky to challenge the idea that there was a single path of advancement that all countries in the global capitalist system would necessarily follow. Trotsky argued that countries did not follow the same series of steps, but picked up from each other in a variety of ways, so that those cast as "less developed" could skip steps and leap quickly: "The privilege of historical backwardness – and such a privilege exists – permits, or rather compels, the adoption of whatever is ready in advance at any specified date, skipping a whole series of intermediary stages."[86] Thus, for example, Russian industry in the period leading up to World War I included large factories based on leading-edge production processes, as employers drew on the latest technical advances achieved elsewhere. There is much to be learned from Trotsky's theorization, though the language of "historical backwardness" still implies that capitalist development involves moving forward. The real history of genocide, ecological destruction, upending of community, suppression of historical self-knowledge and memory as well as imposition of dominant cultures is not in any simple way history moving forward.

This analysis of combined and uneven development offers powerful insights into the ways capitalist sexual formation can follow divergent paths that are nonetheless linked in a contradictory whole. Chris Chitty applied this concept to describe the differentiated forms of queer formation under capitalism: "alternate or queer sexualities – primarily homosexuality, intransitive gender identifications, prostitution and other kinds of sex work – historically emerged under fault lines of transformed property relations in a process of combined and uneven development"[87] The combined and uneven process of sexual formation means that local experiences do not play out in isolation, but are linked through a global capitalist system founded on imperialism, settler-colonialism, dispossession, trade and migration. It is important to understand both specific, local histories and practices and the broader global context. In conditions of global capitalism, local ways of life may be influenced by the coercive colonial imposition of laws and practices, representation through the lens of transnational culture industries, transplanted work practices deployed by transnational corporations and imperialist states, deliberate borrowing by counter-normative communities, and/or human mobility through migration or travel. For Peter Drucker, viewing sexual formation through the frame of combined and uneven social construction "can help us understand how different indigenous starting points, different relationships to the world economy, and different cultural and political contexts can produce very different results – while still producing identifiable elements of LGBT identities in one country after another."[88] The starting point for sexual revolution is this history of sexual formation through combined and uneven social construction, producing very different configurations of gender and sexuality around the world, within particular political, cultural and economic contexts bound together in a complex and contradictory whole by fundamental relations of global capitalism.

In this context of combined and uneven sexual development, the sexual revolution cannot be a single one-time leap in one location within this global system, but will necessarily take the shape of permanent revolution, spreading and taking new forms as required in a variety of circumstances created by histories of standardization and differentiation, including processes of gender, racial, sexual, national and colonial class formation. Trotsky developed the idea of permanent revolution seeking to explain the consolidation of bureaucratic power over and above the working class and the destruction of emergent forms of workers' democracy in the years following the Russian Revolution of 1917. He argued that the internal dynamics of the Stalinist counter-revolution were ultimately grounded in the isolation of the revolution, despite the promising spread of a global wave of insurgencies in 1910–26. Trotsky argued that the successful revolutionary transformation of society required a permanent revolution, an ongoing process through which insurgencies grounded in the particular soil of their locale would deepen and weave together to overturn the global system of alienation and dispossession.

At the core of Trotsky's theory of permanent revolution was the conception of successful insurgent uprising as the starting point rather than end of the revolutionary process: "The conquest of power by the proletariat does not complete the revolution, but only opens it."[89] The system of capitalist relations cannot be overturned by a revolution in one place, which would remain subject to military threat and economic competition given the global scale of production:

> The completion of the socialist revolution within national limits is unthinkable ... The socialist revolution begins on the national arena, it unfolds on the international arena, and is completed on the world arena. Thus, the socialist revolution becomes a permanent revolution in a newer and broader sense of the word; it attains completion, only in the final victory of the new society on our entire planet.[90]

This revolution will not take a single form in all places, but will result from immediate locations in very different locations within global capitalism: "Different countries will go through this process at different tempos."[91]

The sexual revolution, as a crucial dimension of a broader social transformation, will take the form of permanent revolution, meaning that it will require an extended process of deepening, learning and spreading. People will develop new ways of living, beginning immediately in the mobilization of mass insurgency and continuing through the development of new forms of democratic decision making linked to widespread discussion and debate and many experiments in living. This process will not track a single path towards a predetermined end, but will open up engagement grounded in solidarity based on recognition of different starting points and divergent wants and needs. The revolution will necessarily start with the inherited legacy of the past in such areas as life-making ideas and practices, built forms, intergenerational trauma from dehumanization, patterns of global connection, technologies and environmental destruction. Some of this will change rapidly as people transform themselves and develop new capacities through the mobilization of mass insurgency. Others will take more time as people develop new forms of collective and democratic control over processes of life-making, developing new forms of social, ecological and built infrastructure to support mutuality and reciprocity. Through this process, people will play, experiment and evaluate in the erotic realm, finding ways towards the realization of queer utopias that extend beyond the narrow realm of sexualities as the legacies of alienation and dispossession are overcome.

Permanent sexual revolution must include reparation, reconciliation and the right of return to address the historical and ongoing inequities of colonization, enslavement, gendered violence and other practices of differentiating dehumanization. The specific forms that redress takes will vary tremendously depending on the specific character of historical dispossession and dehumanization experienced by particular groups. The Palestinian right of return and the Indigenous demand for land back on Turtle Island resonate with each other, but are not identical. It is those who have experienced colonization, violence and dehumanization who must set the terms for the process of reparation. The permanent revolution frame is founded on the understanding that all participants do not enter the transformational process from the same location, and the process must continue until the needs of all are addressed.

One of the most striking contributions to utopian revolutionary thought in recent years has been a flowering of new work on the abolition of the family. These writers and activists argue that Family Abolition would be necessary for ending compulsion in our intimate lives and opening up many experiments in erotic engagement, caregiving and child-raising grounded in communal support. In the words of M.E. O'Brien, "The abolition of the family must be the positive creation of a society of generalized human care and queer love."[92] The development of new forms of collective and democratic control over life-making grounded in mutuality and reciprocity is an essential element of permanent sexual revolution. People who have freed themselves from the fetters of alienation and dispossession will be able to deliberately direct their creative transformative activity towards the integral fulfillment of wants and needs, centrally including erotic realization. We cannot know exactly what this will look like, as the unleashed world-making of people who have liberated themselves is necessarily open-ended. We have had a preview, however, in the inventive life-making from below associated with freedom struggles throughout the history of capitalism.

Notes

1 INTRODUCTION: EROS AND ALIENATION

1. Stonewall, *Stonewall Top 100 Employers 2016*. (London: Stonewall, 2016), p. 7.
2. Gary Kinsman and Patrizia Gentile, *The Canadian War on Queers: National Security as Sexual Regulation* (Vancouver: University of British Columbia Press, 2010).
3. José Estaban Muñoz, *Cruising Utopia: The Then and There of Queer Futurity* (New York: State University of New York Press, 2009), p. 27.
4. See Judith Butler, *Who's Afraid of Gender?* (Toronto: Knopf Canada, 2024), p. 6.
5. Muñoz, *Cruising Utopia*, p. 1.
6. Herbert Marcuse, *Eros and Civilization: A Philosophical Inquiry into Freud* (Boston: Beacon Press, 1966).
7. The twenty-first-century burgeoning of queer marxism includes: Chris Chitty, *Sexual Hegemony: Statecraft, Sodomy and Capital in the Rise of the World System* (Durham: Duke University Press, 2020); Peter Drucker, *Warped: Gay Normality and Queer Anti-Capitalism* (Leiden: Brill, 2015); Kevin Floyd, *The Reification of Desire: Towards a Queer Marxism* (Minneapolis: University of Minnesota Press, 2009); Jules Joanne Gleeson and Elle O'Rourke, *Transgender Marxism* (London: Pluto Press, 2021); Rebecca Hennessy, *Profit and Pleasure: Sexual Identities in Late Capitalism* (New York: Routledge, 2000); Gary Kinsman, *The Regulation of Desire: Homo and Hetero Sexualities* (Montreal: Black Rose Books, 1996); Holly Lewis, *The Politics of Everybody: Feminism, Queer Theory and Marxism at the Intersection* (London: Zed Books, 2016); M.E. O'Brien, *Family Abolition: Capitalism and the Communizing of Care* (London: Pluto Press, 2023).
8. Karl Marx, *Economic and Political Manuscripts of 1844* (Moscow: Progress Publishers, 1977), p. 68.
9. Susan Ferguson, *Women and Work: Feminism, Labour and Social Reproduction* (London: Pluto Press, 2020), p. 16.
10. Marx, *Economic and Political Manuscripts of 1844*, p. 74.
11. Bryan Palmer, *Cultures of Darkness: Night Travels in the Histories of Transgression* (New York: Monthly Review Press, 2000).
12. Ellen Ross and Rayna Rapp, "Sex and Society: A Research Note from Social History and Anthropology," *Comparative Studies in Society and History* 23, no. 1 (1981), p. 51.
13. Marcuse, *Eros and Civilization*; John Holloway, *Crack Capitalism* (London: Pluto Press, 2010).
14. Sigmund Freud, "An Outline of Psycho-Analysis," *The International Journal of Psycho-Analysis* 21 (1940), p. 31.
15. Ibid., p. 33.

16. Ibid., p. 33.
17. R. Danielle Egan, "Desexualizing the Freudian Child in a Culture of 'Sexual-ization': Trends and Implications" in Emma Renold, Jessica Ringrose and R. Danielle Egan (eds.), *Children, Sexuality and Sexualization* (Houndmills, Bas-ingstoke: Palgrave Macmillan, 2015), p. 109.
18. Jeffrey Weeks, *Sexuality* (second edition) (London: Routledge, 2003), p. 3.
19. Allison Moore and Paul Reynolds, *Childhood and Sexuality: Contemporary Issues and Debates* (London: Palgrave Macmillan, 2018), p. 1
20. Floyd, *The Reification of Desire.*
21. Ross and Rapp, "Sex and Society," p. 55.
22. Kinsman, *The Regulation of Desire*, p. 28.
23. Tithi Bhattacharya, "Introduction: Mapping Social Reproduction Theory," in Tithi Bhattacharya (ed.), *Social Reproduction Theory: Remapping Class, Recen-tering Oppression* (London: Pluto Press, 2017).
24. Johanna Brenner, "21st Century Socialist-Feminism," *Social Studies/Études socialistes* 10, no. 1 (2014).
25. Saidiya Hartman, *Wayward Lives, Beautiful Experiments: Intimate Histories of Social Upheaval* (New York: W.W. Norton, 2019), p. xv.
26. M.E. O'Brien, "Trans Work: Employment Trajectories, Labour Discipline and Gender Freedom," in Jules Joanne Gleeson and Elle O'Rourke (eds.), *Transgen-der Marxism* (London: Pluto Press, 2021).
27. Jordy Rosenberg, "Afterword. One Utopia, One Dystopia," in Jules Joanne Gleeson and Elle O'Rourke (eds.), *Transgender Marxism* (London: Pluto Press, 2021); Sue Ferguson and David McNally, "Precarious Migrants: Gender, Race and the Social Reproduction of a Global Working Class," *Socialist Register* (2015).
28. Jules Joanne Gleeson, "How Do Gender Transitions Happen?" in Jules Joanne Gleeson and Elle O'Rourke (eds.), *Transgender Marxism* (London: Pluto Press, 2021), p. 71.
29. Nat Raha, "A Queer Marxist Transfeminism: Queer and Trans Social Reproduc-tion," in Jules Joanne Gleeson and Elle O'Rourke (eds.), *Transgender Marxism* (London: Pluto Press, 2021).
30. Jeremy Atherton Lin, *Gay Bar: Why We Went Out* (New York: Little, Brown, 2021).
31. Richard Seymour, "An Alien Power" (2023), www.patreon.com/posts/alien-power-83889273 (accessed June 5, 2023).
32. Marx, *Economic and Political Manuscripts of 1844*, p. 147.
33. Karl Marx and Frederick Engels, *The German Ideology* (Moscow: Progress Pub-lishers 1976), p. 48.
34. Marx, *Economic and Political Manuscripts of 1844*, p. 128.
35. E.P. Thompson, *William Morris: Romantic to Revolutionary* (Oakland: PM Press, 2011), p. 806.
36. Pamela Haag, *Consent: Sexual Rights and the Transformation of American Liber-alism* (Ithaca: Cornell University Press, 1999).

37. Rosemary Hennessy, *Fires on the Border: The Passionate Politics of Labor Organizing on the Mexican Frontera* (Minneapolis: University of Minnesota Press, 2013).

38. Haag, *Consent*.

39. Katherine Angell, *Tomorrow Sex Will Be Good Again* (London: Verso, 2021); Amia Srinivasan, *The Right to Sex: Feminism in the Twenty-First Century* (New York: Farrar, Straus and Giroux, 2021).

40. John Bellamy Foster, *The Ecological Revolution: Making Peace with the Planet* (New York: Monthly Review Press, 2009), p. 180.

41. Leanne Simpson, *As We Have Always Done: Indigenous Freedom through Radical Resistance* (Minneapolis: University of Minnesota Press, 2017), p. 8.

42. Hennessy, *Profit and Pleasure*, p. 132.

43. Karl Marx, *Capital, vol. I* (New York: Vintage, 1976).

44. Mary K. Shenk, Mary C. Towner, Emily A. Voss and Nurul Alam, "Consanguineous Marriage, Kinship Ecology, and Market Transition," *Current Anthropology* 57, no. 13 (2016), p. S176.

45. Ibid., p. S176.

46. See David Halperin, *How to Do the History of Homosexuality* (Chicago: University Chicago Press, 2002), p. 28.

47. Weeks, *Sexuality*, p. 4.

48. See Drucker, p. 63.

49. Lewis, *The Politics of Everybody*, p. 29.

50. Brenna Bhandar and Rafeef Ziadah, *Revolutionary Feminisms: Conversations in Collective Action and Radical Thought* (London: Verso, 2020), p. 3.

2 ALIENATION AND THE MAKING OF SEXUALITIES

1. Karl Marx, *Capital, vol. I* (New York: Vintage, 1976), p. 283.

2. Oxford English Dictionary, *The Shorter Oxford English Dictionary* (London: Oxford University Press, 1955), p. 2448.

3. Karl Marx, *Economic and Political Manuscripts of 1844* (Moscow: Progress Publishers, 1977), p. 73.

4. Ibid., p. 74.

5. Ibid., p. 71.

6. Ibid., p. 71.

7. Ibid., p. 71.

8. Marx, *Capital, vol. I*, p. 284.

9. Peter C. Reynold, "Language and Skilled Activity," *Annals of the New York Academy of Sciences* 280, no. 1 (1976), p. 164.

10. Judith M. Burkart, Sarah B. Hrdy and Carel P. Van Schaik, "Cooperative Breeding and Human Cognitive Evolution," *Evolutionary Anthropology* 18 (2009).

11. Adrian V. Jaeggi and Michael Gurven, "Natural Cooperators: Food Sharing in Humans and Other Primates," *Evolutionary Anthropology* 22 (2013), p. 193.

12. Ibid., p. 193.

13. Burkart et al., "Cooperative Breeding," p. 177.

14. See Lise Vogel, *Marxism and the Oppression of Women: Towards a Unitary Theory* (London: Pluto Press, 1983), p. 139.

15. Susan Ferguson, *Women and Work: Feminism, Labour and Social Reproduction* (London: Pluto Press, 2020), p. 112.

16. Vogel, *Marxism and the Oppression of Women*, p. 156.

17. Ferguson, *Women and Work*, p. 115.

18. Michael Leibowitz, *Beyond Capital: Marx's Political Economy of the Working Class* (London: Palgrave Macmillan, 1992), p. 52.

19. David McNally, "The Dual Form of Labour in Capitalist Society and the Struggle over Meaning," *Historical Materialism* 12, no. 3 (2004), p. 198.

20. Meg Luxton, *More than a Labour of Love: Three Generations of Women's Work in the Home* (Toronto: The Women's Press, 1980), p. 17.

21. Kate Doyle Griffiths and J.J. Gleeson, Kinderkommunismus: A Feminist Analysis of the 21st Century Family and a Communist Proposal for Its Abolition (2015), https://isr.press/Griffiths_Gleeson_Kinderkommunismus/index.html (accessed June 6, 2022).

22. M.E. O'Brien, "Communizing Care," *Pinko* 1 (2019), https://pinko.online/pinko-1/communizing-care (accessed October 18, 2023).

23. M.E. O'Brien, *Family Abolition: Capitalism and the Communizing of Care* (London: Pluto Press, 2023), p. 4.

24. Saidiya Hartman, *Wayward Lives, Beautiful Experiments: Intimate Histories of Social Upheaval* (New York: W.W. Norton, 2019), p. 60.

25. Hugh Ryan, *When Brooklyn Was Queer* (New York: St Martin's Press, 2019), p. 138.

26. Ibid., p. 138.

27. Jules Joanne Gleeson, "How Do Gender Transitions Happen?" in Jules Joanne Gleeson and Elle O'Rourke (eds.), *Transgender Marxism* (London: Pluto Press, 2021); Jeremy Atherton Lin, *Gay Bar: Why We Went Out*; Nat Raha, "A Queer Marxist Transfeminism: Queer and Trans Social Reproduction," in Jules Joanne Gleeson and Elle O'Rourke (eds.), *Transgender Marxism* (London: Pluto Press, 2021); Jordy Rosenberg, "Afterword. One Utopia, One Dystopia," in Jules Joanne Gleeson and Elle O'Rourke (eds.), *Transgender Marxism* (London: Pluto Press, 2021).

28. Alan Sears, "AIDS and the Health of Nations: The Contradictions of Public Health," *Critical Sociology* 18, no. 2 (1992).

29. O'Brien, "Communizing Care."

30. Raha, "A Queer Marxist Transfeminism," p. 102.

31. Marx, *Capital, vol. I*, p. 283.

32. Ibid., p. 270.

33. Marx, *Economic and Political Manuscripts of 1844*, p. 74.

34. Aaron Jaffe, *Social Reproduction Theory and the Socialist Horizon: Work, Power and Political Strategy* (London: Pluto Press, 2020), p. 47.

35. Ibid., p. 47.

36. Marx, *Economic and Political Manuscripts of 1844*, p. 73.

37. Ibid., p. 75.

38. John Rechy, *The Sexual Outlaw* (New York: Dell, 1977), p. 300.

39. Bertell Ollman, *Alienation: Marx's Conception of Man in a Capitalist Society* (Cambridge: Cambridge University Press, 1972), p. xv.
40. Ibid., p. xv.
41. Mario Mieli, *Towards a Gay Communism: Elements of a Homosexual Critique* (London: Pluto Press, 2018), p. 255.
42. John Holloway, *Crack Capitalism* (London: Pluto Press, 2010), p. 119.
43. Ibid., p. 123.
44. Sigmund Freud, *Civilization and Its Discontents* (New York: W.W. Norton, 1989), pp. 746–7.
45. Herbert Marcuse, *Eros and Civilization: A Philosophical Inquiry into Freud* (Boston: Beacon Press, 1966), p. 35.
46. Ibid., p. 35.
47. Ibid., p. 46.
48. Ibid., p. 199.
49. Ibid., p. 45.
50. Ibid., p. 47.
51. Ibid., p. 202.
52. Ibid., p. 201.
53. Ibid., p. 210.
54. Ibid., p. 215.
55. Audre Lorde, "Uses of the Erotic: The Erotic as Power." in *Sister Outsider: Essays and Speeches* (Trumansburg, NY: Crossing Press, 1984), p. 49.
56. Ibid., p. 53.
57. Ibid., p. 52.
58. Kay Gabriel, "Gender as an Accumulation Strategy," *Invert Journal* (2020).
59. Ibid.
60. Georg Lukacs, *History and Class Consciousness: Studies in Marxist Dialectics* (Cambridge: MIT Press, 1971), p. 135.
61. Kevin Floyd, *The Reification of Desire: Towards A Queer Marxism* (Minneapolis: University of Minnesota Press, 2009), p. 41.
62. Ibid., p. 24.
63. Gary Kinsman, *The Regulation of Desire: Homo and Hetero Sexualities* (Montreal: Black Rose Books, 1996), p. 28.
64. Max Horkheimer and Theodor W. Adorno, *Dialectic of Enlightenment: Philosophical Fragments* (Stanford: Stanford University Press, 2002), p. 191.
65. David McNally, *Bodies of Meaning: Studies on Language, Labor and Liberation*, (Albany: State University of New York Press, 2021), p. 44.
66. Ibid., p. 11.
67. Ibid., p. 12.
68. Marx, *Capital, vol. I*, p. 163.
69. Ibid., pp. 163–4.

3   SEXUALITIES AT WORK

1. Carolyn Steedman, "Prison Houses," in Martin Lawn and Gerald Grace (eds.), *Teachers: The Culture and Politics of Work* (London: Falmer Press, 1987), p. 127.

2. Tamsin Wilton, *Sexual Disorientation: Gender, Sex, Desire and Self-Fashioning* (Houndmills, Basingstoke: Palgrave Macmillan, 2004), pp. 99–100.

3. Laura Roberson, "Grunt Work You'll Enjoy," *Men's Health* 28, no. 1 (2013), p. 44.

4. Dorothy E. Smith, *The Conceptual Practices of Power: A Feminist Sociology of Knowledge* (Toronto: University of Toronto Press, 1990), p. 28.

5. Ibid., p. 18.

6. Ibid., p. 18.

7. Ibid., p. 18.

8. Judith Halberstam, *Female Masculinity* (Durham: Duke University Press, 1998), pp. 57–8.

9. Ibid., p. 58.

10. Maurice Merleau-Ponty, *Phenomenology of Perception*. Donald A. Landes (trans.) (London and New York: Routledge, 2012), p. 154.

11. Ibid., p. 160.

12. Chris Chitty, *Sexual Hegemony: Statecraft, Sodomy and Capital in the Rise of the World System* (Durham: Duke University Press, 2020) p. 34.

13. Kevin Floyd, *The Reification of Desire: Towards a Queer Marxism* (Minneapolis: University of Minnesota Press, 2009), p. 57.

14. Gibson Burrell, "Sex and Organizational Analysis," *Organization Studies* 5, no. 2 (1984), pp. 98–9.

15. Ibid., p. 99.

16. Ibid., p. 108.

17. Floyd, *The Reification of Desire*, pp. 57–8.

18. Ibid., p. 63.

19. E.P. Thompson, *Customs in Common: Studies in Traditional Popular Culture* (New York: New Press, 1993), p. 358.

20. Ibid., p. 358.

21. Ibid., p. 388.

22. Ibid., p. 388.

23. Jonathan Martineau, *Time, Capitalism and Alienation: A Socio-Historical Inquiry into the Making of Modern Time* (Leiden: Brill Historical Materialism Book Series, 2015), p. 132.

24. Chitty, *Sexual Hegemony*, p. 125.

25. Antonio Gramsci, *Selections from the Prison Notebooks*. Quintin Hoare and Geoffrey Nowell Smith (eds. and trans.) (New York: International Publishers, 1971), p. 297.

26. Ibid., p. 300.

27. Wayne Lewchuk, "Men and Monotony: Fraternalism as a Managerial Strategy at the Ford Motor Company," *The Journal of Economic History* 53, no. 4 (1993), p. 848.

28. Ibid., p. 833.

29. Ibid., p. 828.

30. Ibid., p. 830.

31. Atina Grossman, *Reforming Sex: The German Movement for Birth Control and Abortion Reform, 1920–50* (Oxford: Oxford University Press, 1995), p. 6.

32. Dan Irving, "Normalize Transgressions: Legitimizing the Transsexual Body as Productive," *Radical History Review* no. 100 (2008), p. 55.
33. Hanan Hammad, *Industrial Sexuality: Gender. Urbanization, and Social; Transformation in Egypt* (Austin: University of Texas Press, 2016), p. 28.
34. Ibid., p. 45.
35. Ibid., p. 47.
36. Christopher L. Foote, Warren C. Whatley and Gavin Wright, "Arbitraging a Discriminatory Labor Market: Black Workers at the Ford Motor Company, 1918–1947," *Journal of Labor Economics* 21, no. 3 (2003), p. 494.
37. Ibid., p. 494.
38. Ibid., p. 494.
39. Clarence Hooker, "Ford's Sociology Department and the Americanization Campaign and the Manufacture of Popular Culture among Assembly Line Workers, c. 1910–1917," *Journal of American Culture* 20, no. 1 (1997), p. 50.
40. Allan Bérubé, *My Desire for History: Essays in Gay, Community, and Labor History.* John D'Emilio and Estelle B. Freedman (eds.) (Chapel Hill: University of North Carolina Press, 2011), p. 263.
41. Ibid., p. 263.
42. Ibid., p. 263.
43. Kate Doyle Griffiths, "Queer Workerism against Work: Strategising Transgender Labourers, Social Reproduction and Class Formation," in Jules Joanne Gleeson and Elle O'Rourke (eds.), *Transgender Marxism* (London: Pluto Press, 2021), p. 135.
44. Anne Balay, *Steel Closets: Voices of Gay, Lesbian and Transgender Steelworkers* (Chapel Hill: University of North Carolina Press, 2014), p. 77.
45. Ibid., p. 39.
46. M.E. O'Brien, "Trans Work: Employment Trajectories, Labour Discipline and Gender Freedom," in Jules Joanne Gleeson and Elle O'Rourke (eds.), *Transgender Marxism* (London: Pluto Press, 2021), p. 49.
47. Ibid., p. 49.
48. Ibid., p. 54.
49. Ibid., p. 57.
50. David Roediger and Elizabeth Esch, *The Production of Difference: Race and the Management of Labour in U.S. History* (Oxford: Oxford University Press, 2012); Lisa Lowe, *Immigrant Acts: On Asian American Cultural Politics* (Durham: Duke University Press, 1996).
51. Lauren Berlant and Michael Warner, "Sex in Public," *Critical Inquiry* 24, no. 2, (1998), p. 548.
52. Adrienne Rich, "Compulsory Heterosexuality and Lesbian Existence," *Signs: Journal of Women in Culture and Society* 5, no. 4 (1980), p. 659.
53. Lorraine Hansberry, "Letter to The Ladder," *The Ladder* 1, no. 11 (1957), p. 28, https://documents.alexanderstreet.com/d/1003347890 (accessed August 26, 2024).
54. Chitty, *Sexual Hegemony*, p. 134.
55. Ibid., p. 134.
56. Ibid., p. 134.

57. Ellen Ross and Rayna Rapp, "Sex and Society: A Research Note from Social History and Anthropology," *Comparative Studies in Society and History* 23, no. 1 (1981), p. 69.

58. Ibid., p. 69.

59. Ibid., p. 69.

60. Raffaella Sarti, "'All Masters Discourage the Marrying of Their Male Servants, and Admit Not by Any Means the Marriage of the Female': Domestic Service and Celibacy in Western Europe from the Sixteenth to the Nineteenth Century," *European History Quarterly* 38, no. 3 (2008), p. 439.

61. Bohata, "Mistress and Maid: Homoeroticism, Cross-Class Desire, and Disguise in Nineteenth-Century Fiction," *Victorian Literature and Culture* 45, p. 341.

62. John D'Emilio, *Making Trouble: Essays on Gay History, Politics and the University* (New York: Routledge, 1992), p. 8.

63. Ross and Rapp, "Sex and Society," p. 71.

64. Gayle Rubin, *Deviations: A Gayle Rubin Reader* (Durham: Duke University Press, 2011), p. 89.

65. Ned Katz, *The Invention of Heterosexuality* (New York: Dutton, 1995).

66. Michel Foucault, *The History of Sexuality Volume 1: An Introduction* (New York: Vintage, 1980), p. 26.

67. See Chapter 5 for a detailed discussion of state formation and capitalist restructuring in this period.

68. Lisa Duggan, "The New Homonormativity: The Sexual Politics of Neoliberalism," in Russ Castronovo and Dana D. Nelson (eds.), *Materializing Democracy: Toward a Revitalized Cultural Politics* (Durham: Duke University Press, 2002), p. 179.

69. Johanna Brenner, "On Gender and Class in U.S. Labor History," *Monthly Review* 50, no. 6 (1998), https://monthlyreview.org/1998/11/01/on-gender-and-class-in-u-s-labor-history/ (accessed June 8, 2022).

70. Ibid.

71. Sue Ferguson and David McNally, "Precarious Migrants: Gender, Race and the Social Reproduction of a Global Working Class," *Socialist Register* (2015), p. 2.

72. Johanna Brenner, "21st Century Socialist-Feminism," *Social Studies/Études socialistes* 10, no. 1 (2014), p. 33.

73. Gowri Vijayakumar, "Is Sex Work Sex or Work: Forming Collective Identity in Bangalore," *Qualitative Sociology* 41 (2018), p. 340.

74. Ibid., p. 340.

75. Melissa Gira Grant, *Playing the Whore: The Work of Sex Work* (London: Verso, 2014), p. 116.

76. Chi Adanna Mgbako, "The Mainstreaming of Sex Workers' Rights as Human Rights," *Harvard Journal of Law and Gender* 92 (2020), p. 95, https://ir.lawnet.fordham.edu/faculty_scholarship/1092/ (accessed December 14, 2021).

77. Sarah Beer, "Action, Agency and Allies: Building a Movement for Sex Workers' Rights," in E.M. Durisin, E. van Der Meulen and C Bruckert (eds.), *Red Light Labour: Sex Work Regulation, Agency, and Resistance* (Vancouver: UBC Press, 2018), p. 330.

78. Melissa Farley, "'Bad for the Body, Bad for the Heart': Prostitution Harms Women Even if Legalized or Decriminalized," *Violence Against Women* 10, no. 10 (2004), p. 1089.

79. Ibid., p. 1116.

80. Ibid., p. 1117.

81. Melinda Chateauvert, *Sex Workers Unite: A History of the Movement from Stonewall to SlutWalk* (Boston: Beacon Press, 2013), p. 4.

82. Kimberly Kay Hoang, *Dealing in Desire: Asian Ascendancy, Western Decline, and the Hidden Currencies of Global Sex Work* (Berkeley: University of California Press, 2015), p. 107.

83. Ibid., p. 108.

84. Ibid., p. 105.

85. Emily Van Der Meulen and Elya M. Durisin, "Sex Work Policy: Tracing Historical and Contemporary Developments," in E.M. Durisin, E. Van Der Meulen and C Bruckert (eds.), *Red Light Labour: Sex Work Regulation, Agency, and Resistance* (Vancouver: UBC Press, 2018), p. 43.

86. Ibid., p. 43.

87. Elya M. Durisin, "Perspectives on Rape in the Canadian Sex Industry: Navigating the Terrain between Sex Work as Labour and Sex Work as Violence Paradigms," *Canadian Woman Studies* 28 (2010), p. 130.

88. Ibid., p. 130.

89. Ibid., p. 131.

90. Heather Berg, *Porn Work: Sex, Labor, and Late Capitalism* (Chapel Hill: University of North Carolina Press, 2021), p. 127.

91. Ibid., p. 131.

92. Ibid., p. 132.

93. Ibid., p. 65.

94. Ibid., p. 65.

95. Ibid., p. 75.

96. Ibid., p. 91.

97. Ibid., p. 90.

98. Ryan Patrick Murphy, *Deregulating Desire: Flight Attendant Activism, Family Politics, and Workplace Justice* (Chapel Hill: University of North Carolina Press, 2016), p. 22.

99. Ibid., p. 29.

100. Ibid., p. 22.

101. Angela Davis, *Blues Legacies and Black Feminism: Gertrude "Ma" Rainey, Bessie Smith and Billy Holliday* (New York: Vintage, 1999), p. 5.

102. Saidiya Hartman, *Wayward Lives, Beautiful Experiments: Intimate Histories of Social Upheaval* (New York: W.W. Norton, 2019), p. 61.

103. Bérubé, *My Desire for History*, p. 267.

104. Ibid., p. 267.

105. Ibid., p. 300.

106. Ibid., p. 310.

107. Ibid., p. 311.

108. Ed Jackson and Stan Persky, *Flaunting It!: A Decade of Gay Journalism from the Body Politic: An Anthology* (Vancouver: New Star Books, 1982), p. 225.

109. Gary Kinsman, *The Regulation of Desire: Homo and Hetero Sexualities* (Montreal: Black Rose Books, 1996), p. 312.

4 MARKET MODEL SEXUALITIES

1. Pamela Haag, *Consent: Sexual Rights and the Transformation of American Liberalism* (Ithaca: Cornell University Press, 1999), p. 178.

2. Ibid., p. xviii.

3. Angela Davis, *Women, Race and Class* (New York: Vintage, 1981), p. 175.

4. Ibid., p. 175.

5. Bettina Aptheker, *Woman's Legacy: Essays on Race, Sex, and Class in American History* (Amherst: University of Massachusetts Press, 1982), pp. 62–3.

6. Ibid., p. 62.

7. Ibid., p. 62.

8. Saidiya Hartman, *Wayward Lives, Beautiful Experiments: Intimate Histories of Social Upheaval* (New York: W.W. Norton, 2019), p. xv.

9. Haag, *Consent*, p. 181.

10. I draw on conceptions of mutuality and reciprocity from Leanne Simpson, *As We Have Always Done: Indigenous Freedom through Radical Resistance* (Minneapolis: University of Minnesota Press, 2017); and Marshall Sahlins, *Stone Age Economics* (Chicago: Aldine-Atherton, 1972).

11. Brenna Bhandar, "Status as Property: Identity, Land and the Dispossession of First Nations Women in Canada," *darkmatter Journal* (2016), p. 8, www.darkmatter101.org/site/2016/05/16/statusaspropertyidentitylandandthedispossessionoffirstnationswomenincanada/ (accessed December 8, 2022).

12. Elaine Freedgood, "What Objects Know: Circulation, Omniscience and the Comedy of Dispossession in Victorian It-Narratives," *Journal of Victorian Culture* 15, no. 1 (2010), p. 87.

13. Ibid., p. 99.

14. Christina Simmons, *Making Marriage Modern: Women's Sexuality from the Progressive Era to World War II* (New York: Oxford University Press, 2009), p. 105.

15. Ibid., p. 12.

16. John D'Emilio and Estelle B. Freedman, *Intimate Matters: A History of Sexuality in America* (second edition) (Chicago: University of Chicago Press, 1997), pp. 265–6.

17. Simmons, *Making Marriage Modern*, p. 6.

18. Eva Illouz, *Why Love Hurts: A Sociological Explanation* (London: Polity, 2012), p. 41.

19. Christopher Chitty, *Sexual Hegemony: Statecraft, Sodomy and Capital in the Rise of the World System* (Durham: Duke University Press, 2020), p. 36.

20. Illouz, *Why Love Hurts*, p. 42.

21. Ibid., p. 44.

22. Adam Greenfield, *Radical Technologies: The Design of Everyday Life* (London: Verso, 2017), p. 50.

23. Kate Doyle Griffiths, "Crossroads and Country Roads: Wildcat West Virgina and the Possibilities of a Working Class Offensive," *Viewpoint* (2018), www. viewpointmag.com/2018/03/13/crossroads-and-country-roads-wildcat-west-virginia-and-the-possibilities-of-a-working-class-offensive/ (accessed August 26, 2024).

24. Kelly Moore, "Fear and Fun: Science and Gender, Emotion and Embodiment under Neoliberalism," *Scholar and Feminist Online* (2013), http://sfonline. barnard.edu/gender-justice-and-neoliberal-transformations/fear-and-fun-science-and-gender-emotion-and-embodiment-under-neoliberalism/ (accessed August 26, 2024).

25. Rebecca Reid, "Dear Guys, This Is Why You Should Never Wear a FitBit during Sex," *Telegraph*, 2017, www.telegraph.co.uk/women/sex/dear-guys-should-never-wear-fitbit-sex/ (accessed February 12, 2018).

26. Moira Weigel, *Labor of Love: The Invention of Dating* (New York: Farrar, Straus and Giroux, 2016), p. 8.

27. Ibid., p. 9.

28. See the discussion of reification of desire in Chapter 2.

29. Bruce Alexander, *The Globalisation of Addiction* (Oxford: Oxford University Press, 2008), p. 61.

30. George Bernard Shaw, "Preface," in *Getting Married* (1908), www.gutenberg. org/cache/epub/5604/pg5604.txt (accessed August 26, 2024).

31. Ibid.

32. Edmund White, *States of Desire: Travels in Gay America Revisited* (Madison: University of Wisconsin Press, 2014), p. 268.

33. Alain de Boton, "Why You Will Marry the Wrong Person," *New York Times*, 2016, www.nytimes.com/2016/05/29/opinion/sunday/why-you-will-marry-the-wrong-person.html (accessed March 20, 2017).

34. Susan Ferguson, *Women and Work: Feminism, Labour and Social Reproduction* (London: Pluto Press, 2020), p. 116.

35. Ibid., p. 116.

36. Sébastien Rioux, Genevieve LeBaron and Peter J. Verovšek, "Capitalism and Unfree Labor: A Review of Marxist Perspectives on Modern Slavery," *Review of International Political Economy* (2019), p. 1, doi:10.1080/09692290.2019.16500 94.

37. Saidiya Hartman, *Scenes of Subjection: Terror, Slavery and Self-Making in Nineteenth Century America* (Oxford: Oxford University Press, 1997), p 62.

38. Charles Mills, "Body Politic, Bodies Impolitic," *Social Research* 78, no. 2 (2011), p. 602.

39. E. San Juan Jr., *Racism and Cultural Studies: Critiques of Multiculturalist Ideology and the Politics of Difference* (Durham: Duke University Press, 2002), p. 61.

40. Dorothy Roberts, *Killing the Black Body: Race, Reproduction and the Meaning of Liberty* (New York: Pantheon, 1997), p. 5.

41. Rosemary Hennessy, *Fires on the Border: The Passionate Politics of Labor Organizing on the Mexican Frontera* (Minneapolis: University of Minnesota Press, 2013), p. 131.

42. Wallace Clement and John Myles, *Relations of Ruling: Class and Gender in Postindustrial Societies* (Montreal: McGill-Queen's University Press, 1994), p. 175.

43. Kay Gabriel, "Gender as an Accumulation Strategy," *Invert Journal* (2020).

44. Bhandar, "Status as Property," p. 2.

45. Ibid., p. 5.

46. Ibid., p. 11.

47. Ibid., p. 9.

48. Ibid., p. 9.

49. Bonita Lawrence, *"Real" Indians and Others: Mixed-Blood Urban Native Peoples and Indigenous Nationhood* (Lincoln: University of Nebraska Press, 2004), p. 45.

50. Ibid., p. 45.

51. Ibid., p. 47.

52. Bhandar, "Status as Property," p. 3.

53. Sara Ahmed, *The Cultural Politics of Emotion* (New York: Routledge, 2004), p. 152.

54. Ibid., p. 152.

55. Jenny Lo and Theresa Healy, "Flagrantly Flaunting It?: Contesting Perceptions of Locational Identity among Urban Vancouver Lesbians," *Journal of Lesbian Studies* 4, no. 1 (2000), p. 31.

56. Sy Adler and Johanna Brenner, "Gender and Space: Lesbians and Gay Men in the City," *International Journal of Urban and Regional Research* 16, no. 1 (1996), p. 32.

57. Elizabeth Lapovsky Kennedy and Madeline D. Davis, *Boots of Leather, Slippers of Gold: A History of the Lesbian Community* (New York: Routledge, 1993), p. 114.

58. Ibid., p. 114.

59. Alex Robinson, "N'tacimowin inna nah': Our Coming in Stories," *Canadian Woman Studies* 26 (2008), p. 197.

60. Carole Pateman, *The Sexual Contract* (Redwood City, CA: Stanford University Press, 1988), p. 118.

61. Ibid., p. 8.

62. Ibid., p. 184.

63. Ibid., p. 164.

64. Evegeny B. Pashukanis, *Law and Marxism: A General Theory*. Barbara Einhorn (trans.) and Chris Arthur (ed.) (London: Pluto Press, 1978), p. 110.

65. Antonio Gramsci, *Prison Notebooks Volume 1*. Joseph A. Buttigieg with Antonio Callari (ed. and trans.) (New York: Columbia University Press, 1992), pp. 155–6.

66. Nicola Gavey and Charlene Y. Senn, "Sexuality and Sexual Violence," in D.L. Tolman and L.M. Diamond (eds.), *APA Handbook of Sexuality and Psychology: Vol. 1. Person-Based Approaches* (Washington, DC: American Psychological Association, 2014), p. 339.

67. Ibid., p. 340.

68. Kimberlé Crenshaw, "Mapping the Margins: Intersectionality, Identity Politics, and Violence against Women of Color," *Stanford Law Review* 43, no. 6 (1991), p. 1245.

69. Lewis R. Gordon, "Race, Sex, and Matrices of Desire in an Antiblack World: An Essay in Phenomenology and Social Role," in Naomi Zack (ed.), *Race/Sex: Their Sameness, Difference and Interplay* (New York: Routledge, 1996), p. 127.

70. Ibid., p. 127.

71. Davis, *Women, Race and Class*, p. 177.

72. Yoshimi Yoshiaki, *Comfort Women: Sexual Slavery in the Japanese Military during World War II*. Suzanne O'Brien (trans.) (New York: Columbia University Press, 2002), pp. 190–1.

73. Nahla Abdo, *Captive Revolution: Palestinian Women's Anti-Colonial Struggle within the Israeli Prison System* (London: Pluto Press, 2014), p. 208.

74. Nicola Gavey, *Just Sex? The Cultural Scaffolding of Rape* (London: Routledge, 2005), p. 2.

75. Ibid., p. 3.

76. Ibid., p. 222.

77. Ibid., p. 223.

78. Vanessa Grigoriadis, *Blurred Lines: Rethinking Sex, Power and Consent on Campus* (Boston: Houghton Mifflin Harcourt, 2017), p. xxi.

79. Ibid., p. xxii.

80. Charlene Senn, Misha Eliasziw, Paula C. Barata et al., "Efficacy of a Sexual Assault Resistance Program for University Women," *New England Journal of Medicine* 372, no. 24 (2015), pp. 2326–35.

81. Katherine Angel, *Tomorrow Sex Will Be Good Again* (London: Verso, 2021), p. 27.

82. Ibid., p. 30.

83. Ibid., pp. 38–9.

84. Octavia Butler, *Fledgling* (New York: Seven Stories Press, 2005), p. 48.

85. Jacqueline Rose, "I Am a Knife," *London Review of Books* 40, no. 4 (2018), p. 9.

86. Hannah Frith, *Orgasmic Bodies: The Orgasm in Contemporary Western Culture* (Houndmills, Basingstoke: Palgrave Macmillan, 2015), p. 23.

87. Ibid., p. 41.

88. Gavey, *Just Sex?* p. 124.

89. Tamsin Wilton, *Sexual Disorientation: Gender, Sex, Desire and Self-Fashioning* (Houndsmills, Basingstoke: Palgrave Macmillan, 2004), p. 98.

90. Linda Williams, *Hard Core: Power, Pleasure and the "Frenzy of the Visible"* (Berkeley: University of California Press, 1989), pp. 93–5.

91. L.J. Moore, *Sperm Counts: Overcome by Man's Most Precious Fluid* (New York: New York University Press, 2007), p. 73.

92. Williams, *Hard Core*, p. 101.

93. Ibid., pp. 113–14.

94. Ibid., p. 102.

95. Frith, *Orgasmic Bodies*, p. 41.

96. Ibid., p. 41.

97. Elisabeth Lloyd, *The Case of the Female Orgasm: Bias in the Science of Evolution* (Cambridge: Harvard University Press, 2005).

98. Frith, *Orgasmic Bodies*, p. 23.

99. Lynn Comella, *Vibrator Nation: How Feminist Sex-Toy Stores Changed the Business of Pleasure* (Durham: Duke University Press, 2017), p. 5.
100. Tobin Siebers, "A Sexual Culture for Disabled People," in R. McRuer and A. Mollow (eds.), *Sex and Disability* (Durham: Duke University Press, 2012), pp. 38–9.
101. Ibid., p. 39.
102. Anne Mollow, "Is Sex Disability? Queer Theory and the Disability Drive," in R. McRuer and A. Mollow (eds.), *Sex and Disability* (Durham: Duke University Press, 2012), p. 286.
103. Leila Touil-Satour and Juan M. Leyva-Moral, "Sexual Experiences of Individuals with Spinal Cord Injury: The Somatic-Sexual Transition Framework," *Sexuality and Disability* 40 (2022), p. 430.
104. Ibid.
105. Walter Benjamin, *The Arcades Project*. Howard Eiland and Kevin McLaughlin (trans.) and Rolf Tiedemann (ed.) (Cambridge: Harvard University Press, 1999), p. 42.
106. Ibid., p. 42.
107. Ibid., p. 69.
108. Esther Leslie, "On Making-up and Breaking-up: Woman and Ware, Craving and Corpse in Walter Benjamin's Arcades Project," *Historical Materialism* 1, no. 1 (1997), p. 77.
109. George Lukacs, *History and Class Consciousness: Studies in Marxist Dialectics* (Cambridge: MIT Press, 1971), p. 83.

5   THE STATE AND SEXUAL HEGEMONY

1. This is discussed in more detail in Alan Sears, *Retooling the Mind Factory: Education in a Lean State* (Toronto: Garamond Press, 2003).
2. Lauren Berlant and Michael Warner, "Sex in Public," *Critical Inquiry* 24, no. 2 (1998), pp. 554–5.
3. Jeffrey Weeks, *Sexuality* (second edition) (London: Routledge, 2003), p. 4.
4. Christopher Chitty, *Sexual Hegemony: Statecraft, Sodomy and Capital in the Rise of the World System* (Durham: Duke University Press, 2020), p. 26.
5. Ibid., p. 26.
6. Ibid., p. 25.
7. Ibid., p. 23.
8. Antonio Gramsci, *Selections from the Prison Notebooks*. Quintin Hoare and Geoffrey Nowell Smith (eds. and trans.) (New York: International Publishers, 1971), p. 162.
9. Ibid., p. 162.
10. Karl Marx, *Capital, vol. I* (New York: Vintage, 1976), p. 718.
11. Michael Kidron, *Western Capitalism since the War* (Harmondsworth: Penguin, 1970), p. 24.
12. Christian Topalov, "Social Policy from Below: A Call for Comparative Historical Studies," *International Journal of Urban and Regional Research* 9, no. 2 (1985), p. 259.

13. Philip Corrigan and Derek Sayer, *The Great Arch* (Oxford: Basil Blackwell, 1985), p. 115.
14. Simon Clarke, "State, Class Struggle and the Reproduction of Capital," in S. Clarke (ed.), *The State Debate* (London: Palgrave Macmillan, 1991), p. 168.
15. Paulo Freire, *Pedagogy of the Oppressed* (London: Continuum, 2005), p. 72.
16. Ibid., p. 72.
17. Corrigan and Sayer, *The Great Arch*, p. 2.
18. Ibid., p. 3.
19. Ibid., p. 4.
20. Miguel de Beistegui, "The Government of Desire: A Genealogical Perspective," *Journal of the British Society for Phenomenology* 47, no. 2 (2016), p. 195.
21. Ibid., p. 195.
22. Ibid., p. 195.
23. Ibid., p. 195.
24. Michel Foucault, *The History of Sexuality Volume 1: An Introduction* (New York: Vintage, 1980), pp. 24–5.
25. de Beistegui, "The Government of Desire," p. 200.
26. Ibid., p. 201.
27. John Clarke, "Style," in S. Hall and T. Jefferson (eds.), *Resistance through Rituals: Youth Subcultures in Post-War Britain* (London: Taylor & Francis Group, 2006), p. 148.
28. Ibid., p. 148.
29. See Gary Kinsman, *The Regulation of Desire: Homo and Hetero Sexualities* (Montreal: Black Rose Books, 1996), pp. 108–11.
30. Nigel Harris, "The New Untouchables: The International Migration of Labour," *International Socialism* 2, no. 8 (1980), www.marxists.org/history/etol/writers/harris/1980/xx/untouchables.html (accessed January 20, 2022).
31. Ibid.
32. Colin Barker, "A Note on the Theory of Capitalist States," in S. Clarke (ed.), *The State Debate* (London: Palgrave Macmillan, 1991), p. 182.
33. Ibid., p. 182.
34. Alan Sears, "'The Lean' State and Capitalist Restructuring: Towards a Theoretical Account," *Studies in Political Economy* 59 (1999). See also Harris, "The New Untouchables."
35. Linda Gordon, *Pitied But Not Entitled: Single Mothers and the History of Welfare* (New York: Free Press, 1994).
36. Kitty Jones, "The New New Poor Law," *Politics and Insights* (2013), https://politicsandinsights.org/2013/10/03/the-new-new-poor-law/ (accessed August 26, 2024).
37. Ibid.
38. A.T. Aumeeruddy, B. Lautier and R.G. Tortajada, "Labour Power and the State," *Capital and Class* 6 (1976), p. 48.
39. Harry Braverman, *Labor and Monopoly Capital* (New York: Monthly Review Press, 1974), p. 139.
40. Desmond Manderson, "Symbolism and Racism in Drug History and Policy," *Drug and Alcohol Review* 18 (1999), p. 182.

41. Enid Logan, "The Wrong Race, Committing Crime, Doing Drugs, and Maladjusted for Motherhood: The Nation's Fury over 'Crack Babies,'" *Social Justice* 26, no. 1 (1999), pp. 135–6.

42. E. San Juan Jr., *Racism and Cultural Studies: Critiques of Multiculturalist Ideology and the Politics of Difference* (Durham: Duke University Press, 2002), p. 61.

43. Dorothy Roberts, *Killing the Black Body: Race, Reproduction and the Meaning of Liberty* (New York: Pantheon, 1997), p. 4.

44. Roderick Ferguson, *Aberrations in Black: Towards a Queer of Color Critique* (Minneapolis: University of Minnesota Press, 2004), p. 86.

45. Ibid., p. 87.

46. Sue Ferguson and David McNally, "Precarious Migrants: Gender, Race and the Social Reproduction of a Global Working Class," *Socialist Register* (2015), p. 17.

47. Conely de Leon, "'Pagod, Dugot, Pawis (Exhaustion, Blood, and Sweat)': Transnational Practices of Care and Emotional Labour among Filipino Kin Networks" (PhD Dissertation, York University, 2018), p. 189, https://yorkspace.library. yorku.ca/items/531cdbd8-b52e-4adb-97ba-f2a3ae90d319 (accessed August 26, 2024).

48. Kenneth Ballhatchet, *Race, Sex and Class under the Raj: Imperial Attitudes and Policies and Their Critics, 1793–1905* (London: Weidenfeld and Nicolson, 1980), p. 5.

49. Ibid., p. 5.

50. Ibid., p. 162.

51. Ibid., p. 164.

52. Mousab Younis, "Bitch Nation," *London Review of Books* 41, no. 3 (2019). p. 40.

53. Peter Drucker, *Warped: Gay Normality and Queer Anti-Capitalism* (Leiden: Brill, 2015), p. 41.

54. Sears, "Before the Welfare State: Social Policy and Social Theory," p. 173.

55. Drucker, *Warped*, pp. 115–16.

56. Sears, "'The Lean' State and Capitalist Restructuring," p. 92.

57. Ibid., p. 92; David Guest, *The Emergence of Social Security in Canada* (Vancouver: University of British Columbia Press, 1980), pp. 3–4.

58. Gosta Esping-Andersen, "The Three Political Economies of the Welfare State," *Canadian Review of Sociology and Anthropology* 26, no. 1 (1989).

59. Chitty, *Sexual Hegemony*, p. 173.

60. Drucker, *Warped*, pp. 168–9.

61. Ibid., pp. 182–4.

62. Sears, "'The Lean' State and Capitalist Restructuring."

63. Ibid., pp. 101–2.

64. Drucker, *Warped*, pp. 246–7.

65. Alan Sears, "Queer Anti-Capitalism: What's Left of Lesbian and Gay Liberation?" *Science and Society* 69, no. 1 (2005), p. 102.

66. Chitty, *Sexual Hegemony*, p. 174.

67. Ruth Wilson Gilmore, *Golden Gulag: Prisons, Surplus, Crisis, and Opposition in Globalizing California* (Berkeley: University of California Press, 2007), p. 7.

68. Ibid., p. 89.

69. Ibid., p. 112.

70. Ibid., p. 110.
71. Ibid., p. 110.
72. Kinsman, *The Regulation of Desire*, p. 361.

6   SEXUALITY AND ECOLOGY

1. Jason Moore, *Capitalism in the Web of Life* (London: Verso, 2015), p. 247.
2. Karl Marx, *Capital, vol. I* (New York: Vintage, 1976), p. 133.
3. Ibid., p. 283.
4. Ibid., p. 283.
5. Ibid., p. 283.
6. Leanne Simpson, *As We Have Always Done: Indigenous Freedom through Radical Resistance* (Minneapolis: University of Minnesota Press, 2017), p. 8.
7. Ibid., p. 8.
8. Karl Marx, *Capital, vol. III* (New York: Vintage, 1981), p. 949.
9. Ibid., p. 959.
10. John Bellamy Foster, *The Ecological Revolution: Making Peace with the Planet* (New York: Monthly Review Press, 2000), p. 180.
11. Ibid., p. 180.
12. George Monbiot, "The Lake District as a World Heritage Site? What a Disaster That Would Be," *Guardian* May 9, 2017, www.theguardian.com/commentisfree/2017/may/09/lake-district-world-heritage-site-george-monbiot (accessed August 26, 2024).
13. Andreas Malm, *Fossil Capital: The Rise of Steam Power and the Roots of Global Warming* (London: Verso, 2016), p. 28.
14. Neil Smith, *Uneven Development: Nature, Capital and the Production of Space* (second edition) (Oxford: Basil Blackwell, 1990), p. 54.
15. Ibid., p. 54.
16. Moore, *Capitalism in the Web of Life*, p. 292.
17. Malm, *Fossil Capital*, p. 11.
18. Ryan Jobson, "Dead Labor: On Racial Capital and Fossil Capital," in Justin Leroy and Destin Jenkins (eds.), *Histories of Racial Capitalism* (New York: Columbia University Press, 2021), p. 226.
19. Edward Said, *Culture and Imperialism* (New York: Vintage, 1993), pp. 225–6).
20. Moore, *Capitalism in the Web of Life*, p. 225.
21. Kim Moody, *On New Terrain: How Capital Is Reshaping the Battleground of Class War* (Chicago: Haymarket, 2017), pp. 15–18.
22. Moore, *Capitalism in the Web of Life*, p. 229.
23. Marx, *Capital, vol. I*, p. 375.
24. Mahmoud Darwish, "A Lover from Palestine," in Ian Wedde and Fawwaz Tuqan (trans.), *Selected Poems Mahmoud Darwish* (Cheadle, Cheshire: Carcanet Press, 1973), p. 63.
25. Lisa Foderaro, "In Central Park, a Birders' Secluded Haven Comes with a Dark Side," *New York Times*, September 13, 2012, www.nytimes.com/2012/09/14/nyregion/in-central-park-an-uneasy-coexistence-grows-uneasier.html (accessed August 15, 2018).

26. Ibid.
27. Ibid.
28. Centralpark.com, 2018.
29. Foderaro, "In Central Park."
30. Andreas Malm, "In Wildness Is the Liberation of the World: On Maroon Ecology and Partisan Nature," *Historical Materialism* 26, no. 3 (2018), p. 7.
31. Glen Coulthard, *Red Skin White Masks: Rejecting the Colonial Politics of Recognition* (Minneapolis: University of Minnesota Press, 2014), p. 13.
32. Malm, "In Wildness," p. 10.
33. John Rechy, *The Sexual Outlaw* (New York: Dell, 1977), p. 112.
34. Ibid., p. 113.
35. Ibid., p. 128.
36. Ibid., pp. 176–7.
37. Marcus McCann, *Park Cruising: What Happens When We Wander Off the Path* (Toronto: Anansi, 2023), p. 9.
38. Richard Tewksbury, "Adventures in the Erotic Oasis: Sex and Danger in Men's Same-Sex, Public, Sexual Encounters," *Journal of Men's Studies* 4, no. 1 (1995), pp. 9–24.
39. Ibid., p.14.
40. Gary Kinsman, *The Regulation of Desire: Homo and Hetero Sexualities* (Montreal: Black Rose Books, 1996), p. 358.
41. Malm, "In Wildness," p. 2.
42. Ibid., p. 2.
43. Steven Maynard, "Through a Hole in the Lavatory Wall: Homosexual Subcultures, Police Surveillance, and the Dialectics of Discovery," *Journal of the History of Sexuality* 5, no. 2 (1994), p. 208.
44. Said, *Culture and Imperialism*, p. 226.
45. Ibid., p. 226.
46. John Bellamy, "Third Nature: Edward Said on Ecology and Imperialism," *Monthly Review online*, posted July 18, 2017 at https://mronline.org/2017/07/18/third-nature/.
47. Simpson, *As We Have Always Done*, p. 235.
48. Richard Levins and Richard Lewontin, *The Dialectical Biologist* (Cambridge: Harvard University Press, 1985), p. 4.
49. Ibid., p. 257.
50. Fausto-Sterling, *Sex/Gender: Biology in a Social World* (New York: Routledge, 2012), p. 79.
51. Oyeronke Oyewumi, "De-confounding Gender: Feminist Theorizing and Western Culture, a Comment on Hawksworth's 'Confounding Gender'," *Signs* 23, no. 4 (1998), p. 1053.
52. Ibid., p. 1053.
53. Moore *Capitalism in the Web of Life*, p. 230.
54. Kate Soper, *What Is Nature?: Culture Politics and the Non-Human* (Oxford: Blackwell, 1995, pp. 132–3.
55. Roxanne Gay, "My Body Is Wildly Undisciplined and I Deny Myself Nearly Everything I Desire," *xojane*, April 9, 2014, www.xojane.com/issues/my-body-is-

wildly-undisciplined-and-i-deny-myself-nearly-everything-i-desire (accessed November 16, 2017).

56. Ibid.

57. Ibid.

58. Ibid.

59. Melissa Whitworth, "Victoria's Secret Show: What Does It Take to Be a Victoria's Secret Angel?"*Telegraph*, November 7, 2011, http://fashion.telegraph.co.uk/article/TMG8872623/Victorias-Secret-show-What-does-it-take-to-be-a-Victorias-Secret-Angel.html (accessed January 28, 2018).

60. Ibid.

61. David McNally, *Bodies of Meaning: Studies on Language, Labor and Liberation* (Albany: State University of New York Press, 2001).

62. Mark Greif, "Against Everything," *Verso Blog*, October 6, 2017, www.versobooks.com/blogs/3428-against-exercise-by-mark-greif (accessed October 6, 2017).

63. McNally, *Bodies of Meaning*, p. 12.

64. See Michael Kimmel, "Masculinity as Homophobia: Fear, Shame, and Silence in the Construction of Gender Identity," in Abby L Ferber, Kimberly Holcomb and Tre Wentling (eds.), *Sex, Gender, and Sexuality: The New Basics* (Oxford: Oxford University Press, 2009).

65. Alan M. Klein, *Little Big Men: Bodybuilding Subculture and Gender Construction* (Albany: State University of New York Press, 1993), p. 5.

66. On the development of scientific weightlifting, see Alan Radley, *The Illustrated History of Physical Culture. Vol 1, The Muscular Ideal* (London: Alan Radley, 2001), p. 62.

67. See Varda Burstyn, *The Rites of Men: Manhood, Politics and the Culture of Sport* (University of Toronto Press, Toronto, 1999).

68. David Noble, *Forces of Production: A Social History of Industrial Automation* (New York: Alfred A. Knopf, 1984), p. 36.

69. Ibid., p. 36.

70. Ibid., p. 36.

71. Klein, *Little Big Men*, p. 6.

72. Ibid., p. 6.

73. Leslie Heywood, "Masculinity Vanishing: Bodybuilding and Contemporary Culture," in Pamela Moore (ed.), *Building Bodies* (New Brunswick: Rutgers University Press, 1997), pp. 165–83.

74. Marvin T. Prosono, "Fascism of the Skin : Symptoms of Alienation in the Body of Consumptive Capitalism" *Current Sociology* 56, no. 4 (2008), p. 639.

75. Heywood, "Masculinity Vanishing," p. 165.

76. Prosono, "Fascism of the Skin," p. 650.

77. Frank Mort, *Cultures of Consumption: Masculinities and Social Space in Late Twentieth-Century Britain* (London: Routledge, 1996).

78. Dwight McBride, *Why I Hate Abercrombie & Fitch* (New York: New York University Press, 2005).

79. Klein, *Little Big Men*, p. 244.

80. Ibid., p. 245.

81. Ibid., p. 244.

82. Richard Seymour, *The Twittering Machine* (London: Indigo Press, 2019), p. 89.

83. Donna Haraway, "A Cyborg Manifesto: Science, Technology and Socialist Feminism in the late Twentieth Century," in *Simians, Cyborgs and Women: The Reinvention of Nature* (New York: Routledge, 1991), p. 154.

84. Ibid., p. 152.

85. Ibid., p. 150.

86. Jules Gill-Peterson, *Histories of the Transgender Child* (Minneapolis: University of Minnesota Press, 2018), p. 3.

87. Jordy Rosenberg, "Afterword. One Utopia, One Dystopia," in Jules Joanne Gleeson and Elle O'Rourke (eds.), *Transgender Marxism* (London: Pluto Press, 2021), p. 285.

88. Ibid., p. 286.

89. Gill-Peterson, *Histories*, p. 4.

90. Ibid., p. 4.

91. Ibid., p. 16.

92. Ibid., p. 16.

93. Jordy Rosenberg, *Confessions of the Fox* (New York: One World, 2018), p. 145.

94. Ibid., p. 145.

95. Ibid., p. 150.

96. Ibid., p. 153.

97. Ibid., p. 258.

98. Alan Sears, "AIDS and the Health of Nations: The Contradictions of Public Health," *Critical Sociology* 18, no. 2 (1992), p. 34.

99. Rosenberg, "Afterword," p. 285.

100. Ibid., p. 288.

7   UTOPIA AND SEXUAL REVOLUTIONS

1. Karl Marx and Frederick Engels, *The German Ideology* (Moscow: Progress Publishers, 1976), p. 60.

2. Alan Sears, *The Next New Left: A History of the Future* (Toronto: Fernwood Press, 2014), p. 4.

3. Rosemary Hennessy, *Fires on the Border: The Passionate Politics of Labor Organizing on the Mexican Frontera* (Minneapolis: University of Minnesota Press, 2013), p. 205.

4. Ibid., p. 205.

5. bell hooks, *Outlaw Culture: Resisting Representations* (New York: Routledge, 2006), p. 243.

6. Ibid., p. 244.

7. Ibid., p. 246.

8. Ibid., p. 246.

9. M.E. O'Brien, "Six Steps to Abolish the Family," *Commune* (2019).

10. Kate Hardy and Katie Cruz, "Affective Organizing: Collectivizing Informal Sex Workers in an Intimate Union," *American Behavioral Scientist* 63, no. 2 (2019), p. 257.

11. Ibid., p. 257.

12. Ibid., p. 250.
13. Ibid., p. 251.
14. Hennessy, *Fires on the Border*, p. 100.
15. John Rechy, *The Sexual Outlaw* (New York: Dell, 1977), p. 299.
16. Ibid., p. 301.
17. Ibid., p. 301.
18. Stephen Seidman, *Romantic Longings: Love in America 1830–1980* (New York: Routledge, 1991), pp. 121–2.
19. See Christopher Turner, *Adventures in the Orgasmatron: How Sexual Revolution Came to America* (New York: Farrar, Strauss and Giroux, 2011).
20. James Baldwin, "Freaks and the American Ideal of Manhood," in *Collected Essays* (New York: The Library of America, 1998), p. 827.
21. Michael Warner, "Introduction," in Michael Warner (ed.), *Fear of a Queer Planet* (Minneapolis: University of Minnesota Press, 1993), p. xxxi, n. 28.
22. Kevin Floyd, *The Reification of Desire: Towards a Queer Marxism* (Minneapolis: University of Minnesota Press, 2009), pp. 74–5.
23. Gary Kinsman, *The Regulation of Desire: Homo and Hetero Sexualities* (Montreal: Black Rose Books, 1996), p. 49.
24. Floyd, *Reification of Desire*, p. 78.
25. Sean Egan, "Bolsheviks and the Sexual Revolution," *Irish Marxist Review* 6, no. 17 (2017), https://marxists.architexturez.net/history/etol/newspape/irishmr/vol06/no17/index.html (accessed July 28, 2022).
26. Wilhelm Reich, *The Sexual Revolution: Towards a Self-Regulating Character Structure*. Therese Pol (trans.) (New York: Farrar, Straus and Giroux, 1974), p. 160.
27. Ibid., p. 152.
28. Egan, "Bolsheviks and the Sexual Revolution."
29. Reich, *The Sexual Revolution*, p. 159.
30. Ibid., p. 282.
31. Cat Moir, "Wilhelm Reich and Sexology from Below," *Ber. Wissenschaftsgesch* 45 (2022), p. 643.
32. Harry Braverman, *Labor and Monopoly Capital* (New York: Monthly Review Press, 1974), p. 445.
33. Dennis Altman, *Homosexual Oppression and Liberation* (New York: New York University Press, 1993), p. 107.
34. Ibid., p. 104.
35. Ibid., pp. 107–8.
36. Ibid., p. 108.
37. José Estaban Muñoz, *Cruising Utopia: The Then and There of Queer Futurity* (New York: New York University Press, 2009), p. 26.
38. Frederic Jameson, *Archaeologies of the Future: The Desire Called Science Fiction and Other Science Fictions* (London: Verso, 2005), p. 410.
39. Ernst Bloch, *The Principle of Hope*. Neville Plaice, Steven Plaice and Paul Knight (trans.) (Oxford: Basil Blackwell, 1986), p.136–8.
40. Sheila Rowbotham, *Edward Carpenter: A Life of Liberty and Love* (London: Verso, 2008), p. 389.

41. Jameson, *Archaeologies of the Future*.
42. W.G. Pearson, "Towards a Queer Genealogy of SF," in Wendy Gay Pearson, Veronica Hollingr and Joan Gordon (eds.), *Queer Universes: Sexualities in Science Fiction* (Liverpool: Liverpool University Press, 2008), p. 16.
43. Edward Carpenter, *Towards Democracy: Complete Edition in Four Parts* (New York: Mitchell Kennerley, 1912), p. 5.
44. Marge Piercy, *Woman on the Edge of Time* (London: The Women's Press, 1976), p. 171.
45. Samuel Delany, *Trouble on Triton* (New York: Bantam, 1976), p. 67.
46. Ibid., p. 31.
47. Ibid., p. 31.
48. Ursula Le Guin, *The Dispossessed* (New York: Harper Paperbacks, 1974), p. 17.
49. Delany, *Trouble on Triton*, p. 63.
50. Ibid., p. 153.
51. Piercy, *Woman on the Edge of Time*, p. 64.
52. Ibid., p. 64.
53. Ibid., p. 72.
54. Delany, *Trouble on Triton*, p. 112.
55. Ibid., p. 89.
56. Ibid., p. 93.
57. Ibid., p. 173.
58. Piercy, *Woman on the Edge of Time*, p. 102.
59. Ibid., p.103.
60. Ibid., p. 133.
61. Ibid., p. 74.
62. Ibid., p. 77.
63. Delany, *Trouble on Triton*, p. 108.
64. Piercy, *Woman on the Edge of Time*, p. 134.
65. Ibid., p. 134.
66. Delany, *Trouble on Triton*, p. 136.
67. Piercy, *Woman on the Edge of Time*, p. 116.
68. Ibid., p. 116.
69. Ibid., p. 110.
70. Delany, *Trouble on Triton*, p. 88.
71. Piercy, *Woman on the Edge of Time*, p. 138.
72. Ibid., p. 41.
73. Ibid., p. 116.
74. Ibid., p. 147.
75. Piercy, *Woman on the Edge of Time*, p. 97.
76. Ibid., p. 140.
77. Delany, *Trouble on Triton*, p. 159.
78. Ibid., p. 159.
79. Ibid., p. 89.
80. Octavia Butler, *Parable of the Sower* (New York: Grand Central Publishing, 1993), p. 9.
81. Ibid., p. 33.

82. Piercy, *Woman on the Edge of Time*, p. 105.
83. Ibid., p. 105.
84. Delany, *Trouble on Triton*, p. 67.
85. Ibid., pp. 225–6.
86. Leon Trotsky, *History of the Russian Revolution* (New York: Pathfinder Press, 1980), p. 5.
87. Chris Chitty, *Sexual Hegemony: Statecraft, Sodomy and Capital in the Rise of the World System* (Durham: Duke University Press, 2020), pp. 178–9; see also Peter Drucker, *Warped: Gay Normality and Queer Anti-Capitalism* (Leiden: Brill, 2015).
88. Drucker, *Warped*, p. 63.
89. Leon Trotsky, *Permanent Revolution* (New York: Pathfinder Press, 1969), p. 278.
90. Ibid., p. 279.
91. Ibid., p. 279.
92. M.E. O'Brien, *Family Abolition: Capitalism and the Communizing of Care* (London: Pluto, 2023), p. 246.

Index

queer work, 45–6, 58
  site of activism 58–9

racialization
  desirability of bodies 126
  divisions of labor 44–5, 64
  racial formation at workplace 45
  sexual plasticity 130
  unfreedom 17, 70
  see also Black (people), social
    policy, social reproduction theory
Raha, Nat 28
rape 17, 74–7, 150
  college and university campuses 76
  enslavement 62
  intersectional analysis 75
  military context 75
  sexual violence normalized 74–5
  struggles against 62
Rapp, Rayna 6, 9, 49
Rechy, John, 29, 113–14, 137
reconciliation, 117, 155
Reich, Wilhelm 140, 141
reification
  definition 9
  desire 9, 34, 69, 80–1, 140
  forgetting 34
  orgasmic imperative 80–1
  sexuality 33–6
  see also commodity fetishism
reproductive labor, *see* labor
return
  of/to the land 116, 117, 118, 155
  Palestinian right of 155
revolution 132, 150
  erotic dimensions 137, 140–1, 151
  mobilization from below 132, 134
  permanent 153, 154
  see also sexual revolution
Reynolds, Paul 8, 42
Rich, Adrienne 47–8
rights at work 58–60
  non-discrimination on the basis of
    sexuality 59
  paid maternity leave 59

  partner eligibility for benefits 59
Roberts, Dorothy 70, 95
Robinson, Margaret 73
Rose, Jacqueline 76
Rosenberg, Jordy 129, 130–1
Ross, Ellen and Rayna Rapp 6, 9, 49
Rowbotham, Sheila 144
Rubin, Gayle, 49
Russian Revolution 140–1, 153
  changes in sexuality 140–1
  Stalinism consolidated 141
Ryan, Hugh 27

same-sex formation 99–102
  see also homosexuality, social
    policy
Said, Edward 109, 116
San Juan, E. 70, 95
Sayer, Derek 87–8
schooling *see* education system
science fiction 144–5, 151
  visions of sexual liberation 144,
    151
scientific management 43, 66
  applied to own bodies 66, 122–3
  fitness industry 123
  time-motion studies 66
  see also management strategies
second nature *see* nature
Seidman, Stephen 138
Senn, Charlene 74–5, 76
settler-colonialism 69, 153
  property relations 71
  resistance 72
  wilderness, in relation to 113, 115
sex-positivity 142
  gay male community 142
sex reformers 65
sex work 52
  as work 53–5
  criminalization 55
  debates about agency 54
  porn work 56
  reproductive labour 52
  survival project 52

:4

Thanks to our Patreon subscriber:

Ciaran Kane

Who has shown generosity and
comradeship in support of our publishing.

Check out the other perks you get by subscribing
to our Patreon – visit patreon.com/plutopress.
Subscriptions start from £3 a month.

The Pluto Press Newsletter

Hello friend of Pluto!

Want to stay on top of the best radical books
we publish?

Then sign up to be the first to hear about our
new books, as well as special events,
podcasts and videos.

You'll also get 50% off your first order with us
when you sign up.

Come and join us!

Go to bit.ly/PlutoNewsletter